9½
MYSTICS

9½
MYSTICS
The Kabbala Today

HERBERT WEINER

HOLT, RINEHART AND WINSTON
New York • Chicago • San Francisco

ACKNOWLEDGMENTS

Since these pages represent, not only the effort of many years, but something of a life distillation, I find it difficult to single out names for a special word of thanks. The book itself is an effort to offer such thanks to the teachers and groups it describes. But there are others, who never knew, never suspected how much they taught me through their lives as through their words.

Among those who, over the years, read and constructively reacted to material in this book were gifted editors like Elliot Cohen, Norman Podhoretz, Shlomo Katz, Arthur Cohen, Joseph Cunneen. Gracious help was tendered by Paul Shiman, Dr. Max Gruenwald, Rabbi Julius Rosenfeld and Mrs. Sidney Weinstein. My wife, Shirley, not only shared many of the experiences here recorded but helped to record them. My congregation has been "long-suffering and merciful."

Grateful acknowledgment is made to the following publications and publishing houses for use of material which appears in these pages:

The American Jewish Congress for excerpts from "Braslov in Brooklyn," by Herbert Weiner, *Judaism,* summer 1964; The Theodore Herzl Foundation Inc., for excerpts from "Exercise in Hasidism," by Herbert Weiner, *Midstream,* April 1967; Schocken Books Inc., New York, for excerpts from *Tales of the Hasidim: The Early Masters* by Martin Buber, copyright © 1947 by Schocken Books Inc. Used by permission of the publisher; Schocken Books Inc., for excerpts from "Father of All Worldly Things," by Hillel Zeitlin, in *Language of Faith,* edited by Nahum N. Glatzer. Copyright © 1947, 1967, by Schocken Books Inc. Used by permission of the publisher; Schocken Books Inc., for excerpts from *Zohar: The Book of Splendor,* edited by Gershom G. Scholem, copyright © 1949 by Schocken Books Inc. Used by permission of the publisher.

CONTENTS

PREFACE

This book records a search for the life secrets of a mystical tradition sometimes known as the Kabbala. It describes a series of encounters wherein individuals and groups who claim intimate acquaintance with this tradition are challenged to relate their hidden wisdom to problems of our own day. It also contains a good deal of historic and technical information about Jewish mysticism, but frankly, anyone interested in a purely objective, scholarly account of this latter subject will be better served by other books; this journal is on a more personal and popular level.

I shall not disguise my anxiety as an outsider venturing into an area usually reserved for professional scholars or authentic Kabbalists. That my presentation has resulted in some distortions both of the subject matter and of the personalities described, I do not doubt. For this I am sorry, but I take comfort from a favorite image of the Kabbalists. The primal light, they say, is simply too bright for finite eyes to behold. Paradoxically, it becomes more communicable—if somewhat dulled and altered—as it is "veiled" and transmitted through darkening vessels. The fact is that most people would find it very difficult to establish a direct relationship with either the teachings of the Jewish mystics or the groups who purport to transmit them. There are so many barriers of faith, religious customs, language, technical terminology. My hope is that this journalistic approach will be a kind of mediating bridge, helping through its very strictures to make a precious body of truth and wisdom more accessible to the general public. May this intent soften the final judgment.

—HERBERT WEINER

May, 1969

9½
MYSTICS

1
HE WHO TOUCHES IS TOUCHED

Seek not things that are too hard for thee and search not things that are hidden from thee. The things that have been permitted thee, think thereupon; thou hast no business with the things that are secret.
From the Talmud, Tractate Chagigah

Even now, the motivation for the search recorded in these pages appears so pragmatic, almost crass. I seem to have been looking for a kind of supertreasure whose value would not be affected by economic, social, political, nor, indeed, by any external circumstances. Once I came across a few lines written by a poet named Eli Siegel:

> *substance*
> *is what remains*
> *when everything you can think of*
> *has gone*

That seemed to explain what I was after. But then I found a Hebrew word that expressed it better. The word is *yesh* which means, literally, there is. The old rabbis used it as a synonym for the treasure which awaits saints in the future life. Some of them who liked to play letter-number games pointed out that *yesh* equals 310, which is the number of worlds that underlie and sustain all existence. Since these worlds are continually pulsating with joy, desire, creativity, and power, the *yesh* they offered was far more intriguing than Siegel's rather passive substance.

Still later, I became impressed with the writing and personality of a man who seemed to be a living embodiment of this *yesh*. His name was Abraham Isaac Kook, and he is one of the mystics to be met later in this book. Rabbi Kook once wrote:

> *So long as the world moves along accustomed paths, so long as there are no wild catastrophes, man can find sufficient substance for*

his life by contemplating surface events, theories, and movements of society. He can acquire his inner richnesses from this external kind of "property." But this is not the case when life encounters fiery forces of evil and chaos. Then the "revealed" world begins to totter. Then the man who tries to sustain himself only from the surface aspects of existence will suffer terrible impoverishment, begin to stagger . . . then he will feel welling up within himself a burning thirst for that inner substance and vision which transcends the obvious surfaces of existence and remains unaffected by the world's catastrophes. From such inner sources he will seek the waters of joy which can quicken the dry outer skeleton of existence.

Rabbi Kook's words made me feel better. Apparently, even saints were not above looking for a supertreasure. To be sure, the saints' search often ended up in a strange way—either with the annulment of all desire for treasure be it in this world or the next, or with the conviction that the desire itself, if properly directed, was already the treasure. It may have been something like this that the psalmist was trying to express in the words: "Whom have I in heaven but thee? And besides thee, I have no desire."

In any case, the "thirst for an inner substance and vision which transcends the obvious surface of existence" is not rare in our world. But there are those who thirst more than others, who search with greater effort, and some who claim to have found "the waters of joy which can quicken the dry outer skeleton of existence." Some of these the world calls mystics.

This book is an attempt not only to meet a certain category of such mystics, but to find out if their life-secrets can have meaning even for those who do not share the full intensity of their experience. So we will be talking about mysticism. Therefore, a confession is in order. Though this book is about mysticism, I am far from sure as to what that word means; I do not know if anybody else is. Philologists trace its root to the Greek *myein,* which means to close the lips or eyes. Historically, *mystos* appears to have been a term associated with ceremonies or initiation rites into secret societies that claim esoteric knowledge. Popular usage frequently identifies mysticism with irrationalism or obfuscation, or with the feelings which can be produced by watching a gorgeous sunset. Nor will we get much help from our scholars. A sensitive student of mystical phenomenon, like Rufus Jones, objects to using mysticism as a synonym for the "mysterious" and the occult and prefers to call it "an immediate, intuitive, experimental knowledge of God," which is similar to the Aquinas definition "cognitio dei experimentalia." Both may be right if we are thinking in the context of the Western religions. But what of the non-theistic religions of the East? What of the trances and moods achieved by those who feel no need for positing the existence of a divine being? What of the states of consciousness achieved by those who take LSD or practice yoga deep-breathing exercises?

William James is typical of those who strive for a broader view by suggesting that the mystic achievement is the "overcoming of the visual boundaries between the individual and the Absolute." But, such a definition must confront the fact that some intense spiritual efforts reject the concepts of merging with the Absolute. "Biblical man," wrote A. J. Heschel, "would look upon a claim to union with God as blasphemy. Prophetic consciousness is marked by a shuddering sense of the unapproachable holiness of God."

Shall we then say that the Isaiah who cried out "Holy, holy, holy is the Lord of Hosts, the whole earth is full of His glory" knew nothing of the mystic experience? A Christian scholar like Dean Inge claims just that. The Hebrew knows nothing of mysticism, says Inge. Rufus Jones responds to this by offering the words from Deuteronomy, "And underneath are the everlasting arms," as an example of the quintessential mystical experience. And so we complete a full circle of definition leading nowhere.

No, the term mysticism, although it will have to be used, will not greatly clarify the particular kind of truth or experience that is the goal of the encounters I shall try to describe. One does better by noting in Rabbi Kook's remarks above, the contrast between an inner and external reality, between that which is "hidden" and that which is "revealed." Jewish mysticism deals with inner or hidden matters. In Hebrew, it is often called *chochmat ha nistar,* the hidden wisdom; the mystics are masters of hidden wisdom. Their "speciality" is the effort to understand and personally link themselves with truths, insights, and experiences which are below the surface. They feel this below-surface level to be more important and more real than what is revealed by the outer events of their own lives, or of history, or by the surface reading of a traditional text. Contacting this subterranean reality they think means the acquiring of greater truth and access to the very source-springs of life.

Another word frequently used to describe the Jewish mystical tradition is *Kabbalah,* meaning "that which has been received." The teachings which *m'kubalim* or kabbalists claim to have received were thought by them to date back to antiquity, to Moses, Abraham, even Adam. Their teachings comprise a greatly variegated body of material accumulated over many centuries and in many lands. But, again, what they have in common is a desire to reveal hidden matters—that is, they purport to offer instruction and insight concerning traditional religious texts, laws, legends, customs, and life events that is not readily apparent on the surface. The kabbalists like to use images such as the layers of an onion, or the shell and kernel of a nut, or the outer and inner membranes of the brain to illustrate this contrast between outer and inner layers of truth and reality. They do not deny the plain sense or surface meaning, the *nigleh,* or the revealed aspect of an act, idea, or text; they want only to say that there is also a deeper, less obvious, and more profound significance to the same words or deeds.

One doesn't have to be a mystic to understand why a search for *yesh* makes one look for subsurface reality. Plainly, as far as we can see with our eyes or feel with our hands, there is no supersubstance, not even the white-plumed rock in Frost's "West-running Brook," which can survive the universal cataract of death. In this cataract, "time, strength, tone, light, life and love—and even substance"—all lapse "unsubstantial." If there is something left when all else is gone, then it is a something other than the surfaces which disappear before our eyes. As to the affirmations made by classical religious texts—the claim, for example, that there is an all powerful creator who rewards the good and punishes the evil—how can they be supported? If as Dostoevsky's Ivan Karamazov pointed out, surface logic, surface observation cannot justify the tears of even one innocent child, what shall we say about Hiroshima, and Auschwitz? No, the texts and explanations, if they are not lies, must have a deeper meaning; God's will must be something other than what can be plainly observed. As to those well-springs of joy that are able to remain unaffected by outer catastrophe, they must be located in a layer of existence so deep as to be hidden even from the eyes of faithful believers. The story is told of some students who came to a nineteenth-century Hasidic master in the hope that he could explain the enigma of evil in a world created by a good God. Reb Zusya, they felt, could do this, for he himself was good and pious, yet sick and poverty stricken.

"How, Reb Zusya, do you explain evil," the students asked.

"What evil?" said the rabbi with wide wondering eyes. The students pointed out that Reb Zusya was himself suffering from illness, pain, and poverty.

"Oh that," replied the rabbi, "surely that is just what my soul needs. Our sages have said, a red halter is fitting to a white horse."

The latter part of Zusya's explanation is superfluous. The point is that Zusya had tasted a level of reality where good and evil lost the distinction so apparent to surface vision. Zusya was a saint, a man so flooded by the *yesh* of an inner reality as to be incapable of feeling evil. Few people, however, even among the mystics, can achieve this level of annulment between inner and outer truth, but there are many who feel the need to discover a level of truth and experience which, even if it does not explain good and evil, offers something other and more than what is offered by outer evidence. Perhaps this, the need for "more," is the beginning of the search which may lead to mysticism. And mystics are those who make a strenuous and to some extent successful effort to encounter this "more." And some of them see so much more that they have become the masters, the Kabbala would say, who can turn "darkness into light, bitterness into sweetness."

To be sure, this quest for "more" is not confined to those who look upon themselves as believers in any traditional sense. The editors of a small psychedelic magazine express a similar hunger:

We live in an age when the crucial connection with the Source of all things is in danger of being washed away by the demands of the external world. These contemporary voyagers [the reference is to those who take "trips" under the stimulation of psychedelic drugs] are

*practicing a ritual as old as human history. Their tradition descends
from the ancient practitioners of Tanari and Tibetan Buddhism. From
the conception of the Christian ordeal, the forty days in the desert.
From the rite of passage of the Sioux warrior. From the mushroom
culture of the Aztecs. From the Greek mysteries of Eleusis. . . . What
LSD and other psychedelics offer is the opportunity to re-experience
that awe and these rites of passage without which human life becomes
less than human.*

Surely, much of the contemporary interest in so-called mystical experience is faddist and puerile. Many of those children from middle-
class homes who one day walk the streets of New York and San Francisco ringing Indian bells and preaching "flower power" find themselves better able to "turn on" the next week by participation in an
obscenity-studded riot or by a chemically stimulated inner voyage.
Superficiality, dilettantism, and plain ignorance are characteristics of
much current groping for mystic experiences. Nevertheless, it would
be wrong to underestimate the seriousness of the yearning which so
many have for a substance more substantial than what is offered
by life surfaces. Their thirst leads them to contemplate experimenta-
tions with Zen Buddhism, Indian Yoga, Peyote mushrooms, and other
promising vehicles for experiencing "rites of passage" into interior
realms. Why not fill one's personal "bag" with secrets culled from any
or all religious or ethnic traditions? Why limit one's search for substance to one place or culture? And why of all limitations confine oneself to a confessedly small and parochial area like Judaism?

These are legitimate questions to raise at the beginning of this
kind of journal. And though the purpose of this book is to search for
answers, a few responses might be offered even at this point if only
as hypotheses for future testing.

Why Jewish Mysticism?

As to why we should confine our search for substance within any
one culture, a simple answer would be: how many can successfully
escape such self-limitation? There may very well be some souls whose
breadth of comprehension and talent of empathy may enable them to
be fully at home in many cultures. It was Martin Buber, however,

who once observed that "the mystery of another lies deep within him and cannot be observed from without." And what is true of an individual would seem to be even more true of a history and culture; it takes most people a lifetime to master even the outer subtleties of another culture's language, responses, and moods. As to digging for its *yesh,* its deeply hidden inner substance, that is a treasure hunt for which very few are qualified. Most of us would do well to confine our digging within the confines of that culture to which we have been assigned by natural birth and education—namely, in the general context of Western religious thought, and, in the case of myself, on that location which has been worked over and revealed by the Jewish historic tradition.

That does not mean that one can or should avoid those insights which can be attained by an examination of other mystical systems. As greater ease of communication brings currents of thought from all parts of the world into vigorous contact, comparisons are not only inevitable, but fruitful, but we should be humble enough to admit that such contact is not the same as being deep within. As to the possibility that Jewish mysticism may offer important "secrets" for our day, we may again ask, "Why not?" Judaism is the heritage and life-way of a very small group. Yet, it would be hard to deny that this group has revealed an unusual talent not only for longevity, but for creative existence. To have persisted as an organic and historic tree of life for over three thousand years; to have continually produced new cultural and spiritual shoots as well as mighty offspring like Christianity and Islam; to have survived so many storms of violence and yet retain the energy to recreate a homeland in our day— all this would indicate access to some powerful secrets of life. So why not a "dig" within Judaism.

In addition to these reasons—or excuses—for encouraging an excursion into Judaism's inner world, there are, it seems to me, some characteristics of this world which might be particularly attractive to minds skeptical about incommunicable experiences and sympathetic with Samuel Johnson's reported statement about the fifteenth-century German mystic, Jacob Boehme, "If Jacob saw the unutterable, Jacob should not have attempted to utter it." Johnson was unfair to Boehme,

who is one of the few who communicated both the flavor and content
of mystic insight. But Johnson's point—that lucidity of thought rather
than the "cloud of unknowing" is the test of a valid mystic experience
—reflects the classic Jewish view. It is true, as A. J. Heschel says, that
Ezekiel was so overwhelmed by the glory of God that he fell on his
face, but it is only when he stood up that the Word came to him. A
message which can appeal to logic and mind as well as feeling is the
test to which Jewish tradition would subject all claims to profound
inner experiences. That is why Moses, to whom tradition ascribes those
books of the bible which deal with concrete historic situations and
clear laws, is regarded as the Jewish mystic *par excellence*. Other prophets saw truth "as in an unclear mirror," while Moses saw it as through
"a clear glass"; the very clarity and communicability of his vision reveals it to be a face-to-face knowing of the divine reality.

This insistence on linking the profoundest inner experiences
with a communicable and effective word should prove especially
suggestive today. There also seem to be some important—and very
contemporary—secrets in the Kabbala about engineering a proper and
creative linkage between spirit and flesh, between lofty feeling and
social deed. But these possibilities can only be hinted at here and are
mentioned, frankly, as inducement for struggling with the difficult
barriers of a world that is indeed parochial, sealed off by seven seals
from the casual curiosity of an outsider. At this point, more important
than the uniqueness of Jewish mysticism is a certainty that it shares
with nearly all mystical systems, the belief that its treasures cannot
be discovered without a proper guide.

Find Yourself a Teacher

Hasidim, the mystical folk movement that will be discussed in
the second half of this book, is rich with stories that embody the
abstract teaching of the Kabbala in popular folktales. One of these
tales tells about a disciple who, after returning from a visit with his
Hasidic master, was asked what he had learned.

"I learned," answered the disciple, "the way he tied his shoe-
laces."

It was a serious reply. The innermost truths are glimpsed between the interstices of words that cover up almost as much as they reveal; similarly, the unpremeditated action of a teacher revealed more of his essence and of his relationship to the ideas he affirmed than his speech. Did not Plato also insist that the deepest truths are imparted from teacher to pupil, not by words, but by living together in such a way that a spark of light suddenly springs out of the heart of one and kindles the light in the other? Indeed, the Kabbala, being an inner teaching, can never be fully communicated by words which belong, after all, to the revealed world.

The two subjects which predominate in the mystical discussions of first- and second-century Talmudic rabbis are the work of creation (*maaseh breshit*) and the work of the chariot (*maaseh merkavah*). The first deals with the mysteries of creation adumbrated in the early chapters of Genesis; the second, developed out of the highly abstruse symbolism found in the book of Ezekiel, is concerned, according to later kabbalists, with the laws and processes by which creation was sustained. Moses Maimonides, the great twelfth-century physician-philosopher, sums up the Talmudic rules for the teaching of these subjects with the warning that the teacher must confine his discussions to only one or two pupils at a time. Furthermore, the teacher must give his pupils only the "heads of the chapters," for "he who understands will understand." This last is a strong phrase often found in mystical texts, which seems to accept the paradox of a received personal experience. A teacher must be found, but even when he is found, he can only offer a hint. If this hint does not quicken understanding within the pupil—that is, the student's own inner perception—then the mystery is not for him.

In my initial concern to encourage the examination of the inner wisdom of Judaism, I have perhaps slighted a tradition suggested by the treatment recommended for would-be converts by the early rabbis: "First push him away with your left hand; then draw him nigh with your right hand." After all, the most important reason for trying to find a qualified teacher is that the mysteries of Judaism's *pardes,* or mystical orchard, is not meant for everyone, that unguided and unwise effort to encounter its *yesh* may result in contact with its opposite—the power of nihilism, destruction, and chaos. The time has come, there-

fore, for a measure of caution, and this caution might as well come
from an authentic source—indeed, from the Lord's cherub, whom I
met one afternoon in Jerusalem.

The Warning

Rabbi David ha-Cohen would surely be shocked to hear anyone
call him a cherub. Nor did anyone in Jerusalem call him that. They
had named him the Nazir, because, like the biblical Nazarite, he did
not cut his hair and refrained from drinking wine. At one time, just
after coming to the Holy Land, he had also taken a vow to refrain
from speech. After his marriage, this vow had been modified to fasts
of speech on the Sabbath and during the month that precedes the
High Holy Days. The rabbinical students and visitors who attended
lessons at his home thought of Reb David as a fine scholar and saintly
personality but certainly not as a cherub. Nevertheless, the rabbi
might have understood why such an appellation occurred to me, for
the Nazir, who had once been a brilliant student of philosophy in Europe, was now a student of the Kabbala, which teaches that everything
in the world above has its analogue in the world below. That is why,
say the kabbalists, the bible begins with the second letter of the Hebrew
alphabet, *beth,* which is the equivalent of the number two—to teach
us that God created everything on two levels. And so there is a
heavenly Jerusalem which corresponds to the Jerusalem whose light
and sounds were coming through the windows of the small second-
story apartment where I met the Nazir. There is a garden of Eden
above that is the prototype of the garden that I was trying to enter
below, and just as the upper garden is protected by angel guardians,
so must there be guards below to prevent those who are unworthy,
unqualified, or unprepared from trespassing in the orchard of esoteric
wisdom. There was no mistaking the Nazir's intent to fulfill below the
role of that cherub who guards the heavenly Eden, at least as far as I
was concerned.

Furthermore, there was something cherubic about the Nazir's
appearance. Although no longer young, his bespectacled blue eyes had
an open childlike expression. His complexion was fair to the point of
translucence. Long locks of gray-blond hair reached down to the
shoulders of his red bathrobe and a bushy beard framed his long thin

face. If the conical black silk hat that perched on the top of his head were replaced by a helmet, the brown shell glasses by a visor, and the bathrobe by a suit of armor, he could have played the role of a knight of the round table. Instead, he was playing the role of a cherub, an earthly representation of that cherub whom the Lord had stationed to guard the garden of Eden with a whirling sword of flame.

This role was not apparent at first. When I had knocked at the door and sought permission to enter, Reb David, as his students call him, nodded cordially and invited me to sit beside him at the dining room table. He had set his large magnifying glass down on what looked like a manuscript galley and taken out a pocket watch.

"I can give you a half hour," he said firmly but pleasantly.

"Fine," I quickly replied; "all I wanted was a good definition of Jewish mysticism, an analysis of its major differences from other mystical systems, and advice on how a person could begin its study."

Reb David did not respond to my attempted humor, nor did he answer my questions. Instead, without raising his eyes from the book in front of him, he asked me if I were married, where I had studied, and what work I did. Then, still not looking at me, he told me about another American who had come to him years ago and expressed a desire to study Kabbala.

"For a while we studied in the early hours of the morning. That is the best time; the letters are brighter then. In gematria, Hebrew number symbolism, the word *mystery* is the numerical equivalent of the word *light*. Then the man went on to join a group of kabbalists in the old city of Jerusalem—Beth-El was the name of the synagogue. There he used to practice secret meditations with them. One day word came to me that this young man had fainted during the meditation. When he came to see me the next time, I told him, 'Enough, leave it alone; *Eem poga, noga.*' You understand? If he touches, he is touched, hurt."

With that remark the Nazir had apparently said all he wanted to say about the subject, and I sat wondering how to pick up the conversation.

"Did he leave it alone?" I finally asked.

"No." The rabbi lowered his voice. "There was a tragic ending

—an auto accident. He was killed and left a wife and two children."

"But surely people have studied the Kabbala and not been hurt. Isn't there a way to touch and not be afflicted?"

The Nazir did not reply. I made a last effort.

"But doesn't Rav Kook say that one who feels himself drawn to the well of mystery should seek it out? No other well will slake his thirst."

At the mention of Abraham Isaac Kook, the Nazir raised his head and looked at me directly over his spectacles.

"Then you have read in the writings of *ha-rav,* the rabbi?"

Yes, I had read whatever I could find in print, including the anthologies of Kook's writings that had been compiled by the Nazir.

"You are acquainted with *The Lights of Holiness* and *The Lights of Redemption?* And you know, too, about his commentary to the prayerbook?" The rabbi motioned toward some volumes on the lower part of a shelf-lined, book-filled wall. I nodded.

"*Yofi,* lovely," the Nazir's eyes brightened. "You see the books in this room?" He motioned toward the shelves which covered the walls of the room that served as a combination study, dining room, and synagogue. "Most are enclosed in glass. Do you know why? Because they deal with *nigleh,* the revealed, teachings, laws, and traditions. But you see these shelves?" He pointed to a side of the room completely filled with books. "This bookcase is open because the books in it deal with *nistar,* hidden matter. There is no need to close the shelf. People can open these books, and they'll still find them closed. "Tell me—" Now the whirling sword was really being lowered. "Does the gentleman know the names of the *sefirot?*"

I repeated the names of the ten *sefirot,* the term used in the Kabbala to designate the attributes or manifestations of the hidden God.

"*Keter,* crown; *chochma,* wisdom; *bina,* understanding; *chesed,* grace; *gvurah,* strength; *tiferet,* beauty; *netzach,* victory; *hod,* glory; *yesod,* foundation; *malchut,* kingdom."

"*Yofi.*" The Rabbi nodded and looked at his watch. "All right, I will tell you one thing. Do you know what the Talmudic phrase *to sh'ma* means?"

"Yes," I said. "It means, 'Come, hear.'"

"Correct. To hear, the logic that is based on the sense of hearing rather than seeing, this is what characterizes our teaching. And do you know what the Greek word *theoria,* theory, comes from? It is derived from the Greek word *theatria*." Theory, in Western philosophy, connotes, then, what can be seen, visualized, beheld. But the Hebrew way of apprehending truth is based on the acoustical sense. 'Hear, O Israel, the Lord our God, the Lord is One.' 'Speak unto the children of Israel . . .' Even the word *Semite* is akin to *sh'ma* hear. Does the gentleman understand the difference between the Hebrew and the non-Jewish, Western way of perceiving truth? The latter wants to identify truth with what can be conceptualized, seen—either in the mind or in a bodily sense. To the Jew, identification of truth with that which can be seen is the beginning of idolatry. Do you understand?"

I was not sure that I did fully understand the rabbi's point. It was true the biblical prohibition against picturing any version of divinity had profoundly affected the Hebraic tradition and sharply distinguished it from other religious cultures with their pictures and sculptures of the human form. One might even argue that there has been a deliberate withering of the optic sense in Judaism, resulting in an indifference to esthetic forms that often shocks Western visitors to the Orthodox synagogues of Jerusalem. On the other hand, Hebrew mystical texts often used phrases such as "come, see," rather than "come, hear." Furthermore, they were always talking about visions of divine chariots, cherubs, heavenly palaces, the throne of glory, and the like. I started to mention this seeming contradiction to the Nazir.

"Yes, that requires a long explanation." He cut me off. This explanation would be forthcoming, he said, in a book on Jewish mysticism which he had been writing now for several years. As a matter of fact, he was just going over some of the book's galley proofs. He pointed to one of the pages before him. "Can you read it?"

His finger indicated a quotation on top of the first page.

"Read aloud," he urged.

I read: "Where philosophy ends, there the wisdom of the Kabbala begins."

"And the sources of this statement?" He pointed again.

"*Crown of the Head,* a book compiled by the students of the Gaon of Vilna."

"That is one source, and the second?" His finger again directed me to a line of print.

"The congregation of Rabbi Nachman of Bratzlav."

"Well?" the Nazir waited expectantly.

Again I tried to pass the test. The Gaon of Vilna was a great Talmudic authority of the eighteenth century, a master of *nigleh,* the revealed teachings of Judaism. Rabbi Nachman, on the other hand, was a famous leader of the Hasidim, a mystical folk movement which was vigorously opposed by the Vilna Gaon.

The Nazir's point, I took it, was that Kabbala, Judaism's hidden tradition, was an approved subject of study for all streams of Judaism.

"Good," said the Nazir and turned to another page. "Read!"

Now I was confronted with some lines that discussed the relationship between Platonism and Jewish mysticism. Both systems of thought, the passage explained, assumed that there was a higher world, more real than the one revealed to our physical senses. But, the Nazir had written, where Plato made a sharp distinction between the physical and the spiritual, the kabbalists insisted on an absolute unity. The so-called external world was, for the kabbalist, simply a thickened extension of the more important inner reality, like the shell of a nut or the outer membrane of the brain.

Was the Nazir using his book to answer the questions I had posed earlier? Eagerly, a little too eagerly, I tried to clinch what I thought was the Nazir's point. Did this not mean that the Jewish mystic looked upon everything in this world as Heschel says, as "the jutting edge of what was deeply hidden"? And did this not differentiate the Jewish from other mystical systems? That is, could we not say that while Eastern mysticism tends to regard all phenomena grasped by the senses as *maya,* illusion, Judaism would treat these same phenomena as an allusion, real in itself but, like the visible surface of an iceberg, only part of a greater reality? And did this view not intensify, rather than dilute man's attachment to the real world? I was a bit breathless at the end of my outburst. The rabbi looked at his watch. "Pardon me, but does the gentleman put on *tefillin,* phylacteries?"

The whirling sword was back in position. I tried to satisfy the Nazir's curiosity about my own religious observances.

"And do you know what the Talmud says about the four who entered the *pardes*?"

Obediently I finished the famous rabbinic quotation: "Azzai looked and went mad. Ben Zoma died. Acher 'cut the roots' and denied his faith. Only Rabbi Akiba entered in peace and left in peace. Furthermore," I felt as though I was trying for extra credit now, "the rabbis insisted that no one venture into the realm of the hidden teachings unless he was over forty, married, and had a full stomach—full, that is, with the knowledge of Jewish Law, the revealed Torah."

The Nazir nodded. "Of course, some of the greatest kabbalists did not abide by that rule. For example, the Holy Ari, Rabbi Yitzchak Luria, was a great kabbalist long before he was forty. Moshe Chaim Luzzato wrote his works on the Kabbala when he was a very young man. You know about Luzzato? He is one of my favorites. Of course, both the Ari and Luzzato died while they were still young," the rabbi concluded with a sigh. "I'm only speaking about facts," he added as if to soften his judgment. "He who wishes to enter into these matters must be prepared for some unpleasant experiences."

I rose to leave.

"Just a moment," the Nazir said, holding up a hand. "Is the gentleman perhaps a *cohen,* a priest?"

I told him that I did not belong to that class of Jews.

"Well, I am a Cohen, you know. But anyway, you know the priestly blessing, how it ends."

"May the Lord bless you in peace."

The Nazir smiled. His question was meant as a parting blessing. "But remember," he tapped the book again, "remember the saying of the sages: 'Not a finger is moved here . . .'" He paused waiting for me to fill in the quotation . . . "'but it is noticed above.'"

The Nazir nodded approval.

The Danger

Rabbi David ha-Cohen was not the first student of the Kabbala from whom I sought guidance, but his warning belongs at the beginning of this book because it is the authentic initial response of Jewish tradition to anyone who seeks an acquaintance with its hidden wisdom. In such a framework, one might even try to dissuade strangers from reading this kind of book, arguing that its subject matter, if treated lightly, will not be very meaningful and, if taken seriously, may be harmful.

In brief, the danger consists of the fact that every movement away from the ordered surfaces of life risks an encounter with chaos. The flight from the plain meaning of words and facts, the hunger for a deeper experience than what is offered by everyday reality, the dissatisfaction with the plain meaning of laws is an invitation to anarchy.

It is not difficult to understand why the mystic evokes so ambiguous a reaction from both the social and religious Establishment. Every church realizes its indebtedness to the deposits of mind and spirit which have been bequeathed by those who seek new meanings; its day-to-day existence, however, depends on loyalty to sacred texts, patterns of worship, traditions, and laws. These are the elements which help to bind individuals into a community and link this community with an historic past and future. The mystic experience, on the other hand, is intensely personal and therefore difficult to share, and its emphasis on the hidden rather than the literal meaning of words, traditions, and laws undermines canonical authority. The mystic may begin by affirming the validity of a sacred text or tradition, but his dissatisfaction with surfaces tends to make him look upon them as external shells which enclose a deeper and more important kernel of truth, and people who think they have found the kernel are inclined to discard the shell. Religious leaders are, therefore, very diligent about warning those who talk about inner truths not to stray too far from norms which can be checked by an external authority.

The Jewish suspicion of those who are drawn to subjective, subsurface experience is partly based on such reasoning, as well as its already mentioned suspicion of the ineffable. An incommunicable experience not only seems socially worthless, but it may become an action for antisocial and destructive deeds.

"There is probably no difference," says Dr. Henry Slonimsky, "between the subjective feelings of awe and mystery which grip a Jeremiah when he offers his prophecy, and the inner feelings of the

Aztec priest as he cuts out the heart of his sacrificial victim." The difference between the Aztec priest and Jeremiah lies in the life goals to which they harness their emotions. Inner ecstasies, a sense of mystery and of union with the Absolute, can be evoked as easily by acts of destruction as by acts of mercy. The officials of the Spanish Inquisition, who broke the bones of heretics on torture racks, perhaps tasted a variety of mystic rapture. It is the accessibility of the so-called mystic experience to devil and sinner as well as to saint, to psychotic and drug addict as well as social genius, that makes the traditional Jew cautious about such a subjectivist religiosity. Here again the mystic experience of Moses is praised as a positive alternative, since it is associated not only with clarity of expression but with very concrete and externally verifiable laws. It is as if the Jewish religious genius was saying: "Subjective experience? Fine. There is no religion without it. Religion is a yearning for the living God. 'As the hart thirsts for the water brooks, so does my soul thirst for Thee.' Nevertheless, the important thing is not what you feel but how you act right here on earth."

The psychiatrist would also remind us that the border line between hallucination and mystic vision is very thin. The personality structure of a sensitive individual can easily be cracked by an untutored exposure to the fire of intense psychic experience. Sexual aberrations have frequently resulted from unwise experience in the garden of the esoteric; as we shall see, no phenomenon is more appealing to the mystic as a paradigm of the truth and experience he seeks than the act of love and physical procreation. Eroticism can wreak as much, if not more, havoc when it assumes the guise of spirituality as when it is directed through physical channels.

These considerations help to explain the Nazir's attempt to find out if I had a stable marriage and was sufficiently disciplined by a commitment to the structuring laws of a life-centered tradition to survive the heady perfume of the kabbalist's garden.

In short, the guardian of Judaism's orchard will look upon an individual who would approach its mysteries as an atomic engineer might regard a visitor to a desert proving grounds. He is moving into areas which contain great powers—for creation or destruction. He must obtain certain knowledge, obey rules, and above all be accompanied by a competent guide. Then, like Rabbi Akiba, he may "enter and emerge in peace." Otherwise, *eem poga*—if he touches, *nogah*—he may be touched.

Now that the goal of the quest has been stated and the warning given, how shall we begin? Many are the paths which promise entrance into the *pardes*. Rabbi Isaac Luria defended the variations of prayer which existed in the Orthodox world of his own day with the argument that each of the twelve tribes of Israel had its own gate into the Holy Temple. Every Israelite should seek out the particular entrance which belonged to his tribe. In fact, said the Safed Rabbi, there were six hundred thousand letters in the Torah, corresponding to the number of Jews who left Egypt. Thus every Jew, along with his descendants, is rooted in a particular letter of the Torah. To find a teacher who could show him his particular gate and offer him the spiritual diet required for the nourishment of his specific soul-root ought to be the great quest of life.

While keeping this counsel of the Holy Ari in mind, we should look for some openings into the *pardes* which have been already made for us by talented seekers who have gone before us. Some of these gates, used by past generations, are guarded by individuals or groups whose appearance, language, and attitude toward an outsider is far from encouraging. We would make a mistake, however, in not trying them. Indeed, say one of these groups, the Hasidim of Rabbi Nachman, the presence of obstacles is already a sign of the nearness of treasure. Just as an earthly king will set up his toughest guards near the main treasury, so does the king of kings set up high obstacles about his dearest treasure.

I found this to be so when I approached my first gate—in a basement on East Broadway.

2
A MYSTIC ON EAST BROADWAY

In the beginning, when the King's will began to take effect, He en-
graved signs into the ethereal sphere. A dark flame issued from its inner-
most parts from the mystery of the Infinite, like a mist forming in the
unformed, enclosed in the ring of that sphere, neither white nor black,
neither red nor green, of no color whatever. Only when the flame began
to assume size and dimension, did it produce radiant colors. For from the
innermost center of the flame sprang forth a well out of which colors is-
sued and spread upon everything beneath, hidden in the mysterious hidden-
ness of the Infinite. The well broke through and yet did not break through
the ether (of the sphere). It could not be recognized at all until a hidden,
supernal point shone forth under the impact of the final breaking through.
Beyond this point nothing is knowable, and that is why it is called reshith,
beginning, the first of those creative words by which the universe was
created.

From the *Zohar*, "The Book of Radiance"

John Tepfer, a professor of Talmud in New York, first told
me about Mr. Setzer. I had explained what I was after, not only a
scholar but a genuine kabbalist, who could explain the secrets of
Jewish mysticism to an outsider. Dr. Tepfer did not know Setzer
personally, but he had read some of his Hebrew and Yiddish essays,
and a friend, a professor of mathematics, had told Tepfer that Setzer
had drawn some interesting comparisons between the kabbalistic and
the mathematical concept of infinity. "But," Tepfer warned, as he gave
me Setzer's phone number, "the rabbis like to surround the mystic
orchard with thorny fences. You may find this man difficult to approach." By way of encouragement, however, the professor told me
that Setzer had himself breached one of the three conditions which
the Talmud lays down for those who want to deal with secret matters.
While he was, as the rabbis demanded, over forty—indeed he was
then seventy years old—and while his "stomach was filled," as required,

with Talmudic knowledge, Setzer was a lifelong bachelor and, as such, a transgressor of the rule that only married men may study Kabbala.

That Setzer was not easy to approach became apparent on my first telephone call. A high-pitched voice answered and quickly refused my request for an appointment to discuss arrangements for studying the Zohar. I was referred, instead, to some articles which Setzer had published in a Hebrew journal. On my third call, however, I received an invitation to his office which was located on East Broadway in lower Manhattan.

Setzer's "office" turned out to be a basement store which was approached by descending several steps below street level. When I arrived for my appointment at eleven o'clock at night, I could see through the storefront window a man sitting alone over a pile of books and papers. He appeared to be tall, but it was mostly his extreme thinness and long face that gave the illusion of height. His suit was brown, ancient, and formless, in sharp contrast with the frayed but clean, starched shirt. He seemed tired, and his discolored nose and red-rimmed eyes showed that he was suffering from a cold. Despite his extended hand and high-pitched, tense greeting, his manner was somewhat suspicious as he motioned me to a chair near the table. I said I had heard of his unusual understanding of the Zohar and asked if he would be willing to make professional arrangements for teaching me.

He ignored my proposal, but grunted at the word "understanding."

"Yes, understanding," his long face twisted in bitterness, "they all talk about it, but the Zohar is the only book that people dare to translate without understanding it. Thirty years ago, I spoke with Ginsburg, you know, who wrote the articles on Jewish mysticism in the *Encyclopedia*. Even then he said to me," here he imitated Ginsburg's voice, "of course, Mr. Setzer, I haven't read in the Zohar as much as you." He grunted again. "*Then* he hadn't read as much as I had—and that was thirty years ago, yet. He tried later to get me a subsidy for work on the Zohar."

He seemed to warm up a bit at his recollection of this compliment and absentmindedly accepted the cigarette I offered him. He broke it in two, placing one half in his upper jacket pocket and pushing the other into his cigarette holder.

"No," he finally returned to my proposal, "I haven't the time to give lessons in the Zohar. Years ago I gave them a chance. It's one of our precious pearls, one of the most beautiful treasures of the Jewish spirit, and they know nothing about it at the seminaries. We have such big schools, why shouldn't one of them have at least a chair in Jewish mysticism?"

Disappointed, I asked Setzer why he had first refused to see me and then changed his mind.

It was his "mystic philosophy," he replied. "When a call comes in once or twice, I ignore it. When it comes in three times, it is possible that they are involved."

"They," I later learned, was Setzer's designation for the hidden, but ultimately controlling power of the "other" domain. "They," however, were evidently not yet telling Setzer to agree to my request. I waited for a while, as the old man continued to brood over the way Jewish institutions neglected both Kabbala and Setzer. Only as I was about to leave did he agree to see me again, specifying that I must come only in the evening, after seven o'clock.

Later I learned the reason for his unusual working hours. Years before, after a long siege of illness, Setzer had found himself without an office. A charitable organization, which leased the premises on East Broadway, agreed to keep his books and provide him with a temporary address until he located himself. When I visited him, this arrangement had been in effect for twenty years. Since, however, the office was available to him only after the paying tenants left, Setzer had developed an unusual schedule, commuting from Seagate in farthest Brooklyn in the evening and returning home in the early hours of the morning. The people who used the office during the day had become accustomed to seeing the shelves crammed with pamphlets and books, although Setzer tried to clean off the table before he left.

The very next evening I returned to the office on East Broadway and this time was received a little more warmly. Setzer again began to complain, especially about the difficult circumstances that kept him from working properly. He showed me shelves piled high with thousands of copies of *Das Wort,* a magazine he wrote, published, addressed, stamped, and mailed once a month to the surviving members of the Setzer Pen Club. "Look," he pointed to the debris, "how can I do anything here? It's all so mixed up. I just have no time. Last week I got an order from a man who wants some of my books at a discount. Who can bother? I told him to take his own discount."

I offered my help in cleaning up the office. He seemed to respond, and I decided to broach again the subject of our studying together.

I told him that he should certainly be teaching the Zohar in a Jewish institution but, unfortunately, the only institution whose support I could personally obtain was my own temple. I was being facetious and was about to continue and suggest private instruction, but he surprised me by saying, "Nu—so all right—so let them do it. Only put a notice in the papers and send a notice about the class to the Hebrew journals." I was worried by this sudden turn and expressed some doubts about the attendance that could be secured for a class in the Zohar, to be conducted in Hebrew and Yiddish, at a Reform temple. Setzer reassured me: "Just announce it in the papers. Don't worry, the name of S. Setzer is not so unknown."

The announcements were duly made, and the class began on schedule at the temple. Setzer was the teacher; I was the only pupil. He made no comment, but turned to the first page of the Zohar; sitting alone in an empty classroom, we began our studies.

The Sefirot

By this time, I had acquired some information about the Zohar —for example, that it was really a group of books, including not only scriptural interpretations and legends but theosophic theology, mythical cosmogony, mystical psychology, and anthropology. According to the distinguished scholar, Gershom Scholem, most of the Zohar is written in an exalted style of Aramaic, the language spoken in second-century Palestine. Some of its books or tracts are terse and enigmatic; other portions flow like a novel, recording conversations carried on in the circle of disciples who followed Rabbi Simeon bar Yochai and his son Eliezar, as they wandered about second-century Palestine. Much of their discussion is carried on in a kind of code whereby terms like moon, sky, or Israel refer to the interrelationships of the *sefirot*.

The term *sefira* is first found in the *Sefer Yetzira,* a mystical text which Scholem believes was written between the third and sixth centuries. Here it is used to describe the ten elementary and primordial numbers, *sefirot,* as the book calls them, and the twenty-two letters of the Hebrew alphabet. These together represent the mysterious forces whose convergence has produced the various combinations observable throughout the whole of creation. They are the "thirty-two secret paths of wisdom: through which God has created all that exists."

The names, definitions, and characteristics of these *sefirot* undergo many changes in the history of the Kabbala, but throughout, the *tree of the sefirot* represents a dynamic, pulsating "world of divinity which underlies the world of our sense data and which is present and active in all that exists."

This subsurface reality is used by kabbalists to explain a problem, perhaps *the* problem of all medieval philosophy, the relationship between an all-perfect, all-knowing creator, and his finite creation. How can the perfect create something imperfect, such as our world? How can we say that an all-knowing God responds to prayer, reacts to injustice, is moved by the appeal of a broken heart? Does this not imply that God changes, and does not all change imply a lack? Indeed, how can finite minds say anything at all about the unknowable, undefinable "hidden root of all roots?" Kabbalists tried to resolve these problems by positing a dimension of reality mediating between the *ein sof,* the infinite source of all being and our own world.

The kabbalists believed that knowledge of the manner in which *sefirot* function could bring about a flow of *shefa,* life-sustaining grace, from the upper realms into our world. The *sefirot* themselves were arranged in various diagrams, the most popular of which began with an upper *sefira* called *keter,* or Crown, a level of reality quite beyond human perception. Indeed, so pure and undifferentiated was this *sefira* that it was altogether eliminated from some countings of the *sefirot.* The next lower level of this "tree" consisted of *chochma,* or wisdom, on the right and *bina,* understanding, on the left. Below them came *chesed,* grace, again on the right, and *gvurah,* strength, on the left. Below these and in the center was the *sefira* called *rachamim,* mercy, sometimes called *tiferet,* beauty. A final triad at the bottom consists of *netzach,* lastingness, on the right, *hod,* glory, on the left, and *yesod,* foundation, in the center.

The final level or *sefira* which is the recipient of all the *shefa* that flows from above, is called *malkut,* kingdom. Some diagrams have another *sefira* called *Daat,* knowledge, which is imagined as a kind of spine or center running through all the *sefirot.*

The human body is sometimes used to diagram the tree of the *sefirot.* The top of the head corresponds to crown; the head, heart, and spine to the upper triad; the upper limbs and body to the second level triad; the lower limbs and sexual organs to the final triad. At other times, the *sefirot* are pictured as concentric circles. Then the upper *sefirot* are closer to the inner core, while the lower *sefirot* are represented by the outer circles.

That the study of the Kabbala without an understanding of these *sefirot* and their dynamics was impossible, I knew. On the other hand, I must confess that, when I began my studies with Setzer, all this terminology seemed to be more of a hindrance than a help to my goal. What I really wanted to know was why and how the Kabbala or a book like the Zohar had been able to feed the souls of earlier Jewish generations.

A First Lesson

I had brought an old copy of the Zohar bound in worn leather with rough green pages spotted by the wax of candles held by previous readers. Setzer asked me to open the book to its Introduction. He spent a few minutes reviewing the order of the ten *sefirot* and told me to read the opening lines. My voice faltered through the first sentences of the Zohar, while his hand tapped impatiently on the table:

Rabbi Hizkiah opened his discourse with the text: "As a lily among thorns, etc." (Song of Songs, 2:2). "What," he said, "does the lily symbolize? It symbolizes the community of Israel. As the lily among thorns is tinged with red and white, so the community of Israel is visited now with justice and now with mercy; as the lily possesses thirteen leaves, so the community of Israel is vouchsafed thirteen categories of mercy which surround it on every side.

At this point, Setzer interrupted to point out some associative connotations of the terms I had just read. Red, I was told, is the color of vigor, a characteristic of the *sefira gvurah,* strength; white is the color of *chesed,* grace. Thirteen refers to the thirteen attributes of God mentioned in the biblical phrase, "God is merciful and gracious, long-suffering and abundant in goodness." The "third mention of Elohim" refers to the fact that God is mentioned three times in the opening sentences of Genesis before the divine fiat, "Let there be light."

But this type of association was given only passing attention by Setzer; it was the sort of thing that one took for granted in a student of the Zohar. So the Zohar was soon set aside while, in a mixture of English, Hebrew, and Yiddish, Setzer pointed out that the book's central concern was "the mystery of the creator and the creation, and the relationship between them." The mystery of an infinite God cannot, of course, be fully fathomed by a finite mind, yet questions can be asked. To ask "what?" already implies a certain degree of knowledge. To analyze the nature of "what" is to reveal the existence of a nonmechanical personal power and thus to replace the "what" with a "who." To go further into the nature of "who" makes even this pronoun inadequate for the reality; the "who" falls away, and there remains only a soundless question, more akin to awe and inarticulate wonder, yet still implying a certain knowledge of the existence and nature of Something.

But how can we finite creatures know anything about that infinite which is ultimately responsible for our existence?

The unspoken but necessary assumption, Setzer went on, is that in his creation a creator reveals something of his personality; touched by him, it must bear his stamp. The Zohar tries to proceed from speculation about the creation to speculation about God; similarly, it tries to analyze God's manner of creation by analyzing the creative process in nature and man. It is concerned with the tensions, antagonisms, and oppositions which necessarily precede any synthesis and creative unification. It probes the mystery of nothing becoming something by drawing analogies from the manner in which an immaterial thought or urge becomes materialized in words or even in flesh and blood.

In contemplating the subtleties of creativity, the Zohar turns

to man in all his functions, physical as well as spiritual, for its analogue. The phrase from Job 19:26, "And I shall behold God out of
my flesh," is one of the many biblical sentences used to prove that the
body of man and its functions can provide a hint of the divine process.
The Zohar sees nothing unspiritual about examining the human body,
and particularly the sex act, as a paradigm of the hidden spiritual
universe from which all existence draws its life. For that reason, the
sefirot are sometimes compared to the various limbs of the human
body. At other times, the world of the *sefirot* is visualized as a mystical
organism with both feminine and masculine tendencies. Wisdom, the
giving element, is thus labeled masculine and given the name *father*.
Its opposite on the left side, understanding, is considered feminine because it is a receiver, and it is called *mother*. The next to last *sefira*,
foundation, is also masculine, and associated with the male sex organ.
The lower *sefira*, which receives the seed, is called both kingdom
and *shekina*, the feminine presence of God. *Zivvug*, coupling, is a
Hebrew term which can be applied to the sex act, as well as to the
unifications of the *sefirot*. *Zivvug* is the goal of all the movements of
the *sefirot* in the upper world. To be sure, the acts of unification are
preceded in that world as in this by a dialectic of tensions between
the polarities which evoke the flow of life-giving seed and prepare the
receiver, but unification represents the fulfillment of the plan. What
the Zohar is teaching, therefore, is that grace, life, or joy cannot flow
through the inner worlds and permeate lower or external worlds until
the proper couplings take place, the all-important principle that "what
happens above depends upon what happens below."

"The perfection of the upper worlds waits upon the perfection
of the lower worlds. . . . Adam and Eve must be turned face to face
before the upper union is perfected." The total scheme is much more
complicated; the practical meaning is always the same. The thoughts
and acts of man in our world are invested with implications stretching
far beyond the immediately visible scene. All acts of unification, including sexual acts, become not just symbols but instruments which
enable the upper worlds to function.

The use of erotic imagery for spiritual symbolism is not, of
course, unique to the Zohar; it is found in the prophets, the Song of
Songs, and indeed, throughout the bible. In the Zohar, however, the

eroticism is at times so daring and provocative as to make clearly understandable the law which requires a student of the Kabbala to be stabilized in his emotional and physical life by marriage and by a commitment to the revealed structure of the commandments. Setzer was a tactful teacher, not avoiding these erotic explanations, but communicating them always in a delicate multiallusional form which did not overemphasize their physical association. Nevertheless, there were passages where the old man did not offer an explanation, and I did not ask.

Some Personal Associations

Most kabbalistic writings are taught through hints, which can set off an inner train of associations that might be blocked by too explicit an explanation. Because of poor dentures and a habit of swallowing words, it was often unclear whether or not Setzer's explanations were intended to be full exposition. As our lessons progressed, however, symbolism that had once seemed empty of meaning began to take on manifold connotations. What at first had appeared to be only poetic imagery—a tree and its fruit, a moon and its light, a word and its significance when the letters were reversed—became psychological and philosophical truths equally valid on many different levels. All the levels, biological, sociological, psychological, philosophical, were associated "like the links of many chains all connected with each other so that when one link is touched, all respond." Thus, the biblical phrase in the story of creation, "the tree of life yielding fruit, whose seed was in itself," referred literally to the story of creation, but the tree and the seed also symbolize the physical creative process in man. At the same time, they refer to the intellectual and spiritual fructification of a human being by the seed of divine wisdom, and the passage also suggests the mysterious process by which fruit comes from seed, and seed comes from intangible thought, and thought from the realm of the unknown and the unknowable.

Trying to analyze why Setzer's explanations made previously abstruse passages suddenly pregnant with contemporary insight, I came to the conclusion that it was his way of "psychologizing" the Kabbala. This was no abstract speculation about the nature of God and the relations of God and man, but a probing of the human psyche which

was in turn a mirror of the cosmic psyche. How such understanding
came from Setzer's half-swallowed sentences and allusions, I'm still
not sure. Perhaps it was his paucity of explanation that left room
for personal trains of thought, even some rather absurd associations.
I remember, for example, Setzer trying to explain why the hidden
source of life could not become manifest in our world without the
descending chain of the *sefirot*. "It's like a chemical," he said, "which
is too strong for the container. It has to be diluted before it can be
handled."

The memory of smelly chemical laboratories in college came to
my aid. Were there not chemicals that had to be diluted, poured from
vessel to vessel, perhaps divided and made less strong, before they could
be bottled and used? Suddenly, I understood the kabbalistic references
to the "breaking of the vessels" because the "initial light was too
strong," and why the Kabbala sometimes spoke of the need for thick-
ening the vessels in order to reveal the content. The frequent paradoxi-
cal assertion of the Kabbala, "the more intense the revelation, the more
concealment there had to be," also became clear.

When Setzer began analyzing the function of the *sefirot*, my
associations were even more outrageous. "Obviously," Setzer explained,
"there can be no existence, no reality in terms that we can comprehend,
unless there is both a yes and a no, a giving and a stopping. Thus,
the right side, grace, represents the giving impulse, while the parallel
sefira on the left side represents *din*, judgment, which has to say
'No—not beyond this point.' "

To further illustrate his point, Setzer offered a Talmudic
analogy of this necessary interplay between the yes and no of the
creative process: "First, the Holy One, Blessed be He, tried to create
the world according to the measure of mercy [grace] but it fell apart.
Then he tried to create it according to the measure of justice [*din*,
judgment] but that too fell apart. What did he do? He took an
equal measure of mercy and mixed it with an equal measure of justice
and the result was our world."

When Setzer spoke of the inability of the giving impulse to
assume form without the negative pull of *gvurah*, strength, on the
left side, I thought of those ice-cream machines which poured their
contents on to the cone below, the shape being only able to form when

the machine stopped. What would happen if there were no stopping? Why, there would be no shaped ice cream cone, only an ever-changing blob.

My associations, I knew, were ridiculous, but they seemed to help me understand why, according to the Kabbala, the left side is always associated with destruction and death, for it is from the left side that the no must come. This no may be necessary for form and structure, but it is also a no to the life-giving impulse and, begins on the very highest levels of creation with the *sefira* called *bina,* understanding.

According to the Zohar, the quality of negation runs through all the *sefirot* of the left side, beginning with *bina* and ending with *malkut,* kingdom. In its earliest stages of manifestation, the power to say no simply functions as a differentiating factor; it is needed in order to analyze or break into comprehensive entities the undifferentiated, intuitive flash of insight which comes from *chochma,* wisdom. Obviously, there can be no thought without such analysis, but, by identifying the will to say no with the analytic process, the Kabbala implies that every act of analysis involves a measure of destruction and death. And since, ultimately, the left side, like the right, is rooted in the source of all the emanations, the kabbalist is brought close to a heretical thought, that the quality of negation, death, and evil, are actually rooted in God. Here one has the beginning of the gnostic idea that there is a fundamental cleavage in the ultimate ground-spring of the cosmos. This was how the Kabbala tried to answer the old question, where does evil come from? There was also a pragmatic aspect to this picture of reality, involving the problem of communication and creation. What is it that gets in the way of converting inner thought into outer expression? What dries up the stream of creative flow and diverts it into destructive channels? Listening to Setzer, I began to be convinced that the author of the Zohar had something to say to us today about creative blocks and destructive drives.

Of course, the Zohar is not primarily a systematic exposition of philosophic and psychological ideas. Like other classic Jewish texts, the Talmud, Midrash, and even the bible, it is written in that style which, like the trunk and the limbs of the tree, flows along a central line but also shoots out in all directions. Indeed, its refusal to be bound by a system of logic may be one reason for its attractiveness to nonspecialists. Isaiah Tishbee, a professor at the Hebrew University in Jerusalem, has pointed out that the Zohar mingles "secrets of the soul and of the divine on one hand, and folk beliefs about evil spirits and sorcery on the other, dreams of redemption and the end of days in one place, and the search for guidance in the complications of man to man and man to woman relationships in another. The small, confused, half-expressed and articulated wanderings of the spirit and mind," he writes, "along with inchoate primal feelings which are not considered worthy of inclusion in the structure of a system because of their pettiness, or because they cannot be expressed in abstract fashion or through systematic thought, are just what find expression in the compositions of the Zohar. Their vagueness and opaqueness in content and form are the vagueness and opaqueness of life, which casts up refuse and dirt in its very frothing."

The borders between heaven and earth, logic and dream, are constantly blurred. Rabbi Simeon bar Yochai, the hero of the Zohar, is a "great tree who stands in both worlds." He teaches his students in this world and is also a visitor in the academies on high. At times, the inhabitants of these heavenly academies descend on earth to hear a particularly choice explanation of the Torah; on other occasions, it is the scholars below who make a visionary ascent to the heavenly academy. Setzer's comment on this dreamlike logic at work was subtly perceptive: "If you were sleeping and someone touched you lightly, but not enough to waken you, then something in your dream would reflect that touch. It would, of course, be reflected in your own dream language, but still would be connected somehow with that touch. Often the Zohar is like that: Simeon bar Yochai or one of his comrades quotes a biblical text and asks its secret. Then they seem to go off into a different world, with its own language and symbols, but which is connected with the original text, just as the dream is connected with the touch."

A Reluctant Teacher

After a few weeks, Setzer faced up to the fact that no one else was going to join our class in the temple, and I began again my late evening visits to his office in East Broadway. I would arrive about eleven, when the streets were empty and the building completely quiet except for the occasional scurrying of mice in the ceiling. Our first hour was spent in reviewing the plans which Setzer had for publishing his writings or arranging for an office where he could carry on his work in more comfortable circumstances. After this, we would study a few lines in the Zohar. More and more, however, Setzer's frustration with the fact that his plans remained unfulfilled broke into our studies. Even his satisfaction at the successful elucidation of a subtle passage was touched with bitterness. "Nu," he would ask, "now you understand, yes? On this point sixteenth-century kabbalists like Ari and the Cordovero [Moses ben Jacob of Safed] struggled and struggled and finally came up with nothing. It took me thirty years to understand it, and now I've given it to you in five minutes." He could not suppress a note of regret at parting so easily with knowledge so painfully acquired.

As the weeks passed the time given to the Zohar grew less, and discussion of Setzer's present problems and past experiences expanded. He began to talk about his fine collection of books; it pained him to think of leaving them to one of the institutions that had been so indifferent to him. He talked facetiously about taking the books with him, and he seriously considered trying to make a commercial arrangement with some hotel owner: he would exchange the books, which he estimated were worth about three thousand dollars, for three years of board and room. It would be a good risk for the hotel, he pointed out, for if he died before the three years, the books would still go to the hotel, and they would profit on the arrangement. He also became increasingly reluctant to give away his hard-won knowledge by writing articles on the Kabbala. "Why should I give it to them so easily?" With his few material possessions, however, he was far from miserly. Apart from a small subsidy from a foundation, and a few dollars earned from an occasional article or the sale of some of his old books, Setzer had almost no income, but he responded to every monetary appeal and always distributed some charity on the eve of holidays.

Naturally, he was bitter about being ignored. In Europe he had been literary editor of one of the first Hebrew quarterlies and one of that dedicated circle that helped to bring about a renaissance of the Hebrew language. His name and his articles were known to almost every reader of the Jewish and Hebrew press, and he had published over a dozen well received books on Jewish thought and history. Now, almost unknown and unhonored, he had only this meager, borrowed office on East Broadway. The labor of writing, addressing, and mailing his pamphlets was burdensome, even though he had worked out a system whereby his time was not completely wasted; he placed a large folio of the Talmud on his left and had trained himself to read from it while automatically addressing and stamping the pamphlets piled on his right. But the feeling of frustration grew; more and more of the pamphlets mailed to members of the Setzer Pen Club came back marked "deceased" or "unknown," and most of the two hundred fifty remaining recipients had for years neglected to send in their three dollar subscriptions. Even that small satisfaction which used to be his at being recognized by the Yiddish and Hebrew readers of the neighborhood had disappeared. Once, a bearded rabbi of the neighborhood walked into the basement office in error, and noticed that Setzer was bent over the sacred text of the Zohar and was not wearing the usual head covering. Rebuked by the rabbi for handling so sacred a text without proper respect, Setzer exclaimed: "You—you are the one who should be ashamed, not me. You come in and see somebody sitting alone and studying Torah for the honor of Torah. You don't think to yourself how good it is that in these days it is still possible to find a man who sits alone at night and studies the holy word. All you can think about is a hat."

Reminiscences

Little by little, from scattered remarks and a few articles, I learned the outlines of my teacher's past. He was born in Novgorod-Volhynsk in the Ukraine, the cradle of the eighteenth-century Hasidic movement which sought to bring a new enthusiasm and mystic immediacy to Jewish piety. In an environment abundant with keen Talmudists, he was early recognized as an *ilui,* a child prodigy. His reputation as an unusually brilliant student brought him the friendship of Mordecai Zeeb Feierberg (1874–1899), a leader and intellectual spokesman of the enlightened Jewish youth of that period. Feierberg had written a semiautobiographical novel in Hebrew, *Whither,* in which he described the searchings of a soul that had been uprooted from the soil of traditional Judaism but was unable to place its roots anywhere else and was therefore disintegrating. Under Feierberg's influence, Setzer became a leader of the town's young intellectuals.

Those days in Novgorod-Volhynsk were days of excitement and happiness, full of study and enthusiastic discussions. "We used to go walking in the evenings to the edge of the city and there in the fields carry on our discussions till early morning. We would lie down for a few hours of sleep, only to rise again and continue the talk." Setzer came to be known far beyond the local environs for his angry attacks on the philosophies of Achad Ha'am and Spinoza. Toward Spinoza he was particularly bitter. "I could never forgive him," he told me one evening. "His bowing and scraping before Christianity, his constant attacks on Judaism and his apologies for Christianity. I could never forgive him his lack of feeling for the martyrdom of the Jews, which he himself witnessed. And I had no respect for him because he borrowed much of his philosophy from the atmosphere and thought of the Zohar—and never acknowledged or mentioned it by a single word."

Setzer's literary star rose rapidly when he went to Zhitomir and later to Warsaw, but he was back with Feierberg when the latter died at the age of twenty-five and was chosen to deliver the eulogy over his grave. The picture of his friend's end remained deeply etched in Setzer's memory. During the last moments, Feierberg had asked him for the time and Setzer, looking at the clock, saw that it had stopped. He did not tell this to his dying friend, for he remembered that the clocks had also stopped when the Baal Shem Tov, founder of Hasidism, died.

"They" Again

As the months passed, Setzer began to talk more and more about his past life. Two episodes stood out in his memory, not only because they were occasions when he was close to death, but because both times he was particularly conscious of the intervention of "them," of some higher design in the affairs of his life. Of course, the whole of life, as Setzer saw it, revealed a purpose of which we are not usually conscious. Even as a person who is under the influence of a posthypnotic suggestion goes about his business for what he thinks are his own reasons but is actually following a pull that is not revealed to him, so all the events of life are unconsciously carrying out the will of the hidden powers whom Setzer referred to as "them."

The first occasion, however, on which Setzer was almost perceptibly conscious of their guidance was during a pogrom in Zhitomir. He blamed that episode on the Western Jewish writer and Zionist, Max Nordau. Setzer had read an essay of Nordau's in which a leader is described as one willing to go ahead of his people. This simple and uncompromising definition so impressed Setzer that when an emissary was needed to approach the pogromists and attempt to dissuade them from their designs, he found himself stepping forward. As he approached the hooligans, however, his optimism evaporated: "When I saw the violence in their faces, I knew it was no use, but I kept on walking." When he had come close enough, one of the mob stepped forward and struck Setzer over the head with a heavy piece of wood. His friends managed to bring him to a doctor, where it was discovered that the blow missed being fatal by only a fraction of an inch. During the whole episode, however, Setzer had no fear, since he felt that "they" did not want him to die yet.

He had the same confidence and sense of "their" wanting him to live when in 1914 he became ill with a rare disease that the doctors declared was incurable. Setzer was proud of the fact that his disease seemed to strike only millionaires and intellectuals, but he was unwilling to accept the pessimistic prognosis of the doctors.

"The first few months at the hospital they told me to lie still, and so I was still; I didn't want to cause them any bother. But then I saw that I wasn't getting any better and I said to myself, "*Vus, meshugah bin ich,* am I crazy to die at such a young age?" I just wasn't ready, that's all, and I began to tell them to put me in the fresh air and to give me what food I thought I needed. And then I began to use my will power. This is the key to my whole life: *akshonus,* stubbornness. Every day I took one more step until I finally walked out of the hospital. *Akshonus,* this has been the secret of all my studies, and that is how I began to really understand the Zohar too. I just would not let a sentence or a phrase go without squeezing from it completely what it was trying to say."

It was during those many months in the hospital that Setzer

again took up the Zohar, which he had not seriously read since his
youth. He began to reread it, not only with the iron will that he
used in fighting his illness, but aided by the wide knowledge of
formal philosophy that he had acquired since he had left the yeshiva.
For the first time, the complex symbolism of the Zohar appeared to
yield a logical meaning, and he discovered what seemed to him the
key to its proper understanding. He saw that this classic of mysticism
reflected such classic philosophic problems as substance and attribute,
noumena and phenomena, the finite and infinite; indeed, its probing
anticipated Spinoza and Kant.

"Plato begins with ideas and sees the sensible world as a reflection
of archetypes," Setzer explained. "The Zohar carries its probing further. What precedes the idea? How does the first inchoate, hardly
recognized flash emerge into consciousness? How does it begin to
take form in the mind even before it can be verbalized? And, once this
initial creative flash is put into form, does it not then lose something
of its life?" Setzer saw that such were the themes with which the
Zohar dealt, although never in such abstract terms. It drew upon the
imagery of the *sefirot* or used analogies from the world of nature.
What is revealed at the moment when a seed is no longer a seed and
not yet a plant? Does it not at that moment reveal that nothing which
is really the source from which all life springs? In other words, is not
the *ayin* (which in Hebrew means *nothing,* but which with its letters
transposed can mean *I*) synonymous with what the sages called *yesh,*
the one true richness and treasure of life?

Whatever *yesh* Setzer possessed, however, it was not exchange-
able for rent and food. Besides his donations to charity, the rent for
his room, and the small meal which was at times completely forgotten
and never missed, he needed little, yet his income did not quite match
up to even these needs. At times he rebelled against the pressure of
economics, and his attempts to achieve some financial independence,
if not successful, were often ingenious. At one time, he even decided
to become a race horse gambler.

"After all, I thought, why should it be so difficult? The Talmud is difficult, the Zohar is difficult, but why should it be so hard to
make money? If you really put your mind to it? So I decided to
make money in a way that would leave me the maximum amount of

time for my studies and writings. I developed a system for playing the horses."

The great advantage of gambling on the horses, as Setzer saw it, was that it could be done these days without spending time at the tracks. The bookies circulated about the restaurants on Second Avenue and took bets. Setzer simply gave up a few minutes of study every day, sat at a table in the back of a restaurant, and played his system.

"At first the system had a simple basis, though later I complicated it considerably," Setzer explained. "First, I assumed that they were all *ganovim,* all thieves. Second, I knew it had nothing to do with the *narishkeit,* the foolishness of tracks, clocking . . . and handicaps. After all, if you could win by studying these facts, everybody would win who just studied hard enough.

"In fact, I didn't pay attention at first to the horses at all, but to the owners. After all, I said to myself, these owners like Whitney and others, they have a reputation to keep up. They can't show their faces to their friends if they don't have a certain percentage of winners. With all their fixing, they still have to manage to win a certain number of times. So I used to watch the big owners and their stables all over the country, and after they had a losing streak, I began to play their horses. I used the same system with the jockeys. After all, they have to make a living, and their living depends on their reputations, so they too have to fix up a certain percentage of winners. Later I developed more complicated systems, but for two years I was able to keep ahead of them. I never played less than three hundred dollars a day and sometimes as much as a thousand."

Unfortunately after two years, he wound up with as little money as he had begun with.

"The Mystery of the Sabbath"

About a year after we had commenced our relationship, Setzer's desire to adjust his financial position flared up again. It began with a recording machine I brought to his office to record the chanting of the Aramaic of the Zohar. Setzer was immediately interested in the machine and its possibilities. He wanted to hear how his voice sounded and brought down an old volume of *Das Wort* from some thirty years ago. He read some poems he had written. One began, "I am like a shadow . . . where others go, there am I and yet I am not"; another ended on his desire to "dig a pit between himself and others." When we played back the recording, he was greatly pleased with the way his voice sounded and mentioned the possibility of preparing himself for some lectures with the aid of the machine. Later he asked if a smaller size couldn't be purchased that he might use at home.

"Sometimes a thought comes to my head," he explained, "even when I am shaving, and just the right way to put it into words. If the machine could be going, I could catch it."

A few weeks later, he began work seriously recording a portion of the Zohar called "The Mystery of the Sabbath," a traditional selection which is reproduced in the prayer books of the Hasidim. It is a meditation on the oneness which unites all creation and integrates all souls on the Sabbath and tells how only such integration can evoke the fullest functioning of the creative flow, the fullest contact between creator and creation.

The mystery of the Sabbath, the Sabbath . . . that unites itself through the mystery of the One. . . . And as they unite above, so also do they unite below in the mystery of oneness, in order that the oneness above be a reflection of the oneness below. The holy One, blessed be He, does not sit upon the throne of His glory, until it becomes unified like Him, so that there may be one with one. . . .

Setzer was especially eager for me to understand this passage. He explained that the Sabbath represents the community of Israel, the heavenly counterpart of the people Israel. The Sabbath is also synonymous with *malkut,* the lowest *sefira* which is the throne of God. Being the lowest *sefira, malkut* (or the community of Israel) is most open to attack by evil forces. But these forces of anger and destruction are left behind when *malkut* unites itself and moves toward its unification with the holy One. "Then its face (the face of the community of Israel) shines with the high light. It is crowned by the holy people below, and all are crowned by new souls. . . ."

Gradually, the spiritual dynamics which the Jew tried to set in motion when he recited this text Friday evening became a little clearer. First, there was the striving for integration, the pulling of scattered drives and thoughts, back to a central core. Unless an individual and a community achieved this kind of reintegration, God could not sit upon his throne; there would be no upper coupling of the kind which produces a life flow. In addition to this inward, integrating movement, there had to be a movement upward which would leave harsh judgments and anger behind, invoking the mystery of the Sabbath, lighting up men's faces, extending itself even to the relationship between man and wife who were to be joined in fruitful union below even as the higher union took place above.

Setzer was not only interested in getting me to understand the meanings of this passage, but also in recording his chant of it. After many attempts, he made a version of the chant with which he was satisfied and announced that his recording had commercial possibilities. The more he listened, the more enthusiastic he became, finally venturing the opinion that it was perhaps just for this purpose, to make a commercially acceptable recording of "The Mystery of the Sabbath," that we had been brought together. Unexpressed was the thought: if not for this, then for what did "they" arrange our meeting? For, indeed, there had been no great change in Setzer's life and circumstances as a result of my phone call; we no longer spoke, as we did at the beginning, of publishing a full shelf of books on Jewish philosophy or of arranging for courses on the Zohar sponsored by official institutions. Nevertheless, I expressed doubts as to the commercial appeal of his recording, but Setzer decided to take it to a radio station.

The officials of this station were under considerable obligation to him, for only a month before, without his permission, they had broadcast portions of his book on the Baal Shem Tov and had remained noncommittal as regards financial compensation when Setzer finally asked them. Consequently, they were only too happy to make two records of his tape recording and give them to him as a gift. At first, Setzer was convinced that they were also interested in the commercial possibilities of the record, but after further discussion, they seemed to lose their enthusiasm. Setzer suspected that they were still interested but wanted to find a way of issuing the record without giving him any share of the profits.

Since the tape recorder was kept in my office in New Jersey,

Setzer finally consented to visit me for a weekend. Previously he had resisted my urging, claiming that he had given up all social engagements. "What do I need it for, the tenseness and the strain?" However, in order to complete his recording, he consented to come, and I picked him up Friday afternoon at his office. His overnight clothes were packed in an ancient briefcase, and he himself was carefully dressed in a white and black checkered suit and straw hat. He noticed my interest in his suit and informed me that it came from the 1920s, when they really made good clothes. The suit attracted some attention in temple that evening, where I took him for services, not only because of its unusual, if well-preserved style, but also because it had shrunk considerably around the ankles.

Most of the people at the temple, and especially the young matrons, were quite attentive to their unusual guest when coffee was served after services. He tasted various cakes pressed upon him by the hostesses and seemed flustered but by no means displeased by all the attention. I wanted to protect him from strain in his first venture into social life in years, and when some people invited him out for ice cream, I put them off. Later, when we left the temple, he said to me in a rather hurt tone, "Why did you have to speak for me? It's been so many years since I've been out in company, we could have gone with them."

Approaching the Next World

How is it possible to deal constantly with the theme of oneness and yet remain a bachelor who wanted to "dig a pit between himself and others"? Or again, in the puzzling dialectics of this world, who is more conscious of the need for fusion and togetherness than he who is gripped in the tension of separation and division?

Setzer would have probably called his lonely walking through life independence rather than separation. So eager was he to avoid troubling people that he would lie alone in his room through a week-long siege of illness rather than call for help. But this independence became more difficult with the years. He was not as sure as he used to be that he was not yet ready for death. He thought frequently of moving to Boston, where his only sister lived, but his reluctance to become a source of trouble to anybody held him back. He felt, however, that some change in his living habits had to be made. One evening he proudly announced that his problem was about to be solved. A rich Californian, who knew and admired Setzer's writings and scholarship, had come to visit him, announcing a new Jewish institution of higher learning that was being formed in California, and proposed that Setzer take a position there which would give him both security and time for study. Months passed and Setzer waited for the offer to materialize. "They may force me yet to become rich," he would say when I asked about his wealthy admirer. Then one day he told me that the man from California had died before completing the arrangements, and Setzer was forced to remain in New York.

By the end of our second year together, Setzer was speaking less and less about projects for the future. The scholar's iron will had not left him, but he had been ill and alone in his room a number of times, and the daily travel from Seagate to his office was wearing. More and more of his conversation took the form of philosophic soliloquies about death, which came at the most unlikely moments.

One evening a mutual friend who had just returned from Israel dined with us and began speaking of his trip. Soon we became conscious of the fact that Setzer was also talking, but with no apparent attempt to participate in the general conversation. He was launched on one of his half-whimsical monologues: "I have come to the conclusion lately that something which is completely evil, or almost without any mixture of good, can have a powerful drive for life, for example, a complete murderer or evil genius. But I don't think this is the case with a good person. He must have an admixture of evil to want to live strongly. If he loses it, then he is finished. I know myself that much of my striving and accomplishment and power come from my *yetzer hara,* my evil impulse. Until a few years ago, I used to bathe all year long in the ocean, even in the winter. It was healthy, but I also did it partly because I liked to show off a bit. And when I studied the Zohar, I was interested in it not only for its own sake but also I wanted the satisfaction of knowing that nobody else knew it as well as I. Not that I wanted glory, but I did want that satisfaction. The results were good, but it was the admixture of evil impulse that gave me power. I think about it now because lately I just haven't been concerned with knowing more or less than the other person. The evil is weakening. It's not good."

After such meditations, Setzer would smile in self-amusement, but he was rather serious about them. In fact, he began to make some rather startling changes in his religious habits. Since early youth, Setzer had been unconcerned with the formal ritualistic observances of his tradition, though he was deeply religious in spirit. Whenever one asked why there was so little connection between his personal religious habits and his studies in Jewish Law, he would bypass the question with the admonition to let ritual observances "come naturally without strain"—he liked to drop in on a synagogue when he was in the mood. The year I met him, he began saying the old prayers more regularly and, most surprising of all, he resumed the practice of eating kosher food, something he had abandoned for over fifty years. In announcing his new dietary regime, he was almost apologetic. "After all, I'll have to meet the Cordovero and the Ari soon. Nu, about putting on *tefillin* and praying three times a day, they won't ask me. But to eat *treife* (nonkosher food), it's just not nice."

Jewish tradition encourages little speculation regarding life after death; even the mystics did not let their minds dwell on it. One evening, however, Setzer broke from the tradition and told me a strange story. We had been reading the Zohar at his office, and the hour was sufficiently late for the neighborhood to be very quiet. It had become a custom for him to chant the Aramaic text, after which I translated. The passage we were reading described a mysterious character, Rab Hamnuna, who sometimes appeared on earth in the guise of a donkey driver. I translated, ". . . and Rabbi Eleazar and Rabbi Abba bowed before him, and then they saw him no more. They stood up, looked on all sides, but saw him no more. They sat and cried and could not talk one to the other. After an hour had passed, Rabbi Abba said, 'Is not this what we have learned, that in every path where good men travel, if the words of Torah are between them, then those who have already merited the next world, come before them. . . .' "

Setzer's attention was no longer on the passage. He had risen from the table and was walking back and forth in the quiet office, as if trying to make a decision.

"It should be told in different circumstances," he suddenly began. "This is not the proper atmosphere, but I would like to tell you of an incident in my own life. You know, I am a rationalist, but still, if something actually happens to me, I have to accept it."

It was almost midnight and only the occasional sound of muffled footsteps on the pavement outside could be heard as he spoke.

"I had two sisters. One of them, about five years ago, became seriously ill. One day I was sitting alone in my room and suddenly . . . I am a rationalist, but still, it happened. . . . I saw something dressed in black and it was my sister. She came close to me and kissed me, then suddenly dropped away. Then I heard a voice close by, whispering clearly in my ear, 'Your sister died, your sister died.' The whole next day I heard music, beautiful music of a song I used to know and like very much, but I can't recall it lately. I heard this music so loud and clear that I was sure it was a radio or something which the neighbors also heard, but I found out that they didn't. Then I got a telegram telling me that my sister had died. I figured out the time and hour, and it was the exact moment when I heard the whispering." He paused, and when he sat down again to the Zohar, his long, thin face seemed softer and wearier; he didn't begin reading for a few minutes.

It may be that Setzer was thinking about his dead sister and of the mysteries that mysticism could not unravel. Perhaps he was trying to throw off his mood with a Hasidic phrase of Rabbi Nachman, which he began to use frequently: "It is forbidden to be old."

"That means," Setzer explained, "that one must always continue to make large plans and projects, to look to the future even as a youth."

But I had the feeling as he told this that the battle against oldness was not going well.

A Reading

It was at the end of our second year together that the threads of our relationship began to frazzle and break. One day I told Setzer that I had written an article about him for a prominent Jewish magazine. The old man was not displeased, but a few weeks later he called up the editor and said that he wanted to change some sections.

The editor told him that the article was about him, but it was not his to rewrite. Setzer was never convinced that the article was not his; when it was published, he simply declared, "Well, I've made you famous."

When I sent him the fee I had received for the article, there was no acknowledgment. This was not ingratitude; Setzer simply felt that the article belonged to him, and with it the fee. Although the article resulted in some modest financial benefits for Setzer—a few people sent in contributions to help the aging scholar—his complaints about my failures to carry through on his larger projects grew sharper every week. Finally, I decided to arrange the event which turned out to be the calamitous finale to our relationship.

For many years Setzer had been placing notices in a Hebrew magazine advertising his availability for lectures on subjects such as "The Philosophy of Spinoza," "Crescas," "Maimonides," "The Zohar," and the like. Why he maintained this advertisement I don't know, for he never accepted an invitation to speak, even when it came. It was, perhaps, a phase of his own dream logic that the old man did not want to disturb by exposure to reality. I believed, however, that I could arrange a safe kind of exposure. A group of rabbis in New Jersey wanted to hold a study retreat in Atlantic City. They accepted my suggestion that Setzer be invited as our guest lecturer. To my surprise, Setzer accepted their invitation.

"Only I can't promise now to give the lecture. I'll have to see the kind of people they are."

I drove Setzer out to Atlantic City and introduced him to my colleagues, who went out of their way to make the old man feel comfortable. After a few hours, Setzer told me he liked the men and announced his readiness to give them a reading from one of his essays that evening. I suggested that a lecture might be more in order. But no, Setzer insisted that he liked the rabbis and would favor them by a reading from a chapter in one of his books discussing the difference between sanctification and Nazariteship.

It was not the subject matter which worried me. Setzer's thesis was that the Hebrew concepts of Nazariteship and holiness had common roots; both included the idea of separation from the group and of a voluntary assumption of duties and obligations from which the majority were exempted. The Nazarite, however, Setzer claimed, divided life into two parts, and tended to view this world as all evil. The Hebrew holy man, on the other hand, saw everything as an intermingling of good and bad. "He looks not at the details, but at the 'all,'" and no longer sees two separate divisions. The ultimate root of both good and evil is united in a source that is absolutely good. "It is only that while the root of the good draws its sustenance from the innerness of goodness, the root of evil stems from the outer shell of this goodness."

Setzer was convinced that Christianity favored the Nazarite view of life, and that its concept of sanctification was more concerned with hatred of life than love of God. And "he who denies the holiness of life also denies the reality of the source of holiness, the reality of the holy God." The result of such denial, Setzer argued, is a distortion of faith which opens the way for "a dark and angry mysticism which walks only with terror, with horrors and nightmares that are connected with the drinking of blood, with the agony of a god dying in torture and pain."

Although Setzer's thesis was a good discussion topic, I was a little worried about the idea of giving a reading from his works; such a custom had been high style among Yiddish intellectuals in Seagate around the 1920s, but it was not the sort of thing to which young rabbis were accustomed. Setzer insisted, however, and the rabbis agreed to be good sports.

At nine o'clock that evening, we set up a small table in one of the rabbis' rooms. It was a small room, so several of us had to sit on the bed, and one colleague deciding to be completely comfortable, stretched out on the bed. I finally introduced Setzer who took his seat behind a small table and nervously turned the pages of the book from which he was going to read. Since his dentures were being repaired, he took out his handkerchief and half covered his mouth; then, clearing his throat several times, he began.

Many years have passed since that evening, but I still find it difficult to think of what happened without embarrassment. Incongruity, we are told, is the root cause of humor and laughter. Perhaps that explains it. It *was* incongruous—young American-born rabbis lounging about a hotel room and listening to an old man reading Yiddish with a voice half-muffled by a handkerchief held to his mouth, in the melodramatic tones that had been perfected by Yiddish dramatic readers of the last century. But what started the catastrophe was the rhythmic creaking of the bed. Looking for the cause of the noise, we saw our colleague's round, white-shirted stomach, heaving with barely suppressed giggles.

It must have been the work of Lilith and all her cackling hosts, but suddenly there was an explosion of wild laughter—a terrible paroxysm of giggling which overcame our frantic efforts at self-control. I jumped up and ran to a window, coughing loudly and shouting something about smoke. The others took the cue. Soon everyone was opening windows and doors. Setzer sat at the table, at first bewildered. Then as he realized what was happening, his face became white and his lower lip trembled. In a few moments, we regained control of ourselves and returned to our places. It was too late. Setzer shut the book, rose, and walked out.

We ran after him, trying to explain that it was all the fault of the room, its smallness, the cigarette smoke. He looked as if he wanted to believe us, but shook his head and went to his room. The next morning I drove him back to New York. By mutual consent, we didn't talk about the events of the previous night. It was Setzer's first lecture in more than thirty years. We both knew it was his last.

Finale

After that, I went down a few more times to the office on East Broadway, but we both knew that our relationship had ended. I called from time to time, and one evening Setzer told me his financial worries were completely resolved. He was getting a monthly Social Security allotment that not only was enough for his needs, but covered his charitable donations and even let him save a few dollars.

"Why didn't you tell me about Social Security?" he wanted to know, and I had no answer. Setzer could have been receiving Social Security all these years, had either of us thought about it.

The years passed and our telephone communications were less and less frequent, though we always sent each other cards for the New Year. Then one day, someone called to say that Setzer was in the hospital and wanted to see me. I visited him the next day. He was sitting on the edge of the bed, talking to another visitor, when I walked in. He had always been very skinny, but now the hollows of his cheeks seemed to meet in the center of his long face. Everything about him had shrunk, his shoulders, his chest, even his formerly protruding nose. His hand, when I took it, seemed weightless.

"Ah, ah," he exclaimed in a voice which would have been hearty, if it were not so weak. "I'm glad to see you," and he introduced me to the visitor as his *talmid,* pupil.

"You heard why I'm here, no?" His mouth opened in the suggestion of a smile, but not too wide, for his false teeth were out, a fact which made it even more difficult than usual to understand what he was saying.

"I wanted to take some bicarbonate of soda and, in the dark, instead took Boric acid. An ambulance brought me here three weeks ago, and now they won't let me go."

Before seeing Setzer, I had spoken to the hospital doctor and knew why they didn't want to let him go. An examination of the eighty-six-year-old man had disclosed an advanced cancerous growth, but Setzer didn't know this. The reason he sent for me, he said, was because he had finally decided to leave for Israel. There were some last-minute preparations, and he wanted my help.

From what the doctor had said and from the way Setzer looked, there was little sense in making long-distance travel plans. But I remembered that the iron will of S. Z. Setzer had already made mockery of many a medical diagnosis, and listened carefully to his instructions.

The next few months were hectic and aggravating for all of Setzer's friends who were trying to help him. Finally the day for his departure arrived. I brought a station wagon to Seagate and loaded his luggage. There were three badly scuffed brown suitcases, some string-bound grocery cartons, and the tape recorder I had given him twelve years ago. It appeared to be broken, and I asked Setzer why he needed it. There were some ideas, the old man explained, about the difference between the mathematical ideal of infinity and the idea of the *ein sof,* the infinite as it is understood in the Zohar, that he wanted to record into the machine some day.

"Just think," Setzer mused as we drove to the pier, "soon I will see what Herzl and Feierberg could only dream about."

When I brought Setzer into the cabin, a white-haired man who had been resting on one of the beds in the room sat up in alarm. I understood his concern. The man who was scheduled to be his roommate for a two-week sea voyage looked as if he would never survive the trip. A baggy brown suit hung loosely about the thin frame of his body. His long face, always thin, was now skeletal in appearance and completely colorless, except for the red-rimmed eyes. He sat on the bed, resting against the wall, while I pushed two rope-bound, tattered suitcases and several cardboard cartons into a corner of the cabin. A few other friends had come to bid Setzer farewell, and while they were talking to him I walked over to his worried roommate and told him that he was going to travel with a great Hebrew scholar.

"Oh," said the man doubtfully. "But he must be over 90."

"Not quite," I replied. "Only 86."

The man did not seem reassured.

"He was a contemporary of Theodore Herzl, the founder of the Zionist movement," I added. Setzer's roommate remained unimpressed. I made one more attempt.

"He is also a kabbalist—you know, a mystic." I was hoping, I suppose, that Setzer's connections with the mysterious spheres would relieve his roommate's anxiety.

"And you," asked the man, "you're from his family?"

"No," I said. "Only a friend, and," I remembered Setzer's introduction at the hospital and gave myself permission to say the words, "his pupil."

I never saw Mr. Setzer again. I did receive a card written during the voyage and saying, "What blessings and happiness," and later, from Israel, a New Year's card. An American who visited him in Israel told me that he had quarreled with friends who had put him in a hospital and also with the doctors, insisting on returning to his own room. A few months later, an article in the Yiddish press told of Setzer's death. Later that evening, I reread a passage from one of Setzer's articles which the old man had instructed me to insert in the magazine piece I had written about him. "You might call it," he said, "the prayer of a mystic."

The prayer comes from an essay in which Setzer describes the experience of the mystic as being like that of the boy Samuel in the bible. The young lad heard a call, but at first refused to yield to its implications, for it seemed to be at variance with his reason and experience. But the voice called again and again, until he could not deny its reality. So it is with the mystic.

And even as he [the mystic] attempted at first to be untouched by this other will which wanted to place him under its rule, even as in the beginning he struggled stubbornly not to perceive the mystic truth which wanted to force itself upon him, so now he hastens to take upon himself the discipline of this will.

Even as at first he made himself deaf and blind to the voice of God which had sounded in his ears, and to the signs and proofs which He had shown him, so now are his ears quickened all day to absorb the word of God that is sent to him, and his eyes are opened wide continually to the different signs shown him from the heavens.

But his heart cries. Within him he is filled with despair and his spirit is bent. And it happens that at the moment of his sorrow, at the hour when he remains without guidance, and his soul knows not how to turn—and at certain moments in life he finds it impossible to decide which path to take—that then, these wondrous hints for which he waits, which might guide him through his straits, fail to come.

And at times it happens that the "inspiration of spirit" which had been given him is not wholly removed. The different "hints" for which he waits continue to appear to him. He still hears the voice of God reverberating in his ears. But it is impossible to fathom the meaning of these hints. It is impossible to combine the sounds into words. He knows they seek something from him but he knows not what they seek. And he summons all his strength and strains to lift the veil before him, but his effort peters out in confusion and emptiness. His striving leads him only to sadness of heart and hollowness of soul.

And he feels crushed, desolate, and abandoned—and a prayer of the heart, broken and torn, then bursts from his mouth.

O cause the flow of Thy graciousness to descend upon me, and show me the way which is for me to follow. Enlighten, my God, my eyes, that they may see and understand your wonders and signs; that I may know how to save my soul from the heaviness of this oppression which Thou layest upon me.

May the flow of blessing from above be drawn forth to descend upon me, that I may be able to do the will of my Father Who is in Heaven, that I may be able to properly assume the yoke of His kingdom, and fulfill all that He asks of me.

Grace me, my God, with the understanding and knowledge to find the meaning of the wonders and signs which I see, to comprehend the intent of all those things from out of which you speak.

3
THE ACCOUNTANT

Many talents are required of the person who wants to enter into this world and into this research. I doubt if all of them are to be found in me. But I do testify to two qualities which have accompanied my work in the past and will be there, I hope, in the future: courage and humility. Courage to dare, to pioneer, to ask, and humility before the facts and conclusions, whether or not they suit my theories. . . .

Historical criticism is a modest tool, not inclined to exaggerate its own value or see itself as a panacea. It is not a key which opens all the closed chambers. There are insights which see more. There is intuition; there is contemplation which penetrates (or claims to penetrate) to the depths. Against these, historic criticism seems to be a rather unimpressive matter. And still, how great its power! For it guards against the illusions and self-deceptions which we all love. It may not be much, but we have nothing better and, in a generation which makes a fuss about "existential analysis," it is fitting for a scholar in the humanities to announce where he stands. Anyone who denies the method of historic criticism and makes little of its conclusions or tries to escape from them, builds on air and he will, in the end, pay the price of his position. Intuition and faith are fine in their place. Historical science stands and falls with historical criticism.

—Gershom G. Scholem *in* Molad, *April, 1962*

Even while studying with Setzer, I thought of myself as having yet another teacher. Gershom G. Scholem who, until his retirement in 1965, was professor of Jewish mysticism at the Hebrew University in Jerusalem, never realized I was his pupil. Occasionally, seeing me at a class in Jerusalem or at a public lecture in America, a flicker more of bewilderment than recognition would furrow his brow. For I never formally registered in his classes. But I always understood that an individual in our day, looking for entrance into the *pardes* would find his most accessible gate through Professor Scholem whose superb scholarship is recognized in academic circles throughout the world. And even in Meah Shearim, the Orthodox quarter of Jerusalem, where pious Jews are unusually unimpressed by the world's standards, Scholem's mastery of his field receives acknowledgment. One afternoon in Jerusalem the Nazir, while displaying his collection of rare kabbalistic texts, showed me a copy of the *Book of Creation,* but made a point of folding down a corner of the book's face page.

"Can you guess whose name is written on this page?" he asked. Then he turned up the corner to reveal Scholem's signature.

No one can deny Scholem's immense knowledge, not only in the field of Jewish mysticism and history, but in comparative religion, philosophy, history, literature, and even science.

One of Scholem's friends, an individual of cautious statement, respectfully classified the professor of mysticism as "one of the ten great minds in our generation." But then, he regaled me with an anecdote. During the First World War Scholem, though a pacifist at the time, was drafted into the German army. The military authorities found themselves with a soldier who apparently had forgotten all his German and spoke only Latin. Scholem's performance, and evidently the quality of his Latin, were so convincing that the Army hastily discharged him. "And if you have ever seen Scholem's facial contortions, you will understand their decision," my friend concluded.

I understood my informant's allusion. Gershom Scholem's tall, gangling figure gives the appearance of continuous disjointed motion. Even when he is sitting behind a desk and delivering a lecture, there is a perpetual writhing of hands, arms, and legs. His facial grimaces are a completely uninhibited expression of his outer and inner environment. A sudden unexplained noise in the classroom can evoke the look of a hunted victim. The description of a complex idea may be accompanied by a contortion of the brows which makes the observer feel that the thought is being physically squeezed out of his skull. Professor Scholem is fully aware and even delighted at the consternation his physical appearance may arouse, especially from those who have a different image in mind of how a professor of mysticism should look.

The subject came up only a few moments after I began to interview him one summer afternoon in New York. He had responded to my telephone call by inviting me to visit him in an office of the Jewish Theological Seminary. I found him sitting at a desk on which lay a

Hebrew manuscript and a box of chocolates. I introduced myself as one
of his unofficial pupils, but told him that the questions I wanted to ask
were not directly related to the subject of Jewish mysticism. They had
to do with himself and the genesis of his own interest in the Kabbala,
for, I explained somewhat apologetically, people expected a higher cor-
relation between subject matter and teacher in a topic like mysticism
than they would in fields like physics and history.

Scholem leaned back in his chair and raised his eyebrows in mock
apprehension. "Maybe I ought to roll my eyes more," he said, gazing
upward to demonstrate the pious pose people expected.

We both laughed at the prospect of Gershom Scholem trying
to look more mystical. Scholem came forward in his chair, reached into
the box on his desk, grabbed three chocolates, popped two in his mouth
and laid one aside for reserve. Then he leaned back again, cupped
his hands behind his head, and with evident pleasure, tried to answer
my questions.

His interest in Jewish mysticism, he began, was not something
that he had gotten from his family. "They were good German Jews,
quite assimilated and in the printing business." He had not been
given a Jewish education in his youth. Indeed, he first began studying
Hebrew in his late teens. When, in his early twenties, he "returned"
to Judaism, he had joined the extremist Orthodox religious party, all
the while harboring secret communist leanings. "They would have
been shocked had they known, but I saw no necessary contradiction."
He had taken his degree in mathematics at a German university and
only later decided to devote himself to the field of Jewish mysticism.

"Wasn't the mixture of mathematics and mysticism rather
strange?"

Scholem shrugged. "Perhaps my mathematical training helps me
to insist on more precise definitions. Also, maybe it lets me be more
scientific or objective in my weighing of data. In any case, my decision
to study Jewish mysticism came the day I visited the home of a
famous German rabbi, a person with reputation for scholarship in the
Kabbala—I shall not mention his name. Seeing on his shelf some
mystical texts with intriguing titles, I had, with all the enthusiasm
of youth, asked the rabbi about them. " *'Dieses quatsch,* this junk!' the
rabbi had laughed at me. 'I should waste time reading nonsense like

this?' It was then," Scholem raised his eyebrows in amused reflection, "that I decided here was a field in which I could make an impression. If this man can become an authority without reading the text, then what might I become if I actually read the books?"

"But wasn't there an attraction of a more personal sort that drew you to Jewish mysticism?"

"I will tell you," there was a mischievous smile on his lips, "I did in my youth write a book about Kabbala from the personal point of view, but you won't be able to get it."

"Why not?"

"Because I bought up all the copies," Scholem grinned and threw another chocolate into his mouth. "But you know, it's a hot day." The professor took out a handkerchief and mopped his brow. "Once on a day like this I was sitting alone in the seminary library upstairs reading some kabbalistic manuscripts. It became so hot that I stripped myself completely of clothes and sat there naked—after locking the door, of course." His tone indicated that there were to be no more personal revelations that afternoon. The rest of our hour was spent in discussing the monetary miserliness of certain publishers and the difficulty he always had in persuading them to pay proper royalties.

The next summer, while visiting in Jerusalem, I once more called for an appointment. This time the professor invited me to his home. Again it was a hot day, and Scholem met me at the door wiping his forehead with a handkerchief. The living room adjoined a room whose walls were covered with what must be the world's best private collection of books and manuscripts on the subject of Jewish mysticism. I suddenly thought of a comment Martin Buber had made about Scholem once when I had visited him: "Scholem is a great scholar; he has made a science out of the Kabbala." It was not clear from Buber's expression whether or not he meant his remark as criticism or compliment.

There was no mistaking Scholem's feeling toward his Jerusalem neighbor, however. "Buber's glory and fame are assured." He grinned. "But he certainly has a talent for making cloudy anything that is clear."

I mentioned Buber's remark about Scholem making a science out of the Kabbala. Was it possible to use a scientific approach to something so subjective as mysticism?

Before answering, Scholem led me into the living room where

his wife brought us some cookies and cups of hot chocolate. He saw me looking at a painting hung on his wall—a portrait of a face with round, staring eyes, wide mouth, prominent nose—more a caricature than a picture.

"Yes," he happily affirmed, "that's me—the clown." The professor's delight at the entrance of Fanya, his good-looking and personable former student, was evident. He teasingly invited her to sit with us and was at least as concerned with the effect of his remarks on her as on me. Rapidly finishing a cup of chocolate, he returned to my question. "The one thing that I pride myself on," he said, utterly serious for a moment, "is a willingness to bow before the facts, even if that means giving up my own cherished opinions."

But was there also not some personal involvement with the subject of Jewish mysticism? Surely it was not just a matter of scientific scholarly curiosity.

"Oh, of course. By now I imagine that anything I say or do has the influence of the Kabbala in it. But the main thing I try to maintain is distance. Without distance, there can be no real scholarship. I must be ready and have been ready to change my views if the facts have proven me wrong. This is the main virtue that I claim for my scholarship."

Seeing that I was still not satisfied with his answer, he wriggled his large fingers in the air. "Listen," he said, "I've done my research in this history of the Kabbala simply because I loved Judaism and wanted to show that mysticism was a legitimate part of this Judaism. Not some strange flower, but an indigenous growth. However, if you want to know about my feelings on this subject, I mean my personal feelings, I will tell you a secret." Scholem and his wife looked at each other as if relishing this moment of teasing disclosure. "It is all written down, but only in the form of incidental remarks—hints, scattered through my writings."

As I left Scholem's home, I realized that there had been a measure of impertinence in my questions. Scholem has never claimed to be a mystic, only a student of mystic phenomena. Analyzing my own curiosity as to the influence of the Kabbala on Scholem's personal life and thought, I recalled a remark which I once heard a Jerusalem rabbi make about all so-called scientific scholars in the field of Jewish mysticism.

"They are accountants," the old man had said. "That is, like accountants, they know where the wealth is, its location and value. But it doesn't belong to them. They cannot use it."

Would Scholem be satisfied with such a characterization of the objective scholarly approach to Jewish mysticism? Can a mysticism from which a man insists on keeping his "distance," yet speak, as the Quakers would say to his condition.

These were the questions to which I hoped Scholem would yet respond to directly. Meanwhile, all I had was the promise of hints in his account. And there was the account itself which, whatever it might disclose of Scholem's personal views, is the best introduction to the varieties of Jewish mystical expression.

The Account

Major Trends in Jewish Mysticism, Scholem's grand summary of this field, is a deceiving book in that its fine organization disguises the depth and width of research which undergirds every paragraph, for Scholem is an accountant who has discovered much of the data he records. He has pieced together long-forgotten scraps of manuscripts, stripped pseudoauthors of their disguises, revealed subversive heresies lurking within innocent-looking hymns, and destroyed long-accepted theories about the origin and dating of classic kabbalistic documents. He has established logical causal connections between such seemingly diverse phenomena as the Kabbala, the French Revolution, and early Reform Judaism.

Scholem begins by insisting that "there is no such thing as mysticism in the abstract . . . there is only the mysticism of a particular religious system—Christian, Islamic, Jewish mysticism, and so on." Historically, mystical tendencies are often connected with the attempt of fresh religious impulses to reconcile themselves with an inherited religious system and its classical formulae. Thus, for the mystic "the substance of canonical texts, like that of all other religious values, is melted down and given another form as it passes through the fiery stream of the mystical consciousness." It is hardly surprising that, "hard

as the mystic may try to remain within the confinements of his religion, he often consciously or unconsciously approaches, or even trans-
gresses its limits, becoming then an either recognized or unrecognized
heretic."

This heretical upsurge is unconsciously aided by the fact that
the mystic, in his rebellion against the carefully demythologized classical concepts of his faith, opens himself up to the power of long-
suppressed spiritual cravings. The bible, later the rabbis, and most of
all the Jewish philosophers of the Middle Ages, fought every evidence
of pagan mythology. But this eagerness to achieve a completely demythologized, monotheistic faith paid a heavy price for its disdain of
the primitive levels of human life. It ignored the terrors from which
myths are made, as though denying the very existence of the problem.
This feeling for the reality of evil and the power of the demoniac
found its expression through the Kabbala, which also became a vehicle for the reentrance into Judaism of old pagan superstitions, theur-
gic rites, and gnostic heresies.

"The Kabbala," Scholem points out, "was not, as is still sometimes supposed, a unified system of mystical and specifically theosophical thinking. There is no such thing as 'the doctrines of the kabbalists.'
Actually, we encounter widely diversified and often contradicting mo-
tivations, crystallized in very different systems or quasi-systems."

Scholem reserves the term *Kabbala* for these manifestations of
the mystical impulse that appeared during and after the Middle Ages,
but his point about the variegated nature of Jewish mystical phenomena is apparent throughout the book. For instance, the pre-Chris-
tian era groups such as the Essenes or Theraputae that formed covenant communities that lived by organized mystic traditions. Later came
the Descenders of the Chariot mentioned in the Talmudic literature
of the early centuries, small circles of initiates whose visions are described in mystical tracts such as the *Greater Chambers* and the *Lesser
Chambers*. These visions are replete with descriptions of heavenly
palaces, hierarchies of angels, thrones, and the like. It is a mysticism
which stresses God's otherness. Its major moods are "majesty, fear, and
trembling."

In the Middle Ages, the mysticism of the Hasidim, the pious
ones, of northern Europe, led by the thirteenth-century Rabbi Yehuda

ha-Hassid, was still interested in the fiery imagery of heavenly chariots, palaces, and cherubs, but also stressed God's immanence and saw Him as a "dear Friend." It preached a fervent love of God, humility, personal asceticism, and an equanimity that would enable man to be undisturbed by either pain or joy, wealth or poverty. These early Hasidim combined their spiritual strivings with a belief in the semi-magical efficacy of prayer and holy words. This belief in the power of words was the foundation for the reverence that later mystical movements in Judaism show for a *baal shem,* a master of the word. It also became the basis for a mystical legend such as the golem, the homunculus supposed to have been created in sixteenth-century Prague by the famous Rabbi Loew.

Much more orderly and systematized is the metaphysical speculation which characterized Jewish mystical movements in southern France and Spain during the Middle Ages. Here, too, there were various schools of mystical thought, including one headed by Abraham Abulafia, who is unusual in his willingness to describe his inner experiences. Abulafia developed a system of meditation in thirteenth-century Spain which would interest enthusiasts of yoga and modern psychologists. The soul, said Abulafia, has knots and seals, which enable it to function in a finite world, for the flood of the divine stream, if let freely into the soul, would overwhelm and blind it. Thus, the problem of man is to learn how to untie the knots of his soul, to retreat from the world of multiplicity into the world of unity without being utterly dissolved by the divine light. To accomplish this, Abulafia developed techniques for concentrating on the Hebrew alphabet, arranging, balancing, and harmonizing its letters as carefully as a composer would work with notes. The goal of his "play" with the letters and their numerical equivalents was not only to imprint their mystic meaning on the soul but to use them as a device for dissolving all mental and sense images, the forms which prevent man from vivid contact with the cosmic intellect and force. Abulafia and his followers left numerous how-to manuals and personal testimonies of their success in achieving the state of consciousness which the Jewish mystic calls *dvekut,* an intimate clinging to God.

Thirteenth-century Spain also produced the Zohar, and Scholem's discussion takes on the excitement of a mystery story as he attempts to trace the ideas of the Zohar to their original sources. The hunt leads to southern France and two individuals, Rabbi Abraham ben David and his son, Isaac the Blind. These men, in turn, seem to have received their secrets from the East via a family that came from Italy. The "chain of the Kabbala" then leads from the Provence to Gerona in Spain and from there to the author of the Zohar.

The authorship of the Zohar is a major problem for the historian of Jewish mysticism, and its resolution usually differentiates the believing kabbalist from the objective scholar. Was the Zohar, or large sections of it, written, as kabbalists claim, by the second-century Rabbi Simeon bar Yochai? Or was it composed by a man named Moses ben Shem Tov de Leon, who lived in Avila, Spain, during the middle of the thirteenth century? Scholem's first hypothesis, which opposed the theory of the scholarly establishment of his day, was that portions of the Zohar did go back to the time of Simeon bar Yochai, but continued research and use of modern philological techniques made him "bow before the facts," and conclude that it was completely the work of de Leon.

Following his chapters on the Zohar, Scholem's descriptions deepen as he discusses the intricate theosophical system of the sixteenth-century Isaac Luria, the Holy Ari. The latter's theories form the basis of the movements which quite plainly hold a special attraction for Scholem, namely, the Shabbatai Zevi heresy and its amazing aftermath, the Jacob Frank Movement.

Shabbatai Zevi was born in Ismir, Turkey, where he studied the Kabbala as a young man and was considered strange. According to Scholem this behavior was the expression of a manic-depressive psychosis. Shabbatai Zevi could be a pleasant companion and a fairly diligent rabbinic student one day, and could, the next day, fall into a state of utter hopelessness. It was probably to find a remedy for this condition that Shabbatai Zevi, when he came to the Holy Land, visited a man known as Nathan of Gaza, who had a reputation for helping people. In the kabbalistic terminology of the day, Nathan could prescribe the proper *tikkun,* repair or therapy, that a person needed in order to "lift the spark" or bind his soul "to its roots." It was Nathan, Scholem suspects, who confirmed Shabbatai Zevi's suspicion that he was the Messiah. To be sure, there have been few periods of Jewish history without some kind of a messianic outburst. The difference was that, in this case, during the years 1664 and 1665, large numbers of sensible and practical burghers in cities such as Amsterdam, Frankfurt, and London began to sell their possessions and acquire white silk garments in preparation for their journey to the Near East where the Jewish king-Messiah was supposed to announce the arrival of the messianic age. Jewish communities and their responsible leaders quivered with expectation. Rumors of the coming event even excited Christian journalists, who went East to cover the story and send back descriptions and drawings of the "Jewish king." To be sure, there were aspects of this Messiah that disturbed even his own followers. Nathan tried to offer kabbalistic explanations for some of Shabbatai Zevi's "strange acts." The precise nature of these acts is uncertain. They probably were episodes that would disturb good Orthodox Jews, such as pronouncing the name of God, a right accorded only to the high priest during the days of the Temple, or abrogating the traditional fast on the ninth of Av, the commemoration of the destruction of the Temple. Later, after the Messiah and Nathan had gathered some disciples, there were some truly strange events, including Shabbatai Zevi's marriage to a woman of sordid reputation.

The most difficult test for Nathan's powers of explanation ensued after Shabbatai Zevi appeared before the Turkish sultan, who was disturbed by the social and religious ferment of the new messianic movement.

The sultan offered Shabbatai Zevi two alternatives. He would either put on the green turban, sign of the Muslim faith, or lose his head. Shabbatai Zevi donned the turban. At this point, by all logical considerations, the Shabbatai Zevi movement should have died. Instead, it entered into its most interesting and dangerous stage. The "Messiah," now a Muslim, continued to receive visitors and hold court in the Gallipoli prison castle to which he was confined for fifteen years. There he would sing songs and listen to music—music was one of his outstanding talents—while his disciples, led by Nathan of Gaza, propagated a religious theory explaining why it was necessary for the Messiah to become a Muslim. So successful was this explanation that in some communities faithful Jews followed his example and became Muslims, at least on the surface.

In eastern Europe, in the early part of the eighteenth century, the explanation of the Shabbatai Zevi apologists became the ideology of a Jewish group led by Jacob Frank, a power-mad genius. On one occasion the Frankists announced their readiness to convert to Catholicism. To all appearances, they became faithful Christians, but made one reservation: they would not cut off their beards. After all, how could a good Jew cut off his beard? For these people were in their minds good and faithful Jews. The proof of their faith and trust was their readiness to assume the most tragic of fates, apostasy. The Frankists undertook other unusual proofs of their "faithfulness." They not only broke the laws of the Torah, their ceremonies were said to include incestuous sexual orgies. The Frankists were, to be sure, an extremist offshoot of the followers of Shabbatai Zevi. Most of the latter were content to go on pretending that they were Orthodox Jews like the rest of the community. Only in intimate gatherings and in carefully disguised writings did they reveal their belief in the "new Torah." There is a further sequel to this chain of events which is no less surprising than what has so far been described. According to Scholem, from these circles, and motivated by their ideology, came some of the French Revolution's most fervent fighters. These groups also produced, by a dialectical development, some of the pioneers of rational "enlightened" Reform Judaism.

Scholem's book then proceeds to a description of Hasidism, the latest "phase in the development of Jewish mysticism," and ends with a tale which, he suggests, sums up the history of the Hasidic movement.

When the Baal Shem, the Master of the Name, as the founder of Hasidism was called, had a difficult task, he would go to a certain place in the woods, light a fire and meditate in prayer—and what he had set out to perform was done. When a generation later, the Maggid of Meseritz was faced with the same task, he would go to the same place in the woods and say: "We can no longer light the fire, but we can still speak the prayers"—and what he wanted done became reality. Again a generation later Rabbi Moshe Leib of Sassov had to perform this task. And he, too, went into the woods and said: "We can no longer light a fire, nor do we know the secret meditations

*belonging to the prayer, but we do know the place in the woods to
which it all belongs—and that must be sufficient," and sufficient it
was. But when another generation had passed and Rabbi Israel of
Rishin was called upon to perform the task, he sat down in his golden
chair in his castle and said: "We cannot light the fire, we cannot
speak the prayers, we do not know the place, but we can tell the
story of how it was done." And, the storyteller adds, the story which
he told had the same effect as the actions of the other three.*

Not only Hasidism, suggests Scholem, but Jewish mysticism
too, finds itself today in a position where all that remains of mystery
is the tale. But "the story is not ended, it has not yet become history
and the secret life it holds can break out tomorrow in you or me. Under what aspects this invisible stream of Jewish mysticism will again
come to the surface, we cannot tell—that is the task of prophets, not
of professors."

The Lurianic Mythos

I did not know, when I first read Scholem's closing sentence, that
I would one day hear him move beyond the "task" of professor to dare
some speculations on just how the "secret life" of the Kabbala might
be surfacing in our time. But, it always seemed to me that of the
many riches preserved through Scholem's magnificent scholarship, one
set of ideas which developed about Rabbi Isaac Luria in the sixteenth
century, was particularly promising for its potential insight into peren-
nial life problems. Luria, called by his followers the Holy Ari (ari
means lion) came from Egypt to Safed, a city in the northern hills of
the Holy Land, and died there during a plague before he reached the
age of forty. Even during his lifetime, folk legends began to enshroud
him in a semimagical garb which grew in luster and detail with succeeding generations. He left no books or essays, only a few poems. The
outlines of his teachings were copied by a few disciples who revealed
them only to their own small circles. Nevertheless, only a few years
after his death, his system of thought had spread to all corners of the
Jewish world and became what Scholem calls the "true theologia mystica of Judaism. . . ."

It is difficult to explain why the Kabbala of the Ari achieved such popularity. His ideas are extremely abstruse and intricate. There were always only a very few who fully understood them. Scholem's explanation of the powerful effect of the Ari's ideas is that they offered the Jew an answer to his basic historic predicament, the conflict of being a chosen people whose chosenness appeared to bring upon them exile and suffering. Although the ideas were delivered in a philosophic and technical shorthand which took for granted a mastery of sources quite beyond the grasp of the masses, the details added up to a kind of pictorial drama or mythos.

According to Scholem, much of the Kabbala draws its power from a kind of mythos that was embodied in gnostic heresies which official Judaism tried to suppress. Gnosticism is a term used to describe a large variety of religious ideas and expressions. *Gnosis* means knowledge, and the gnostic sects in and around the fringes of Judaism and early Christianity held out a promise of salvation through the acquisition of a secret body of knowledge. Most gnostic movements also offered their followers a picture of creation which involved the concept of a fall, the fall of a soul or even of God from higher regions into the dark lower prison of our world, from which depths it tries to free itself and ascend. The more heretical gnostic myths also assign the world to the control of a lower power or demiurge, a concept which can easily flow over into that Manichean teaching which Judaism calls the heresy of the two powers, the denial of God's omnipotence. Scholem sees what he calls the Lurianic mythos as a clear example of gnostic doctrine in Judaism. It involves a catastrophic fall and would-be ascent of holy entities. It speaks of a non-Godly power, hints at the possibility of a basic dualism in the very nature of the Godhead, and sees redemption as a process of freeing the soul from its imprisonment in the lower regions. If this is gnosticism, then the Lurianic mythos has gnostic characteristics. But the Jew who accepted this mythos did not consciously sense in it any heresy. To him it was a dramatic explanation of the world's creation drawn in a mystical yet sharply visual imagery. I take the liberty of presenting it in a style for which Scholem cannot be held responsible.

The protagonists of this drama are God, the cosmos, and man. The language used in relating the myth is not that of the usual storyteller; indeed, if one were to attempt a visual abstraction of what takes place, one might begin with a blank canvas. But it is not really blank: it is a symbol of a universe coextensive with God. There is only God—nothing else. Then there is a movement. A space opens up, as if within God himself; it is as if God "contracts" himself. The result is an area empty of God. That is the first act of the drama, an act which is called *tzimtzum,* that is, concentration or withdrawal.

The next act involves the reentry of God into the empty space. Obviously, it will not be that kind of reentry which restores completely the condition that existed before, otherwise the drama will cease. It is only a partial reentry. A line or charge from the divine is extended into the empty space. This is the second step of the action, called *hitpashtut,* and it is the opposite of the first act, the breathing out which succeeds the breathing in. Now, something begins to happen in the space which was made by the withdrawal of God.

What actually occurs is a subject for endless speculation on the part of the kabbalists, but its result is a terrible catastrophe. The something which had just begun to be formed is shattered. The outer husks or shell of what has been formed is broken and the inner light, the creative life-charge of these emerging forms, is scattered in two directions. Some of this light, called *holy sparks,* returns to its source, that is, upwards to the divine root of light, to God. But other sparks are entangled with the shattered husks, which are called *klipot,* and fall with them. The divine harmony has been broken: "things are not in their place." This is the end of the third action which sets the stage for the entrance of man.

The tension of the action has now been established. The sparks yearn to return to their source and the husks to their place, both want to be lifted to the roots so that the primordial unity may be reestablished. The process of "lifting the sparks" to their roots and effecting a *tikkun* or "repair" is the task of man, a task in which all generations can play a role. Man must separate the sparks from the shells, free them from their imprisonment so that they can reascend. These sparks are embedded in all levels of creation: the mineral, vegetable, animal, and human. Thus, when man turns over the soil he can help lift the divine sparks in the soil to a higher level of existence in the vegetable order. In the same way, he can release the spark from the vegetable and embody it in a human being, a still higher level. Through his

life and deeds, he can also enable the sparks in the body and soul of
man to ascend to its root, which in mystical cosmology is identified
with the image of a primordial man—Adam Kadman.

The process of gathering the sparks does not always go
smoothly. There are moments when it is almost completed and then
comes another fall, another catastrophe. It is when the time for the
Great Tikkun, the final redemption, approaches that there is the greatest danger. Why? Because this redemption involves the liberation of
those holy sparks and shells which have fallen into the deepest abyss.
The Great Tikkun cannot be completed without the lifting up of
these sparks, for they are the holiest of the sparks. Their very power
has carried them farthest away from their originating source, and
the man who seeks to redeem them must descend into those depths
where the power of darkness rivals the power of light. Here, the
klipot, the husks which come to symbolize the nonbeing element, have
their realm of power. Terrible and difficult is the struggle which
must take place in these depths so far from the divine effulgence. It
may be that man will have to use stratagems to prevail in these dark
forces. He may have to fight with Satan, so to speak, on the latter's
terms. He may even have to pretend that he is "one of them" in order
to bring about that final act of freedom, and he may be himself caught
in the abyss.

Application of the Mythos

It can easily be seen how this mythos could become a cornuco-
pia of meaning or "hints" for each age or person according to need.
For example, Scholem explains how the descendants of those exiled by
Spain in 1492 were able to draw comfort from this Lurianic theology.
Since to kabbalists all history is but the outer representation of an inner spiritual process, expulsion from Spain of the Jews was seen as the
outer covering of the real catastrophe that is still taking place in the
inner world. The seeming absence of God, which the Jews of Spain
experienced was analogous to the primal withdrawal of God. Israel is
in exile just as God is in exile. But there is a purpose to this scattering
of the Jews; they are to go everywhere to gather the sparks and prepare the world for its Great Tikkun. The condition of the Jew, therefore, is not the result of an accident and certainly not a challenge to

the claims of his ancestral faith. On the contrary, his condition of exile is proof of the cosmic mission which devolves upon every individual Jew and upon the people of Israel as a whole. The world will not be restored or redeemed unless the Jew performs his task.

The Lurianic mythos became, therefore, an explanation of the Jewish exile, and since this exile was the predicament not only of Spanish but of all Jewish communities, its attraction was obvious. In addition, it was an explanation of reality on a universal or purely personal level. It could, for example, say something to the person who sought an explanation for the evil in a world which had been created by an all-good and all-powerful God. The image of God withdrawing could also offer some sort of an answer to a mind struggling with abstract theological questions, such as how can there be creation when all is already filled with God? The Lurianic mythos also offered comfort by suggesting that not only man but God, too, was in exile. Man and God were partners in fate, and God needed man to redeem Him from His exile. This latter theme became the most important element of the Jewish religious consciousness.

"I do not ask not to suffer," cried a Hasidic master, "I ask only that there be a reason for my suffering." The theory of a God in exile, of a catastrophic divine fall which waited for man's redeeming effort, filled man's work and pain with cosmic purpose. The lifting of the sparks lent new meaning to the minutiae of the ritual commandments. The act of eating bread, putting on phylacteries, making love, involved a "higher need," as the kabbalists phrased it. Every gesture, every act, every accident could now be illuminated and suffused with a mystic intent, *kavannah*.

The theory of the sparks and the Great Tikkun also opened up new avenues of human relationship along lines which are not dissimilar from what we would call psychotherapy. Some people were more gifted than others in being able to perceive the "essential spark" in a person's soul. They could prescribe the particular Tikkun which that soul needed in order that its spark might move on the higher levels. Here was an ideology ready-made for wise men or "seers"—those who could see the spark as well as for charlatans.

In this way, the symbolism of the Kabbala offered not only an explanation for historic phenomenon and theological problems, but also a technique for "untying the knots and unsealing the seals" of a man's personal existence. It promised him secrets which could increase the flow of life and grace into the world, but it did this at the risk of bringing him close to "the abyss in which the freedom of living things is born," the realm where the holy sparks are enclosed by thick husks and Satan's power is formidable. Fecundity, creativity, the drive of life forces for full expression, these are always but a hair's breadth away from anarchy: "the line of division between the holy and the satanic is as thin as a hair." That is why the image of the seed which must die in the ground before it can be reborn in a new burst of life has always drawn the religious imagination. Every creative act must pass through a moment when it is neither seed nor flower, through the abyss which the mystics called *ayin,* that nothingness which is the hidden source-spring of everything. Such a passage is fraught with danger, however, for the pull of the abyss, of anarchy, formlessness, and chaos, is strong as death.

The Pull of the Abyss

One does not have to be a mystic to want to transcend the prosaic and chaining demands of "you must do this" and "the Law says." Who has not felt at moments the pull of the demoniac, the urge to break, to destroy, to taste "freedom"?

Ecstatic, a word which literally means to leave the body, is a term frequently used to describe the mystic experience. Such leaving may, indeed, result in a vision of deeper truth, but it also involves a degree of disconnection with the world of common reality. The mystic may very well return to that world, but then again, he may not.

Scholem explores the anarchic potentialities of the abyss as a way of explaining the Shabbatai Zevi and Jacob Frank heresies. The messianic dream has always involved a yearning for the freedom promised by a "breaking of the shells." And there have been times when the Jews were eager not only to yearn but to taste something of this world-to-come. When this desire was especially strong, a Messiah often appeared. With his appearance, the tension between the inner felt truth and the outer reality reached an extreme. That there is a difference between the outer and inner truth is one of the oldest of Jewish religious claims. Not the strongest and the most powerful, but the weakest, the most persecuted are the chosen of God. The Messiah will appear, not at the head of a glorious triumphant army, but riding on a donkey, and he shall be "ugly and despised of men." This, of course, is the paradox at the heart of Christianity, the paradox of the crucified Christ. This scandal of a faith which proves itself by its very absurdity was pushed to an even greater extreme in the case of Shabbatai Zevi. Shabbatai Zevi would appear to have gone far beyond Jesus in setting up that paradox whose acceptance is the test of faith. Not only was he willingly defeated; he willingly did that which, for the Jews, is much worse than defeat, in the eyes of the world, he became an apostate, a betrayer of the faith.

The groundwork for this paradox was laid by the Lurianic mythos and by the many Jews who came from a Marrano background. The Marranos were Spanish Jews who had to do precisely what Shabbatai Zevi did a century after the Spanish Inquisition. They had to pretend that they adhered to one faith while secretly remaining true to their Judaism. For those who had lived this double life and tasted its bitterness, Shabbatai Zevi's heresy appeared to be a kind of vindication. They understood it not only as a prototype of their own conditions, but as a symbol of that split between outer and inner truth which is characteristic of our unredeemed world.

The Lurianic mythos provided this heresy with an even more powerful and dynamic element by permitting contact with the demoniac. Man could not avoid such contact in the final stage of the Great Tikkun, when the battle to free the sparks had to be carried on in the lowest depths and the prison "forced from within." This ultimate stronghold of Satan could only be taken by someone who knew it intimately; sin would have to be embraced in order that its life force be taken from it. Thus, all the elements were present: the catastrophe; the ideology; the Messiah; and the heady taste of anarchy and nihilism. Of course, no one dared to say this openly, although Nathan of Gaza did point out that the numerical equivalent of the Hebrew word for snake is the same as the Hebrew word for Messiah, a symbolism reminiscent of the ancient gnostic rites, but the official rationale was the old one of the seed being broken before it could bring forth new life. One had to transgress the Law in order to fulfill it. In this way did Nathan the prophet explain the apostasy of Shabbatai Zevi, and a century later the Frankists could begin their orgiastic rites by twisting the ancient rabbinic blessing, "who has released the bound," to "who has permitted the forbidden."

The Orthodox Jewish community in the time of Shabbatai Zevi sought to stamp out its enemy; soon it was impossible to find a Sabbatean or a Frankist who could publicly confess his faith. The movement remained largely buried until Scholem not only uncovered its traces, but followed its influence into the most unlikely of new environments, the French Revolution and the beginnings of Reform Judaism. Junius Frey, who went to the guillotine with Danton in 1794, had been slated to be the successor to Frank; the earliest leaders of Reform Judaism in Hungary came from the followers of Shabbatai Zevi. The link between these "enlightened" movements and the demoniac end-products of the Lurianic Kabbala is another one of those paradoxes which, under Scholem's analysis, represent a perfectly logical ideational development. The revolt against Orthodoxy, the eagerness to cast off husks and reach for the inner spirit, the dream of a world above little law, all of these are, of course, easily turned toward causes like Liberal Judaism and the French Revolution. More complex is the link between the Lurianic image of lifting the sparks and the commitment of early Reform Judaism to a mission which would be achieved by a gradual evolutionary movement toward a better world which could be brought about by man's efforts.

The belief in progress, the idea that the world is of necessity evolving toward good, is not, Scholem shows, a basic element of the Jewish faith. On the contrary, the biblical end of days is sometimes described by the prophets as being preceded by a catastrophe, by a horrible period of destruction, such as the battle of Gog and Magog. A more authentic ideological base for liberal Judaism's belief in progress is the Lurianic mission which assigns to every generation a portion in the process of liberating the sparks and hastening the accomplishment of the final Great Tikkun. Actually, Scholem contends, the seemingly rational faith of both a French Revolutionist and a Reform Jew in man's ability to lift society to a continually higher level has a mystical, rather than a biblical or rabbinic base.

In this way, Scholem takes a number of seemingly unrelated events and, through meticulous analysis and research, shows their causal relationship. It is the feat of a great accountant, a great story-teller, a great scholar.

Making Sense of the Senseless

History, it has been said, is largely a making sense of the sense-less. It is the task of the historian to work out a causal nexus of events, and, clearly, Scholem has an unusual talent in this direction. But a mind which is able to relate the most diverse phenomena can also err by the power of its virtuosity as it exhibited itself one day in a class at the Hebrew University in Jerusalem.

The lecture was attended by gray-haired farmers from the *kib-butzim,* some priests, a nun, a smattering of foreign students and various visitors, as well as native-born *sabra* students. Scholem entered, as was his habit, a moment after the bell rang, glanced frowningly at a student who had not yet put out his cigarette, and turned to his notebook. The theme that morning dealt with the kabbalistic concep-tion of God as the *ein sof,* the infinite source of all existence, beyond any definition or description, even beyond adjectives such as merciful or good. Like Maimonides and other medieval philosophers, the mas-ters of the Kabbala were extremely careful to avoid all personal references to the nature of God.

"The Jewish mystic would not dream of addressing this un-known God in terms of Thou and I," Scholem said with the expres-sion of distaste on his face, as he indulged in a favorite sport, criti-cism of Martin Buber.

The major problem of the Kabbala was to explain how an in-finite and utterly transcendent God could communicate with crea-tures and a world which was capable only of grasping the finite. All creation, Scholem pointed out, is the expression of God's thought and will, but this expression has to be structured in order that it might exist. The clue to the basic structure of creation, says the *Sefer Yetzirah,* the *Book of Creation,* one of the oldest of mystical texts, is the twenty-two letters of the Hebrew alphabet. These letters are not only symbols of the structure; they are the essential expression of God's will and wisdom. All that exists—man, nature, the cosmos—is also God's speech. The Hebrew letters are related to God as ordinary language is related to man. More than his deeds and more than his

physical creations, it is speech and language that reveal a person's inner thought. Similarly, the words of the Torah, God's speech, are the
closest we can get to Him. But just as written words reveal only a
part of man's thought, so the words of the Torah reveal only a part of
God's thought. The spoken word can reveal even more, the idea that
precedes its articulation, even more, and the mental impulse which
is the seed of the thought, even more. The more ineffable the communication, the more it has to say. This is the reason for the Kabbala's
preoccupation not only with the written and spoken word, but with
the voice that is not yet differentiated into letters, and with the silent
breath before it becomes a voice. In short, the more articulate, the
more differentiated the instrument of communication, the less is revealed.

This idea appears again and again in Jewish mysticism, which is
a mysticism utterly engrossed with the word. Since Hebrew letters are
direct expressions of God's thought, the Jewish mystic was interested
in the form as well as the meaning of these letters, a thought which
led a latter-day mystic to suggest that the white space surrounding the
letters was also replete with mystical meaning. This interest in the
sound and form of Hebrew letters as a key to ultimate mysteries of
creation achieves its apogee in the kabbalist's concern with the letters
of God's name.

Toward the end of his exposition, Scholem flailed the air with
his hands and came up with a vivid illustration of the abstract concept he had been trying to delineate. For the kabbalist, the written
Torah is like an "Edison gramophone and its record." A person may
take a record and through its little lines recover something of the
original voice which made the impressions in the record, and from
the voice learn something of the thought. For the kabbalist, the words
of the Torah are such a record. That is, God's voice expressed itself in
the shapes and forms of the Hebrew alphabet and in the conjunctions
of this alphabet which made up words and sentences. By reversing the
process, as the needle reverses the process which engraved the record,
the kabbalist hopes to make contact with the original voice of God.

To be sure, this reversal process has its limitations. The written
word may give us a clue as to the thought, and the thought may provide a clue to the mind and will of which the thought is but a partial

revelation, but sooner or later we come to the *ein sof,* the infinite, the utterly undifferentiated. This problem of what and how much can be revealed at these upper limitations revolves about the so-called higher *sephirot,* which in the kabbalistic diagram of the higher man or primordial Adam correspond to the head and the brain.

Professor Scholem now turned his attention to an explanation of these upper *sephirot.* He spoke about the *Book of Brightness,* another early mystical text, and about Rabbi Isaac the Blind, who lived in eleventh-century Provence and was one of the creators of what later became the Spanish Kabbala. There was a difference between the number of *sephirot* listed by Rabbi Isaac and the number named in the book of the Bahir. Professor Scholem now demonstrated how the later concept developed out of the earlier. He seemed to be perspiring even more profusely than usual as he spoke. Everyone continued to take notes. Scholem's speech faltered slightly, his grimaces became more violent, but the demonstration continued until the bell rang.

Only when the next period resumed did Scholem, with a broad smile, reveal the cause of his perspiration in the previous hour. "I ask your apology, dear sirs, but I made a mistake at the conclusion of my last lecture. I had misplaced three pages of my lecture, but now I have found them again."

What had happened was that Scholem had concluded one page and gone on to another without noticing the missing pages. Obviously the subject, as well as the line of thought, was unconnected, but Scholem had connected them. In earlier years, Talmudists would show their mental ingenuity by sticking a pin through the Talmud, taking the diverse subjects pointed to by the pin and, by a *tour de force,* weave them into an intelligent lecture. Scholem had done the same with the Kabbala.

Having related this episode and preceded it by references to those eccentricities of appearance and behavior in which Scholem seems to delight, a pause must be made to correct a possibly erroneous impression. "What you must understand," one of his disciples, Dr. Rivka Shatz Oppenheimer, pointed out to me, "is that his clowning and bad-boy anti-establishment image which Scholem sometimes presents to the public conceals a 'nazir'—a man whose Nazirite-like devotion to scholarship and historic truth verges on the border of asceticism."

Dr. Oppenheimer's point cannot be overemphasized. Gershom Scholem is an intellectual phenomenon, a giant among scholars whose willingness to "bow before the facts" cannot be seriously doubted. Scholem's ideas, however, as he would be the first to point out, are not immune from the particular *Zeitgeist* of his time. By and large, the twentieth century has tended to see religious development through the ages as progress from unenlightenment to enlightenment. It has also been committed to the belief that events and ideas evolve out of an explicable relationship, that there are no heavenly interventions interrupting the natural, logical flow of phenomena.

But does a phenomenon such as mysticism really fit so neatly into the evolutionary program which Scholem sets up: the "childhood" dream era; the period when institutionalized religion sets up an abyss between God and man; and finally the birth of mysticism which would restore the old unity on a new level? Or does not a vital faith refuse to make easy distinctions between "pure" religion, myth, and superstition? Scholem himself mocks those who attempt to explain spiritual phenomena in terms of ideological schools, but as a scientific historian he cannot believe in mysterious incursions from on high. For him a reference in a kabbalistic document to an "Elijah appearance" may be hallucination, or simply a technical term for designating a doctrine that breaks or disregards an older tradition, but it cannot mean what most kabbalists took it to mean, that Elijah actually did appear with a message. But this raises a question which must be directed not only to Scholem but to all objective historians of faith: have their self-imposed criteria for judging facts made it impossible for them to comprehend the essence of the phenomenon they try to describe?

Tourism in Place of Worship

Since Scholem is not only an accountant of Jewish mysticism but a discoverer of much of the material which has been entered into the account, it is difficult to find a critic of his work in academic circles. There is, however, one man in Israel, a professor of Hebrew literature at Bar-Ilan University in Tel Aviv, who enjoys a reputation as a jouster with Israel's cultural idols. Not long after Scholem published his books on the Shabbatai Zevi movement, Baruch Kurzweil hastened to the attack. Admitting to not being an expert in the Kabbala, the strategy he employed was a frontal assault on all so-called scientific historians of Judaism, using Scholem as an example *par excellence* of this academic camp.

Jüdische Wissenschaft, the so-called scientific study of Judaism, Kurzweil argues, began in nineteenth-century Germany. Its goal was frankly apologetic. It was a time when both the traditional faith and the walls of the ghetto were crumbling. Judaism was challenged to justify itself in terms which were acceptable to civilized human beings; that is, it was asked to prove its compatibility with nineteenth-century liberal ideas. The practitioners of a scientific study of Judaism set out to demonstrate that Judaism could pass this test. Some of them could not convince themselves and accepted the logic of their own conclusions. Thus, a brilliant scholar named Moritz Steinschneider proclaimed that the task of Jewish scholarship was simply to provide Judaism with a "decent burial." Others took a different path. Understanding that Judaism had survived the centuries because of a religious faith, and feeling that this faith was dead, they offered in its stead the "science of Judaism."

"And so there happened to Judaism," wrote Kurzweil, "what happened to other holy places. That which was no longer looked upon as a fountain of life, or a shade for the spirit, or as a reason for existence, became sanctified and set aside for tourism."

At first, according to Kurzweil, this tourism had an intellectual character, but later the scholars built a mountain of paper upon which they ascended and descended like Sisyphus.

And behold, the people, when they saw that the living God failed to appear, gathered around the Sisyphists and said: "Go up and make us a god in place of the God of Judaism, in whose Name we have lived until now—for we no longer know what this Judaism is." And the Sisyphists said unto them: "Take a portion of the gold which is in your houses of commerce and your banks and bring it to us as grants for research, for travel, for congresses—in short, for scientific tourism.

Included in this band of Sisyphists, replies Kurzweil, and perhaps the most talented and important among them is Gershom Scholem. Kurzweil readily grants Scholem's prowess as a scholar but then proceeds to an analysis which verges on the border of psychoanalysis. Scholem is split, claims Kurzweil, between his claim to objectivity and his dislike for the comfortable smugness he senses among scholars of his day. The professor of mysticism has himself criticized the eagerness of modern Jewish historians to compromise with facts in order to harmonize their ideas with the spirit of their age. They are reluctant, Scholem has said, to scandalize the Establishment. And there is nothing, Kurzweil implies, that Scholem likes better than to scandalize the Establishment.

Gershom Scholem has often referred to himself as an anarchist by inclination, but, agrees Kurzweil, this attraction to anarchism has unconsciously caused him to rewrite Jewish history so as to give its heretics and nihilists an importance which they never really had; hence, his interpretation of Jewish mysticism as a veil for forbidden heresies and his view of kabbalists as secret rebels against the law. To be sure, Jewish mysticism without the Law can become a demoniac, nihilistic force. But that is precisely why the Rabbis always insisted on combining the mystic experience with the stabilizing and socially conscious yoke of the commandments. The fact is, Kurzweil says, that Scholem is personally anti-rabbinic, anti-Talmudic and anti-Enlightenment, and this influences his view of Jewish history. It explains his positive delight in claiming that there is no such thing as Judaism. What people call Judaism, Scholem has claimed, is nothing more than a set of ideas which are believed by its authorities in a particular generation and these authorities have said vastly different things at different times. Such a view, Kurzweil points out, deprives Judaism of its *raison d'être,* but its inherent anarchism is more a reflection of Scholem than of historic reality.

Søren Kierkegaard once criticized objective historians of religion for paying more attention "to the frame than to the mirror." Kurzweil's complaint is that Scholem has looked overmuch in the mirror while drawing up his account of Jewish mysticism. The consensus of scholarly judgment would not support Kurzweil's position. There is a line of criticism, however, which has more popular support: This is the claim that a student of mysticism should be able to offer something more than a record of past events. An expert in secrets of the past ought to have discovered some secrets which people can use today.

End of the Striptease?

My own attempts to probe Scholem's feelings on this personal level were, as has been seen, parried by polite and tantalizing referrals to hints scattered throughout his writings. It was with surprise, therefore, that I received an invitation announcing a public lecture by him on "The Possibilities of Jewish Mysticism in Our Day." It was a cold rainy night, but a number of visitors had come from Tel Aviv and other places to Jerusalem's small liberal synagogue to hear what they had been asking Scholem to tell them directly for years and, until that night, without direct reply.

Veteran lecturer that he was, Scholem appeared somewhat nervous, and he referred continually to a small sheet of paper on which he had made some notes. The professor began with the warning that the listeners might emerge with "more doubts than instruction." Although there was no definition of mysticism on which all could agree, he offered his own: "a personal experience of divine matters." What the "divine matters" were, Scholem did not explain.

The paradox of any mystical movement was how a singular experience could be translated into a group experience. This had occurred in the past and made it possible to speak of a mystical movement, but for the last two hundred years, there had not been (unless we think of something like the Subud movement in Indonesia) this kind of communal mystical quickening. There were certainly many individuals with strong and perhaps original mystical experiences, but they had not found a way of translating these experiences into forms which were meaningful to the group. The question of the evening, then, was not the possibility of individual, but of a group kind of mystical expression.

In the Jewish world, said Scholem, many were surprised that the recent Jewish catastrophe in Europe did not have among its reactions the quickening of such a mystical reaction among some groups, even as the kabbalistic movement in Safed of the sixteenth century was a reply to the Spanish expulsion. But, Scholem reminded us, two or three generations intervened between the Spanish catastrophe and the response. The same delay in reaction occurred between the Jewish catastrophes in Europe and the Sabbatean or later Hasidic movement.

There were, however, individuals in our times who could be regarded as authentic expressions of man's mystical capacities. Examples in the Jewish world would be some of the Lubavitcher rebbes, leaders of a Hasidic movement which started in the eighteenth century and still functions today; a Hasidic rebbe called Arele Roth, whose followers can still be visited in Jerusalem; the illustrious former chief rabbi of Israel, Abraham Isaac Kook. The latter, suggested Scholem, is especially interesting in that he tried to understand the meaning of our age's secularism in a mystical way.

But what could the aforementioned individuals mean for people "like us"? Scholem now came to the center of his theme. "For we are not able to be *shlomei emunah,* wholehearted in the faith, of our fathers who accepted the Torah as the word of God, as a revelation from heaven." The Kabbala was built upon the absolute conviction that not only every word, but every dot and even space in the Torah was divinely revealed. For the mystic, there was no such thing as the real meaning of the bible. The meanings of the bible were infinite; therefore, it could be not only an inexhaustible source of new religious insights but could also provide the forms in which these insights could be communicated to the group. It was this acceptance of a common faith in the divine origin of the bible that accounted for the continuity of Jewish history. Without such faith, there is danger of anarchy.

"For, all of us are anarchists," said Scholem, screwing his wide mouth and twisting his hands in the air. "Some know it, and some try to hide the fact."

It was at this point in his address that Scholem began grimacing at his paper and wiping his forehead with his handkerchief. "Is there any hope, then, that a generation lacking this kind of faith in divine revelation can produce a kind of mystic ferment so strong that it could form its tools and vessels of communication, and also draw from the past?" That is, could there be a Jewish mysticism, not just a mysticism of individuals?

"Perhaps"—the audience could feel that Scholem's "perhaps" was very weak—"perhaps, it would be a kind of mysticism related to Kook's attempt to find holiness in the secular."

It might even be, said Scholem, that the impulses which in other generations were involved with religion are today to be sensed in some secular phenomenon. The building of the State of Israel was looked upon by many as involving such an attempt. The poet Walt Whitman and many who pioneered in the *kibbutz* movement, such as A. D. Gordon, had tried to point out this *essential* holiness in the secular.

"For mystical impulses are deeply rooted in the human psyche, only in the future they may be clothed in a naturalistic, rather than a religious consciousness—a consciousness which, on the surface, will not be related to traditional religion." As a final example, Scholem offered a book like *Cosmic Consciousness* by R. M. Bucke as illustration of what he meant by this mystical consciousness.

The lecture ended, or, rather, petered out. There were no questions or invitations to questions on Scholem's part. He left the room quickly with some friends, and it was said that he was sorry about the whole evening. A journalist friend, who had questioned Scholem over the years about his personal views and been put off by vague hints, was especially disappointed. "It's happened. The striptease of thirty years is over. All has been revealed—and there is nothing there. Bucke's *Cosmic Consciousness*? A sophomoric text abounding in rapid, vague discussion—and Scholem accuses others of vagueness. As for the 'mysticism in secularism' with Walt Whitman as an illustration—that is the kind of mysticism anyone can feel on a fine summer morning, if his stomach is in order."

The Gate of Scientific Scholarship

The journalist was unfair, both in his assumption and his conclusions. True, Scholem has said that anyone who delves into the mine of Judaism's hidden worlds will touch "pure gold," but he has never pretended to be either a mystic or a guru. All he lays claim to is "the courage to dare, to pioneer, to ask." What he has done, however, is to cut a gate into the thicket of the Jewish *pardes* which offers not only tourists but would-be settlers a remarkable glimpse of what had always been *terra incognita* to all but a very few initiates. Using this entrance, Scholem has uncovered many profound ideas and insights into the dynamics of the human psyche on both a personal and historic level. If knowledge of the past and understanding of the dialectics of ideas and their interplay with other forces of history have value, then Scholem's research has surely revealed a rich vein of "gold."

Nor is it possible to say that Scholem's hints about the future possibilities of Jewish mysticism are simply a striptease that results in disappointment. There are some very thoughtful and responsible leads for those readers who wish to apply past experiences to future possibilities. Whatever his personal interest in the demoniac and heretical, the professor has gone out of his way to point out the sad results of all messianic movements, while demonstrating the sterility of a Judaism which loses it connection with the darker subterranean force of the psyche. A Judaism thoroughly enlightened and cleansed of all so-called superstition, magic, and theurgy is likely to be a Judaism without vitality. Nor can Judaism be compressed into the framework of ideas and beliefs accepted by the wise men of any particular generation; its mystery is far too profound for such easy definition.

To those who seek to read the future, Scholem merely asserts that the ideas peculiar to Jewish mysticism have a symbolic character, but to effect a flowing of mysticism, these symbols must express deeply felt needs. It was such a coincidence of need and symbol that brought the descendants of Spanish exiles into fruitful symbiosis with the mystical theology of the Safed kabbalists. Such weddings, however, are not arranged on demand; they require a process of natural development, and the trauma of the Jewish holocaust in Europe coupled with the phenomenon of the ingathering of Jews in Israel are events which have not yet found authentic symbolic expression.

Most important of all, however, may be Scholem's simple warning that the main assumptions which produced the Jewish mysticism of the past are no longer present. For modern believers are not *shlomei emunah,* whole hearted, in their faith in the existence of a personal God or in the divine character of His revelations through the medium of the Torah. Can there be a Jewish mysticism without these assumptions? If so, it will certainly have to be radically different from the Torah-centered, Hebrew word-oriented mysticism of the past. Can one find the possibilities of such a mysticism in phenomena which until now has been labeled as secular?

At this point, it may be that Scholem's answers begin to falter, but, surely, this is simply because of honesty. Or is there another reason, suggested by the Holy Ari when he described the relationship between man and the mystery in images taken from the human sphere? There is the knowing of man and woman when both have "their backs turned." Then, there is the level of knowledge when the woman turns invitingly, but the man remains "back to face." There is also the level when the man turns, but the woman is not ready to turn. And there is the full knowing of face to face.

If one applies this image to Scholem, one would have to say that his relationship with Jewish mysticism is certainly far beyond the character of "back to back." Perhaps at some point, there may have been a turning, either on the part of the lady, or the man. But the next step in the process of knowing has to be engagement and not the preservation of distance. The teaching of inner secrets is not revealed to anyone who is worried about getting overinvolved. This, however, is a problem not only for a great scholar like Gershom Scholem, but for anyone who wants to be both a knower and an objective observer, for all those who wish to study Jewish mysticism as a subject which passionately involves the lives of *others*.

On the other hand, those who become personally involved may have to pay a high price. For the lady will not give herself cheaply. Alienation from society, misunderstanding on the part of the world, personal loneliness—this I discovered was often the lot of those striving for a more intimate relationship with their beloved.

4

CHAMBERS WITHIN CHAMBERS

And when such a soul departs from this world, pure, bright, un-blemished, the Holy One, be blessed, daily causes her to shine with a host of radiances and proclaims concerning her: Here is the soul of my son, such and such: let her be preserved for the body from which she has departed.

This is the significance of the words: "And if he espouse her unto his son, he shall deal with her after the manner of daughters." What mean the words, "after the manner of daughters"? It is a secret held solely in the trust of the wise: A palace which is known as the Palace of Love sits amidst a vast rock, a most secret firmament. Here in this place the treasures of the King are kept, and all his kisses of love. Every soul loved by the Holy One, be blessed, enters into that palace. And when the King makes his appearance, "Jacob kisses Rachel" (Gen. 29: 11), which is to say, the Lord discerns each holy soul, and taking each in turn to himself, embraces and fondles her, "dealing with her after the manner of daughters," even as a father acts toward his beloved daughter, embracing and fondling her, and presenting her with gifts.

Zohar: The Book of Splendor

The holy Zohar likens the man who seeks the inner truth to a lover circling a palace which he presumes to be the residence of his beloved—presumes—since he cannot seem to find a gate which will lead him to her. He might altogether despair and give up his search, except that the maiden is aware of his longing for her. What then does she do? She opens a small door of her secret chamber, reveals her face to her lover for a moment, then quickly withdraws it. It is only a fleeting glimpse but enough to rouse him to renewed love, enough to strengthen his will to continue the search—a search which becomes itself a way of life.

It is a chastening illustration. If a seeker of mystic truth in the age of the Zohar had to be satisfied with a passing glance, what can we expect in our day? And where shall we go to attain it?

There are, of course, the books, the "tale," as the Rabbi of Rizhin called it, showing what others did and where they did it. It is also possible to visit a place where one can bring together the tale and the physical location. Safed offers itself as a possibility for such an imaginative exercise. It is still possible to walk through the sixteenth-century streets of this Galilean town and see the courtyard from which Rabbi Isaac Luria and his "holy community" began their Sabbath twilight procession into the fields. Dressed in white, strewing flowers as they went, they would sing a hymn that one of their group had composed, *"L'cha Dodee,"* . . . come forth, my beloved, to greet the Sabbath bride, . . . towards that Sabbath let us go; for she is the source-spring of blessing; welling forth out of that which was first and most ancient; last in creation, but first in conception. . . ."

This hymn has since become a part of the Sabbath evening service in every traditional congregation, but few among those who chant it today realize that the words they are saying have hidden meanings related to the world of the *sefirot*. To Rabbi Isaac Luria's followers, however, these kabbalistic references revealed the inner structure and dynamics of the universe. Through them, man was made conscious of the role he had to play in enabling this universe to function, so that *shefa,* the juices of life, would flow from the upper reservoirs into the waiting vessels below. It was this consciousness that distinguished the life of the mystic from the life of the merely devout Jew. Every thought, every word, every act had boundless repercussions for Israel, for mankind, for the world. Hence the importance of *kavanot,* the inner intentions which sensitized the Jew to the fuller implications of the word he was about to speak or the ritual he was about to perform. That was why the holy community would gather for its Sabbath morning prayers before dawn and sit quietly or lie prostrate for an hour before uttering a word. Even then, they were not ready to say the prayers until they had further prepared themselves.

"Beloved of the soul, merciful Father," each one would quietly chant, "draw Thy servant toward Thy will. Let Thy servant run like a gazelle, let him prostrate himself near Thy glory and Thy love for him shall be sweet, sweeter than drops of honey, than all goodness."

Then, before entering into the main sections of the prayer service, the worshipper would recite the sacred words of the Zohar:

Behold, in fear and trembling, I am prepared to unite the Holy One, blessed be He, with the shekina, *the presence, through this commandment which I am about to fulfill.*

And since the chief commandment is "thou shalt love thy neighbor as thyself," each member of the group would try, before the commencement of the community prayers, to feel this love. Only then, as the light in the sky would begin to outline the hills facing them across the valley, would they join in chanting the opening psalm of morning service.

On the Sabbath, their prayers would be followed by a communal meal. There were three such meals, and each had its own atmosphere. "Now do I prepare the banquet of the full mystery, the key of the holy King; the banquet of the King do I prepare," the holy band chanted before each meal. Then they would sing hymns composed by their leader, the Holy Ari. The Friday evening hymn describes the Sabbath bride being invited to the "table shining with newness and light." She is surrounded on the "right and the left" by the other days of the week, each of which draws their strength from her. Her husband, "the community of Israel," crushes her in his embrace, gives her pleasure. All the angry voices are stilled, faces, spirits, and souls become new. "May it be the will of the holy ancient One," the holy band concludes, "hidden of all hidden, sealed from all, that holy dew may be drawn from Him, to fill the head of the little face and enter the holy garden of apples."

The allusions are kabbalistic, and the eroticism is evident. For Friday night is the time of the holy coupling, both in the world of the *sefirot* and between husband and wife on earth, and these unifying actions induce and stimulate and reinforce each other.

The Sabbath banquets were heavy with erotic imagery. The late morning meal was preceded by a hymn that described a "table enwreathed by precious secrets," where the holy brotherhood heard "sealed words revealing mystery." The third meal, which began with sunset, was the hour when the "children of the chamber of longing" taste the "great peace." This was the last meal of the Sabbath, when the holy Band, reluctant to part with their Sabbath queen, tried to delay her parting by their songs and words of Torah.

It is still possible to visit the places where the Holy Ari and his followers played out the soft drama of their meetings with Queen Sabbath, there to recite the words which they chanted. It must be a solitary exercise, however, since there are no more kabbalists in Safed. Perhaps there are a few old scholars who understand some of the mystic vocabulary, but there is no longer a holy community for whom the unseen world is more real than the seen.

Until 1948, there existed in the old section of the city of Jerusalem the congregation of Beth-El, the house of God. There are people who still remember the silent *kavanot* of this congregation when, by inner movements of mind and emotion, they tried to arrange the *sefirot* in proper conjunction. This community was founded in 1740 by twelve young men, who made a written covenant which they signed in blood:

The Lord in His desire for the repentance of the patient, caused us, the youngest of the flock, to be inspired to band together as one person for the sake of unifying the holy One, blessed be He, and his shekina, *to give pleasure to our creator. . . .*

(The twelve young men promised to) love one another with a spiritual and bodily love, and all this only to give pleasure to our creator by a cleaving of spirit and unity, the only exception being that each one of us shall have his wife separate unto himself. . . .

Yet each one's soul shall be tied to that of the other so that we twelve shall be as one soul of great splendor. Thus, one will be able to raise the other as if he were a rib of himself, of the same soul, of the same being. . . . Under this principle, too, we obligate ourselves by our signature to tie our love with a strong tie, and from this moment on we agree that in the length of days and years in the world to come, we shall spare no effort in that higher world to correct and raise the souls of any of our group. . . .

Driven out during the 1948 Arab-Israeli war, the congregation is now housed in the new quarter of the city. When I visited the building one afternoon, however, all I found were three old men reading a commentary by Haim Vital, the disciple of the Holy Ari who had preserved in writing some of his teacher's words. For an hour I listened to the men mumble on about "worlds of emanation and creation," "heavenly wheels" and "upper" and "lower" faces. It was obvious that they were simply performing a *mitzvah,* a dutifully pious exercise, repeating words that had long ago lost their vital power; apparently no mystic community exists in Jerusalem today.

In the course of time, I heard about other so-called kabbalistic communities or study groups, but each lead ended in frustration. Here and there one could find a learned and pious kabbalist, but the wellspring, if it were there, was sealed, like the secrets he was trying to impart. Either the old secrets had lost their power to feed the roots of modern souls, or there was no individual who could reveal this power. One day, however, hope revived on seeing an advertisement in an Israeli paper which announced the existence of an international Center for Kabbala.

Zohar for the Masses

Those responsible for the announcement had no intention of restricting their activities to a small elite. Hoping to capture a mass audience for an enterprise which they considered completely vital to the future of Israel and the world, they offered regular classes in Haifa and Tel Aviv, as well as in the town of B'nai Brak, where a daily seminar in the Zohar was available to any visitor.

Upon inquiry, I learned that the impetus for this Kabbala project had come from a very fine scholar, now deceased, a Rabbi Ashlag, who was convinced that the time had come when Kabbala ought to be studied, not, as traditionally, after an individual has become thoroughly familiar with Mishnah and Talmud, but at the beginning of one's introduction to Judaism. After his death, his son had decided to pursue his father's goals in a practical way by building a Kabbala center in the town of B'nai Brak.

I decided to sample the perpetual Zohar seminar, and arriving in B'nai Brak one afternoon, asked for the synagogue of Rabbi Ashlag. Someone directed me to a new and still unfinished building. Inside, a dozen men were seated on either side of a long table, looking at copies of *The Ladder,* a commentary on the Zohar by the deceased Rabbi Ashlag. At the head of the table sat a brown-bearded man somewhat past middle age. When I entered he paused in his lesson, bade the sexton give me a copy of *The Ladder* and returned to his instruction.

"Let's go over that again, Reb Yonah," he said in a strained voice to a young man with a small, pointed red beard. "Remember how it has all been arranged. All that has been created is divided into four levels." Then, his dark eyes glancing about unsurely at his students, of whom most were elderly and some dozing, he described the four kabbalistic worlds.

"First, there is the world of *atzilut,* which corresponds in the *sefirot* to *chochma,* wisdom. This is the world which cannot be distinguished from the *ein sof,* the infinite source. It is *neetzal,* which means an emanation from the infinite, but the separateness of this emanation is, in our eyes, annulled as the flame of a candle is annulled before the flaming torch. In this world of *atzilut,* there is hardly any difference between the inner light, the content, and the vessel which contains it. And the characteristic of this world, like the characteristic of the source from which it comes, is completely giving. Do you understand, Reb Yonah?"

Everyone looked at Reb Yonah, who nodded smiling, obviously gratified by the attention he was getting. Rabbi Ashlag—a man sitting alongside me confirmed that it was indeed the son of the project's founder—continued:

"After the world of *atzilut* comes the world of *briah,* creation, and then the world of *yetzirah,* formation. In each of these worlds the vessel grows progressively thicker in comparison with its inner light, and as the vessel grows thicker, it becomes more and more a vehicle for receiving rather than giving. Finally, there is the fourth and last world, called *asiyah,* action, which in the system of the *sefirot* corresponds to *malkut,* kingdom. This world is all vessel, and is completely a receiver. It is separated from the other worlds which share, though in ever-diminishing degree, the quality of giving light, which is the characteristic of the divine source. And everything that has been created is divided into these four worlds, including man. Thus, according to the Kabbala, man has four levels to his soul. The lowest, corresponding to the world of *asiyah* and the *sefira malkut,* is called *nefesh.* Then, above it, are the soul levels, called *ruach,* spirit; *neshama,* soul; and finally, that level of the soul where it can barely be distinguished from its source, the *yichida,* oneness, which corresponds to *atzilut.*"

Reb Yonah was vigorously nodding to indicate his understanding of the explanation, but Rabbi Ashlag looked doubtful. After a pause, he asked another man at the table to continue reading. Haltingly, the man read a few lines from the Zohar and then, in response to Rabbi Ashlag's invitation, attempted to identify the words of the text with the *sefirot*. "Earth is *malkut,* sun is *tiferet,* or the little face —that aspect of God which is called 'the holy One, blessed be He.' And the *zivvug,* the unity, which is spoken of here, is the unity of the holy One, blessed be He, with *malkut,* the *shekina*." Rabbi Ashlag nodded and the man appeared delighted at having successfully matched up the code words with their *sefirot*.

When the lesson was over, I introduced myself. Rabbi Ashlag told me he planned to visit the States the following year to collect money for the completion of his center. He invited me to spend a Sabbath with him at B'nai Brak when there would be better opportunity to study the Zohar and feel the atmosphere of the Kabbala.

Several weeks later I drove into town a half-hour before the chains were put up, closing the streets to traffic. I hurried to the rabbi's house where his wife, a bright woman with a blondish wig and vivacious black eyes, told me that I was expected. She had even baked two Sabbath loaves for me. Racing against the sunset, I ran to a nearby hotel, rented a tiny room, was told when the electric lights automatically shut off for the Sabbath, then rushed back to the synagogue, where Rabbi Ashlag and some twenty men were already engaged in their Zohar studies.

This evening's text in *The Ladder* was concerned with the biblical passage dealing with the freeing of the slaves at the jubilee, which occurred every fifty years. According to the Zohar, this passage referred to the phenomenon of *gilgul ha-nefesh,* the transmigration of souls. In order to lift itself up gradually from the lower level of action to *atzilut,* where it reunites with its source, a soul may have to come back to earth after its death. Here, through performance of the commandments, the thickened bodily vessels in which it has been enveloped are slowly purified.

This evening, Rabbi Ashlag wore a fur-encircled hat and a glossy black silk caftan. He was flanked by his two sons; the older, a husky six-footer also wearing a black silk caftan, and the younger, dressed in Lord Fauntleroy-like black stockings and black knickers. It was clear that Rabbi Ashlag and his sons were trying to play the role of the royal family in a Hasidic Court, but everyone was uncomfortably self-conscious because Rabbi Ashlag was not a rebbe in the Hasidic sense, that is, one descended from a "royal family," and his congregation were not really Hasidim.

The lesson ended about ten in the evening, and I accompanied the rabbi to his home. The table was elaborately set with twelve Sabbath loaves instead of the usual two, in accordance with the mystic formula of the Holy Ari.

"This is the way of Jewish mysticism," Rabbi Ashlag explained. "Everything above must have a counterpart below; we must have a real feast on the table if we speak about a spiritual feast." We sat around the table, the women waiting quietly at the farther end, while the rabbi rapidly chanted Rabbi Isaac Luria's introductory hymn. Then he rose to place his hands on the bread which was the earthly counterpart of the shew bread in the heavenly holy Temple above. The ritualistic motions preceding the cutting of the bread were akin to the ancient priestly sacrificial rites. The bread was going to release its holy sparks, the life which would then be absorbed into the body of man, who would in turn offer his life up to God; it was the reverse process of the chain of descent. Suddenly a four-year-old child at the end of the table began to cry. Rabbi Ashlag, forbidden by ritual law to speak at that moment, indicated by his eyes that the child ought to be removed. Following the blessings over bread, the elder son lifted a brimming wine cup and placed it in his father's hand for the prayer of sanctification. Then he too blessed the wine, as did the younger son, who, after he had finished, offered a limp handshake to the rest of us at the table.

While we were eating the delicious chicken, I asked the rabbi if the Kabbala had any special view about the eating of meat. The Nazir in Jerusalem, I had heard, did not eat it.

"An ignorant man should not eat meat," the rabbi quoted the Talmud. The reason, according to mystic tradition, is that ordinarily man serves as a means whereby the sparks embedded in the lower forms of life can be lifted closer to their source. If man is more animal than human, then the animal elements he eats will not be lifted by

him but will drag him down. This also suggests the importance of
environment, since the scales between the upper and lower elements,
between holiness and secularism, between faith and disbelief were always closely balanced. That is why Orthodox Jews had to be so careful about selecting proper surroundings for their families, and why
he preferred to live in a religious city like B'nai Brak.

The next morning I went to the services at Rabbi Ashlag's
synagogue; despite all the elaborate claims and preparations, they did
not seem to be very different from those of any of the dozens of synagogues in B'nai Brak. Indeed, when the rabbi's two sons faced the
ark and offered a prayer in the form of a nasal duet, the congregation
was obviously more amused than inspired.

I left B'nai Brak with a sense of having witnessed a play. It
contained elements of great beauty and poetry and associated its
performers with some very decent human values, but it was still a
play. What had Setzer told me one evening about the letter *kof*? It
was not among the most respected letters of the Hebrew alphabet.
For one thing, it was the first letter of *klipah,* husk, which the kabbalists associate with evil and death. But *kof* also means monkey, and
these two associations of the letter can be related. Just as a monkey
likes to imitate human behavior, a shell can pretend to be the real
thing, yet is inauthentic.

The analogy is too harsh. Rabbi Ashlag and his family were
sincere. Nevertheless, there was a husklike imitative quality in their
kabbalistic projects and rites. But had not Gershom Scholem compared
Jewish mysticism to a subterranean stream, whose forms of expression
varied profoundly from age to age? The Neoplatonic, moralistic piety
of the German Hasidic mystics was not able to confine its symbolism
to that which was used by the second-century Descenders of the
Chariot. Neither could the originators of the *sefirot* system in the
Spanish Kabbala find outlet for their insights in the symbols of earlier
periods. Why, then, should we expect to find a vital Jewish mysticism
in the kabbalistic symbols and imagery of earlier generations? The
old forms may, like the world from which the divine flash has withdrawn, still contain an impression of the vital force which once in-
habited them, but the power of that impression is no match for the
husks.

There may also be another reason why modern Jews have trouble communicating with the world of the Kabbala. The present generation is asking entirely different questions; it does not seem concerned about the problem of reuniting a perfect and unified creator with a fragmented and disharmonious creation. It is not easy for us to realize that the Descenders of the Chariot or the Holy Ari and his disciples were as fearful of pain and death, or as hungry for love and joy, as modern man. Of course, their imagery is far removed from our thought forms, but in their attempts to combat the dread underside of reality, may they not have discovered some permanently valid secrets buried in the symbolic world of the Kabbala? And may there not be groups or individuals who can bridge the old and the new, who can hear the old secrets and relate them in a way which will capture the attention and understanding of the modern ear. A little later in this book we will examine the claim of Hasidism to be such a community, but are there not also some individuals who can effect this kind of linkage?

The Ideal Teacher

Arthur Koestler describes the ideal writer as one who would immerse his feet in a basin of hot water and sit near an open window. He must be able to look out of this window, yet be careful that he not fall through it. In fact, he should try to keep his feet in the hot water. On the other hand, his immersion in the hot water should not be accompanied by a closing of the windows which would result in the windowpanes becoming completely befogged by the steam rising from his hot water basin.

My search for instructors in the Kabbala had up to now brought me into contact with individuals who tended toward one or the other of the extremes about which Koestler warns. The ideal insider-outsider seemed difficult to find. To be sure, there were gifted individuals such as Gershom Scholem and S. Z. Setzer who combined an authentic and profound knowledge of the Kabbala with an awareness of twentieth-century perspectives, and I had, over the years, become acquainted with other individuals, either personally or through their writings, who seemed able to construct some kind of a bridge between this hidden wisdom and the needs of an individual and of a

community in our time. In Israel, a teacher by the name of Joseph
Schechter has been trying to present his students with a Judaism that
combines intense innerness with the needs of the here and now. In
his writing the Kabbala, Hasidism, the Chinese *Book of Changes,*
Yoga meditative techniques, Kierkegaard, Tolstoy, and the latest experiments in parapsychology are provocatively linked together.
Schechter has even stimulated the formation of a youthful community
which for a while attempted to concretize his ideas in their life and
work. Particularly intriguing is Schechter's argument that a modern
Judaism must rediscover the efficacy and power which a community
acquires through silent meditation, fasting, and purification through
ritual immersion. Young Israelis, Schechter believes, who prefer the
concrete physical expression to verbiage, would be attracted by this
kind of religious expression.

In Canada, Zalman Schachter, an Orthodox rabbi who calls himself a Hasid, has published a how-to-do-it manual telling outsiders how
they can take some first steps toward constructing an interior life based
on mystical techniques. Rabbi Schachter has suggested the formation
of a liturgical society called the Children of Light, similar in its external form to a monastic order but differing from such orders not only in
terms of its faith but by its rejection of the "un-Jewish" vow of celibacy.
His eclectic use of the insights of Indian mysticism, hippie societies,
and the psychedelic underground have made Rabbi Schachter an object
of suspicion in Orthodox Hasidic circles but has also won him many
admirers. There are also unusually gifted writers, such as Eli Wiesel and
I. B. Singer, who have been able to translate their personal experiences
with Judaism's hidden realms into a literature of the highest quality.
Finally, there are scholars who have tried, through translations of
Hasidic and kabbalistic texts, to reveal what Martin Buber has called
"the hidden light."

All these teachers, writers, and translators have had to work
out a relationship between "the basin of hot water" and the "open
windows," and some of them have had remarkable success. For an
insider-outsider, however, success seems to depend on the amount of
strain or even antagonism that he senses between his inner and outer
worlds. The deeper the immersion in Judaism's hidden world and
the wider the windows which open out onto the outside world, the

more powerful will be the resultant mix, particularly if the teacher is unusually gifted in his ability to synthesize and to communicate his insights. It was this premise which made me feel that in Rabbi Adin Steinsaltz I had finally found a teacher.

Adin

I met Rabbi Steinsaltz at a study circle which met Thursday evenings in Jerusalem to read Hasidic texts. The group included Hugo Bergmann, emeritus professor of philosophy at the Hebrew University; Zalman Shazar, soon to be elected president of Israel; as well as several teachers, lawyers, and business men, none of whom would call themselves mystics and some who wondered if they were religious, but all agreed that Adin, as they called their teacher, was a genius. He had, I was told, a degree in mathematics from the Hebrew University and an almost unlimited knowledge of twentieth-century science and literature. At the same time he was recognized by even the most Orthodox scholars of Jerusalem as an *ilui,* a master of Talmudic Law, and this competency in the revealed aspects of Judaism was accompanied by a profound knowledge of its hidden wisdom. Just as unusual as this abundance of knowledge was his capacity for lucid exposition that was able to relate seemingly outdated teachings to the most immediate of modern problems.

The man whom they were describing, when I first saw him, was no more than twenty-six years of age. He had red hair, a straggling reddish beard, and clear blue eyes framed by brown spectacles. Though it was cold he insisted on wearing only a thin suit and an open-collared white shirt. His voice was so soft as to make it difficult at times, even for those sitting near him, to hear what he was saying. Nevertheless, after that first hour in class, I knew that I wanted to hear more and asked him where I could have the opportunity. He graciously told me what other classes he was teaching in Jerusalem and even offered some private hours of instruction.

Adin, I soon learned, was the only child of a staunchly non-religious, socialist family which remained unconverted despite the growing fame of their son. He did not hesitate—he was even a little proud—to describe the situation in his home where he, instead of his mother, lit the candles on Sabbath eve and built up a zone of Orthodoxy. His religious commitment, he told me, did not take place as the result of a conversion experience. At the age of fourteen, he had simply left high school because "I didn't think I was getting anything out of my studies," and he had gone to live for a year with an elderly Hasid in the Orthodox quarter of Jerusalem. Adin's rabbinic knowledge had not been obtained through the usual channels of the yeshiva, but was mainly self-acquired, but neither this fact nor his youth had prevented him from probing some of the most complex aspects of Talmudic Law.

The young rabbi, when I first began studying with him, was still a bachelor, struggling with the problems of loneliness, insecurity in the midst of praise, and frustration between romantic goals and unyielding social realities. A few years earlier, he and a group of friends had gone to the Negev Desert, where they tried to form a covenant type of *kibbutz* in which Hasidic fervor and religious orthodoxy were to be linked with hard physical labor. For two years these young people had tried to achieve their dream, but they had finally broken up. Adin was still not able to speak of this failure without his voice betraying deep disappointment. He longed deeply for the companionship which was being denied him by virtue of the fact that his genius had so early made him a teacher of older people and estranged him from easy relationships with those his own age.

Today, happily married and a father, Rabbi Steinsaltz is engaged in the translating, elucidating, and editing of the sixty-four volumes of the Talmud, a feat which would be considered immensely difficult for even a team of scholars to accomplish in a lifetime. Adin's plan is to finish the work within seven to ten years, and all that prevents him from maintaining his projected schedule is a shortage of financial assistance which would enable him to assign some routine editing and cross-checking tasks to other people. One reason for the absence of such assistance is the ambivalence with which some Orthodox circles regard the phenomenon of a Talmudic genius, who, apparently fully committed to Orthodoxy, is yet able to keep such open windows in terms of personal relationships as well as ideas. Despite this hesitation, the leading Orthodox religious authorities of Jerusalem were present at a reception convoked by President Shazar to celebrate the publication of the first volume of Rabbi Steinsaltz's Talmud in 1967. Representatives of Israel's Socialist Party joined with religious authorities and Talmudic scholars to praise the young rabbi's work. His father, who had once fought for the Spanish leftist government, also attended, paternal pride overcoming his sense of irony. "They say that someone like my son appears only once in two thousand years—and it had to happen to me," he remarked with a smile.

At the Six-in-One Synagogue

One of the places where Adin told me I could attend his classes was a synagogue located on a side street in the Katamon area of Jerusalem. It was a neglected building, with benches and tables slapped together out of old boards. On the Sabbath, when the urinals were not flushed, the stench could become unbearable. The synagogue consisted of five small rooms, each with its own ark, variety of ritual and congregation, and a sixth prayer-quorum, made up of latecomers, conducted services in the hallway. By the end of the Sabbath, the congregational boundaries would disappear, and everyone wandered into whatever room happened to have a service starting at that moment. The result was an astounding concatenation of accents, costumes, and faces. There were Hasidim in the yellow caftans that proclaimed their descent from the old Jerusalem families; Sephardic Jews in black conical hats and striped Arab-style robes; blonde children of European descent running around with the darker offspring of the Eastern communities. There were also young men wearing the little woolen yarmelkes that symbolized adherence to a religious youth movement, or sharply tailored clothes and hat, in the high Levantine style favored by North Africans.

"A regular Noah's ark," one of Adin's students commented, as he saw me staring at the potpourri one day. He was a husky Russian-Jewish engineer who had run away to Israel after seeing the concentration camps in Eastern Europe. He had fought in Israel's War of Independence and now, after his day's work and also on the Sabbath, studied Hasidic texts with young Rabbi Steinsaltz. But there were moments when Adin accused him of reverting to Marxist skepticism; one such relapse occurred during a weekday evening class, as we were reading some references in a Hasidic text to the *seraphim* and the *ofanim*. These mysterious creatures are mentioned in the book of Ezekiel, and included in the daily prayerbook among the celestial hosts that daily praise God's holiness. The *ofanim,* according to the text we were studying, belonged to a lower level of the heavenly hierarchy. *Ofan* is associated with the Hebrew root for wheel and implies a continuous circling; *ofanim* are creatures who are constantly praising God, repeating, "Holy, holy, holy." The *seraphim,* however, belong to a higher level of the heavenly hierarchy. *Seraph* in Hebrew is linked to *flame.* So fiery is the devotion of these *seraphim* that they can only get through the first "holy" before they are burnt up by the intensity of their devotion.

"Look, Adin," the Russian Jew suddenly burst out, after our teacher had finished exploring this idea, "an Army can train only so long, then it has to shoot. When are we going to shoot?" The Russi, as we called him, was always pressing Adin to outline ways in which these mystical secrets could find a practical outlet.

The young rabbi good-naturedly parried the challenge. "Some people spend their time, when they're not working for a living, talking about money and the stock market. We're spending our time here talking about the composition of spiritual worlds above and within us. That very fact already makes a difference in our lives. Doesn't it?"

The Russi did not appear convinced, but looking about at our class, I was intrigued by the face of a bearded Hasid with shrewd, shining black eyes. It was a type I had seen before—vital, sharp, even avaricious. If such a man were turned loose in the market place, he might tear competitors limb from limb; instead, here he was, using all his cunning to accumulate more understanding of the distinction between the *seraphim* and the *ofanim.* Maybe Adin was right; the decision to spend one's time talking about such things as the levels of angelic hierarchy did make a practical difference in life.

During the evening's lesson my mind also went back to a meeting of Israeli farmers I had attended earlier that week, where there had been talk of the current interest in the exploration of the *chalal,* outer space. "We have lost our *shamayim,* heaven," one farmer said. "Today we see up there only *chalal,* empty space, and we speak only about the conquest of space. It seems to me that the reason we speak so much about conquering *chalal* up there is because we feel so much empty space within."

This much was certain: for the Jewish mystic there was no empty space, either "up there" or "within." His heaven was thoroughly crowded with hierarchies of angels, levels of worlds, chambers, palaces, thrones, and chariots. He did not suffer from a sense of interior emptiness. Nevertheless, the Russi's question, "When do we shoot?" had not been fully answered, and one afternoon I presented it to Adin again.

Application of Mysticism to Life

"I've been thinking," he replied, "and sometimes it seems that the world is like a wild forest in which man can do little except make a small clearing." To attempt such a clearing was Judaism's goal, and part of the work consisted in applying lucidity of mind to all subjects, even a subject as cloudy as the Kabbala. This offered an opportunity to ask for a definition of mysticism, and the next day he brought me a slip of paper on which he had written the following:

The goal of Jewish mysticism is the effort (combined with the practice) to come close to things, a yearning for identification. This yearning includes all things, small and large, but its special goal is an identification with the innermost aspect of everything—the divine. Mysticism, therefore, is the desire to remove the outer coverings of things which hide their inner quality. Only through finding innerness in our life, as well as the innerness of all things, will this desire for full identification enjoy any kind of gratification. It is possible, therefore, to perceive two processes at work in mysticism. First, an activity which is mainly speculative—that is, the intellectual effort to remove the shells of reality. Secondly, the activity by which, after the removal of the outer coverings, one binds oneself to this truth. These two processes make up, respectively, the philosophy and practice of mysticism.

Adin warned that there was little in this definition which would help a person to understand the unique character of Jewish mysticism, still less to teach him, as the Russi put it, "How to shoot." The answers to such questions could only come after exposure to specific texts, ideas, and forms of expression. When I asked Adin to offer such exposure during our private lessons, he chose examples almost at random from whatever material happened to be at hand—an old prayerbook, an Hasidic pamphlet, notes from a lecture about application of the Kabbala to women's problems. Remembering that he was a young bachelor, I expressed particular interest in the latter, for I wondered how a young rabbinic bachelor could relate the Kabbala to women; Adin merely smiled and suggested that it was probably easier for him than for a married man to work out a feminine mystique.

Not surprisingly, Rabbi Steinsaltz's theories about ideal womanhood are grounded in Orthodox Judaism. The first prescription which Orthodoxy suggests for women is *zniut,* modesty in thought, word, and behavior. This concern for modesty expresses itself in the separation of the sexes during worship or in any public gathering. The obvious purpose of this separation is to avoid erotic stimulation at the wrong time and in the wrong place, but there is also an inner aspect to this regulation: it gives women a chance to develop their own characteristics rather than to engage in a frustrating imitation of men. It is in his description of these natural feminine qualities that Rabbi Steinsaltz drew upon his knowledge of the Kabbala.

In the tree diagram of the Kabbala, the first of the *sefirot* (*chochma,* or wisdom) is categorized as male and placed on the right side; the second *sefira* (*bina,* understanding) is feminine and on the left. These two *sefirot* are called the "two friends who never part," and as we have seen, their unification produces the life flow that sustains the universe. Translating the characteristics of these *sefirot* into psychological terms, *chochma* can be identified with the primal flash of the mind, the impregnating seed, and *bina* is the vessel in which this seed receives form. *Chochma* is perception attained through the quick flash, the spark of genius, whereas *bina* involves labor and meditation. *Bina* takes the intuitive thought, expands it, analyzes and synthesizes its elements. Therefore, every basic idea which is sown by wisdom must have a period of "pregnancy" in *bina,* a period of development which readies it for outer exposure. Furthermore, *bina* is also associated with the unfolding of emotions, the element of heart.

Out of these abstractions, the young rabbi extracted his prescription for feminine fulfillment. Women will be most successful in developing their indigenous qualities, he suggested, if they choose a field of work which requires neither swiftness of mind nor the dynamic flash of intuition, but rather the effort of quiet and persistent clarification. In the same way, the prayer mood of women ought not to imitate men; it should not aim at dynamic outbursts but a "quiet, warm, logical, and more inner mood."

Another characteristic of ideal femininity might be deduced from the *sefira* called *tiferet,* or beauty, which in the tree occupies a position midway between right and left and upper and lower. It is the harmonizer of opposites. This fact should make women realize that beauty is not something that can be defined in terms of specific facial lines, but their harmonious conjunction. Therefore, suggests Adin, the education of women ought to develop their *tiferet*-like gift for creating harmony in all realms, from furniture arrangement to family disputes.

I complimented the then bachelor rabbi on his prescription for feminine happiness, and we agreed to compare theory with reality after his marriage. I went on to request a study program designed to extract kabbalistic secrets for other life situations, and, as always, Adin was amenable. Soon I was taking notes on how to go to sleep, how to wake up, how to eat, and how to face all kinds of life-situations in accordance with the hidden wisdom.

Our discussions began to range further and further afield. "Did you ever notice that the jackets of Hasidim are buttoned with the right side over the left," Adin asked one day.

We began talking about the Zohar's command to "include the left within the right." The Jew understood this command as his commitment to harness the fiercer, more judgmental forces of the universe to the service of mercy and lovingkindness. That was why, Adin said, the prayer posture of Christians—hands evenly clasped or palms touching each other—would never be adapted by a pious Jew. In fact, knowledgeable Hasidim tried, even when dancing, to always begin with the right foot. "There are cultures in the East where every movement of the dance has symbolic import. In mystical Judaism, this stylization is carried over into every act of life, the most prosaic detail is thus given an expanded consciousness."

Expanded consciousness made me think of the devotees of psychedelic drugs, and Rabbi Steinsaltz had his opinions on this subject. "LSD and other so-called mind-expanding drugs can offer a trip but they cannot provide the contents for this trip. This will be determined by what a person brings or doesn't bring to his experience. Don't forget Aldous Huxley, who saw so much when he took drugs, brought forty years of study and knowledge to his experience."

Nor was Adin convinced by current demands for spontaneity of expression, with or without the aid of drugs. What most people call spontaneity is often only a reaction to a stimulus they have received from the mass media and represents simply the influence of the conscious thoughts of others. He also indicated some skepticism in regard to that brand of Eastern meditation whose goal is "to empty the mind" of all conscious thought. "To empty the mind may be a good first step, but afterwards the mind must be filled with concrete content." In this respect, as in so many other ways, Judaism took the middle way between East and West: "The West might be said to emphasize action—physical sanitation. The East concentrates on perfection of the spirit—spiritual sanitation. Judaism seeks to unite both ideals."

This constant dialectic and mediation between seemingly opposite worlds—spirit and body, the high and the low—was, as Adin saw it, the essence of the Jewish way. On the purely speculative level, it could be seen in the operation of the *sefirot*. One day, pointing to the right and left sides of the kabbalistic tree, Adin explained that the stronger the pull between these opposites, the greater the flow of *shefa* from the upper *ein sof*. The usual number of connections which can be drawn between the *sefirot* make thirty-two channels or hidden paths of wisdom. In the later Kabbala, the channels of connection became much more complex; each of the ten *sefirot* was in turn divided into components so that there was not only the sphere of wisdom, or beauty, but also the wisdom that was in beauty, or the beauty that was in wisdom. This division opened the way for even richer combinations between the *sefirot*—and, as Adin pointed out, the more involved the tensions, the richer the flow. Such a picture of cosmic reality, I told him, could bring comfort to intellectually complex or even split personalities. Adin agreed but promptly showed me a map which could bring even more comfort to simple nonintellectuals. Usually, he pointed out, the unities in the chain of descent involved *sefirot* that are on the same or directly adjoining level. Occasionally, however, a direct vertical union could take place which sidestepped all intermediate steps. For example, there could be a direct connection between *chochma,* the lofty *sefira* which symbolized the knowledge achieved by the flash of intuition, and kingdom, the lowest *sefira,* associated with concrete physical activity. This was the kind of intuition characteristic of prophecy, the truth that comes directly from the most spiritual level but is immediately converted into a concrete word or act without intermediate rationalizing or diluting channels, and intuition is often more available to a simple person than to the sophisticated.

Adin had other insights to reveal through these kabbalistic diagrams. For example, psychoanalytic schools would find it interesting to note that relationships called incestuous and forbidden below, such as those between father and daughter, mother and son, are permitted to take place in the world of the *sefirot* above. But above all, what was stressed in all these diagrams was the ever-present reminder of Judaism that the *shekina,* God's presence, wishes to dwell below in the mundane matters of this world. This was alluded to in the *sefirot* map by the obvious association in imagery between the utterly transcendent *sefira,* crown, and the very lowest kingdom. In some kabbalistic speculations, kingdom actually precedes crown in the sense that every idea has another idea before it. Furthermore, the Kabbala predicts, in the End of Days, the lower *sefira* or *malkut* will actually rise and assume a place above the crown, becoming the "crown of her husband." In other words, this world, though transient and gross, is nevertheless the goal and crown of all creation.

Chambers Within Chambers

The desire of the *shekina* "to dwell below" reminds every student of kabbalistic diagrams that the real purpose of his map is to provide a structural plan outlining the dynamics of daily existence. This architectural view of life is an old Jewish idea. Rabbinic literature pictures God as a master builder, who constructs the world according to a plan outlined in the Torah. The image of God as a builder is also the premise of the *Book of Creation,* one of the oldest kabbalistic texts. This imagery is carried over into the inner world of the mystic, who is forever speaking about palaces, chambers, and gates.

Haim Bialik, the greatest of the twentieth-century Hebrew poets, has compared the Sabbath to a magnificent palace constructed over the course of centuries by builders in a hundred different lands. This palace, built out of twenty-four hours of time, is erected on the laws derived from the bible and Talmud, which outline the basic structure of this day. There are thirty-nine such laws, the fathers of hundreds of others, and they make up the rigid structure of the palace and its various chambers. The interior decorating is done by the poetic legends, songs, prayers and customs which grace each section of the total building.

One day, my young teacher introduced me to *The House of Jacob,* a prayerbook compiled by a controversial eighteenth-century kabbalist, Rabbi Jacob Emden, which vividly illustrates this architectural approach. The weekday prayers are divided into sections called "the main living room, the chapel, the study," and the like. The Sabbath prayers are more delicately compartmentalized. Those offered at sunset, the time for the entrance into the Sabbath, are in a section called the Curtain. After the curtain is drawn aside, we come to the dining room, dealing with the laws, rituals, blessings, and hymns used at the Sabbath meal. This is followed by a move to the royal chamber, and then to the bedchamber.

The Sabbath morning scene is set in a different section of the palace. It begins with a gathering in the hall of the nobles, for on the Sabbath every Jew should conduct himself as a prince. Then all enter into the throne room where they petition the King directly. This period of petitioning (prayer) is followed by a sojourn in the library (referring to that portion of the Sabbath service when the Torah, the book of the Law, is read). From here they go to the wine room, namely to the main meal of the Sabbath which is preceded by *kiddush,* the blessing and drinking of the wine. The afternoon brings everyone to the classroom for instruction in traditional laws and legends. Then there is a return to the chamber of prayer, and finally, a long corridor leading to the chamber of exit.

This palace of the Sabbath is familiar to every Orthodox Jew. What the Kabbala adds is a kind of inner psychic programing of rhythms and moods appropriate to each chamber. There is, for example, the annulment of those divisions which characterize ordinary existence—between man and man, between mind and heart, ideal

and reality. "The mystery of the Sabbath" which must be revealed
is that God is to "sit upon His throne"—that is, unite with the community of Israel. In addition, there must be the effort to unite oneself
with the laws of heaven and earth, which, as in Chinese Taoism,
associate evening with femininity, the mood of passive receiving. In
the latter part of the Sabbath night, masculinity, the will to penetrate
and know, begins to emerge; this is the time for holy coupling, an act
which takes place on an earthly level between man and wife, and
concomitantly, in the world of the *sefirot.* Sabbath morning is quite
different; now it is the male element which predominates. The mood
of the Sabbath morning prayers is bright, outgoing; there is light,
activity, and the study of the Law. Study, knowing, is a kind of male
penetration, as in the biblical phrase, "And Adam knew Eve." Late
Sabbath afternoon is again different: union has taken place and the
seed has been deposited: what is left now is the essence of the experience—peaceful gratitude, lingering recollection, and soft longing. This
is the atmosphere of the third and last meal of the Sabbath, as the
holy *chevraya* sit about the table with their teacher singing melodies
of thanksgiving for the nearness to God which is sensed at this hour
of grace.

The combining of sexual rhythms with the natural rhythms, the
changes of the seasons, and the alteration of light and darkness is also
boldly taught in the Far Eastern religious traditions. Anyone familiar
with the yin and yang imagery of Chinese Confucianism, with the
attempt to link human rhythms with natural confluences in the *Book
of Changes,* or with the inbreathing and outbreathing of Hindu
cosmology, would have no trouble drawing parallels with the inner
Judaism of the kabbalist. Adin enjoyed making such correlations, not
only with themes like the Sabbath, but even in areas that a modern
mind would almost assuredly consider irrelevant, for example, with
the Kabbala's interest in what might be called the alphabet-number
game.

Mathematical Mysticism

Gematria is the technical term for a system whereby letters are
transposed into numbers. *Temurah* is a variation of this word-sport,

which changes the order of the alphabet, substituting *b* for *a* or *c* for *d;* or the first letter of the alphabet may be substituted for the last, the second for the next to the last, and so on. At other times, words and mathematical sums may be worked out by adding up the first letters of the words in a particular phrase. These letter-numbers may also be triangulated, multiplied, divided, and subjected to a variety of mathematical processes.

The attention which Jewish mystical texts devote to this type of mind play had always puzzled me. To be sure, from Pythagoras to Pascal to Gershom Scholem there is ample evidence of a natural affinity between mathematics and mysticism, but the association of numbers with letters was a different matter. One afternoon after Adin had finished drawing some diagrams illustrating the place of the seventy-two letter name of God in relationship to the fifty-two and forty-five letter name, along with their numerical equivalents, I could not help asking if all this wasn't a somewhat mechanical and artificial exercise? The fact that the number forty-five can, in Hebrew, be read as "what" or that seventy-two is the equivalent, in Hebrew, of son (with the letters reversed) may or may not be an interesting coincidence, but why build such coincidences into the status of an insight into the basic structure of the universe?

By way of an answer, Adin pointed out that many mathematicians covered blackboards with formulae and symbols simply for their own amusement, some Kabbalistic word-number play could be understood as the same kind of activity. On the whole, however, this occupation with letters and numbers was based on the assumption that the Torah was a code which could be broken in various ways. Its message was revealed partly by the plain sense of the words, but the decoding process would also require the analysis of the words or their numerical equivalents. Not only gematria, but the whole system of kabbalistic imagery might be looked upon as a system of coordinates of the kind a mathematician would use for drawing a graph; it is simply one of many symbolic ways of describing relationships. By working out these relationships, expressed through patterns of psychic movement, kabbalists believe they can come to a greater understanding of man and the world, the laws of physics, or the insights of psychology.

Kabbala as a Game

Sooner or later, the outsider will inevitably ask himself: Is all this talk about other worlds, and the quickening of the unities above by the quickening of the unities below—is it anything more than the product of imagination? And the rituals which concern themselves with placing six loaves of bread in a specific pattern on the Sabbath table, or the effort to quietly pronounce the first word in the eighteen benedictions at the precise moment of sunrise—are they not a kind of artificial game?

In our day, however, games are beginning to be recognized as serious affairs; the theory of games has become a branch of mathematics, with implications which stretch from atomic physics to military planning. To "drop out of the game" is a favorite phrase of those who would abandon the status or money-oriented pastimes of a conformist society. But we can hardly escape playing our games from the beginning to the end of life. In *Homo Ludens,* Huizinga described certain characteristics of man's "play." It must be a voluntary activity, that is, an act of free-will. It involves a "stepping out of real life" into a temporary sphere of activity. Although different from ordinary life, it also involves setting up certain limits of time and space. All play has its being within a playground marked off beforehand either materially or ideally. Thus the play of religious ritual has its consecrated places and times. So does the "play" of the Japanese tea ceremony, or the "play of athletics." Particularly interesting is Huizinga's point about the tendency of play surrounding itself with an air of secrecy.

Even in childhood the charm of play is enhanced by making a secret act of it. This is for us, and not for "others." What the "others" do "outside" is no concern of ours at the moment. Inside the circle of the game the laws and customs of ordinary life no longer count. . . .

A "spoilsport" is one who not only withdraws from the play world but robs it of its illusions. He breaks the magic world and must be ejected. In the serious game of society, spoilsports are sometimes called "apostates, heretics, innovators, conscientious objectors," etc. It sometimes happens, however, that the spoilsports in their turn make a

new community with rules of its own. The outlaw, the revolutionary,
the kabbalist, or member of a secret society, indeed, heretics of all kinds,
are of a highly associative, if not sociable, disposition . . .

Huizinga makes clear that games need not be frivolous, but may
also enhance life. "In play we may move below the level of the serious,
as the child does, but we can also move above it in the realm of the
beautiful and the sacred." All this makes it easy to look upon the
Kabbala as a game, but how is the quality and direction of life affected by it?

Perhaps we can get some further insight by looking at the
game described in Herman Hesse's *Magister Ludi,* where symbols, or
"beads," are arranged like the notes and themes of a musical composition. The symbols and grammar of the game, Hesse writes, "represent
a type of highly secret language, in which several sciences and arts, in
particular mathematics and music, not to forget the theory of music,
play their part." Hesse's bead game is also a device which comprises
all the values of our culture; it plays with them as, in the springtime
of the arts, a painter may have toyed with the colors on his palette.
The adept of Hesse's game would play upon all that man has produced in philosophy, religion, and art "as an organist plays upon the
organ. . . ." Knecht, the hero of *Magister Ludi,* has a special game
which involves a "rhythmical analysis of a fugue theme, in the midst
of which stirred a phrase, probably from Kung Fu Tze." To prevent
the game from being merely an exhibition of virtuoso technique or
prodigious memory, contemplation was used "to vivify the content
of the symbol intensively and organically."

The game is prepared and played by a scholarly community, for
it involves dangers—weak minds and characters are recommended to
"safer paths." The objective of the players is "to discern opposites correctly, in considering them primarily as opposites but eventually as
poles of a single unit." When properly played, "each symbol and each
combination of symbols led, not hither and thither, not to single examples, experiments and proofs, but towards the center, into the mystery and vitals of the world, into primaeval conscience. . . ."

Hesse's bead game, it seems to me, offers some intriguing parallels to the Kabbala. The abstract symbols and imagery—the names of

God, the references to *seraphim,* the ancient of days, the ten *sefirot,* and the four worlds—are similar to the many-leveled symbolic beads of *Magister Ludi.* Similarly, the kabbalistic acts of concentration and withdrawal are related to the in and out of breathing, to yin and yang, which Hesse also associates with his game. The dialectic of opposites, so much a part of the Kabbala, can be described in Hesse's understanding of polarities which eventually become "poles of a single unit."

But there also are some important differences between Kabbala and Hesse's bead game. For example, Knecht says that "a true bead player should be permeated with serenity like a ripe fruit with sweet juices and, above all, should possess the serenity of music, which is naught else but courage—a serene, smiling, striding and dancing amidst the terrors and flames of the world, the festive offering of the sacrifice." But this is not the mood of the Kabbala; withdrawal and serenity are only part of its dialectic. *R'zto,* going out into the sphere of the timeless, is followed by *shuv,* a return to earthbound reality; life is seen as the constant swinging of a pendulum, hidden mystery to concrete revelation.

There is also a difference between the goal of the kabbalist and the player of the bead game. Both yearn for a vision of that "infinity where the stars reign supreme," but the kabbalist is not satisfied with that orderly and impersonal infinity. His journey through the paths of the *sefirot* takes him from the personal who, into the deeper mystery of the what, and on to the region of the *ayin,* the ultimate nothing, which, although beyond all human definition and even question, is the source of all being. But there, at the very edge of the search, the kabbalist again sets up the image of primordial man, complete with descriptions of eyes, limbs, and hair. The latter may represent the most external emanation of the Godhead, but it is still connected; when removed, it withers and dies. The eyes, however, offer a glimpse into the inner depths.

Although symbolic, this remains an anthropomorphic description of divinity, with shocking Blakeian dimensions, because when the Kabbala relates the human eyes to God's eye, it does so in more than the allegorical sense. The human eye is a fallen version of the divine eye, just as the human body is an infinitely grosser version of the utterly incorporeal divine man, and the limbs of the human body are related "in their roots" to the limbs of God. In similar fashion, the kabbalist insists that the very highest *sefira* is crown, which is beyond all attempts at description; he immediately adds its characteristic is joy and its center characteristic is will. Although the joy and will are "ten times ten thousand times" different from human joy and will, an individual draws his joy and will power by connection with crown, the deepest layer of the world's spiritual substructure. Eyes and limbs and will are also symbols, but the images remain, forever distinguishing from other varieties which would disparage the importance of the body, the yearning for joy, or the value of the human will.

If the Kabbala is a game, therefore, it is one that is played for high stakes; nothing less is involved than the sustenance of God's creation. With the help of an Adin Steinsaltz, some of the meaning of the kabbalist's game may be abstracted from its technical terminology, but such men are rare and words are not enough; the play requires players. Today there are few, if any, communities committed to the Kabbala as it was played in the days of the Holy Ari. There are some communities, however, who claim to have brought the old game up to date. To meet them, let us go to the gate of Hasidism, the movement which, according to Buber, took the Kabbala and made it a "folk ethos."

5

MYSTICISM FOR THE MASSES
Hasidism and Martin Buber

The Hasidic teaching is the most powerful and unique phenomenon which the Diaspora has produced. It foreshadows a renaissance. No revival of Judaism will be possible that does not contain some of its elements.

The Hasidic legend . . . did not grow up in the shade of ancient groves, nor on hills clad with silvery olive trees. In narrow streets and gloomy little rooms, it passed in awkward words to ears that listened in fear; it was uttered by faltering lips, and faltering lips carried it on from generation to generation. I received it from books of the people, from chapbooks, and stray leaves; at times from a living mouth, from the mouths of those people who had themselves heard the faltering words. I received it and I tell the story anew. I have not woven it into a fabric of fables, I have told it afresh as a descendant. I bear in me the spirit and the blood of those who created it; and in my blood and spirit it has become new. I stand in the chain of those story-tellers, a link between links; I tell the story afresh, and if it sounds new, it is only because the new was dormant in it when it was first told.

— MARTIN BUBER, *Jewish Mysticism*

Past expressions of the hidden tradition have shared one characteristic, they were confined to small groups. About the middle of the eighteenth century, however, the Kabbala opened a gate of the *pardes* which was designed to attract the simple, the unlettered, the ordinary folk of Israel. "This is the gate of the Lord," it proclaimed, "let the *tzaddikim,* the righteous ones, enter therein." The righteous in this instance were the rebbes or spiritual leaders of the movement that has come to be known as Hasidism. With their help, the daily lives of the multitudes were transmuted and suffused by the moods, images, and insights of Jewish mysticism. Today Hasidism is a living, creative entity encompassing many thousands of families in all parts of the world; indeed, its teachings, stories, and music have spread far beyond the Jewish world. Mainly responsible for the attention which this East European religious movement today receives in the Western world was a young man who wrote, "The Hasidic truth is vitally important for Jews, Christians and others, and at this particular hour more important than ever before. For now is the hour when we are in danger of forgetting for what purpose we are on earth, and I know of no other teaching that reminds us of this so forcibly. Therefore," Martin Buber declared at the beginning of the twentieth century, "I carry it into the world against its will."

When Martin Buber decided to carry Hasidism into the world, he had already achieved recognition in both the non-Jewish and Jewish community. In Vienna, where he was born, he had shown great promise as an art critic. He had been a warm supporter of the Zionist movement from its inception and was asked by Theodore Herzl to edit its new journal, *Die Welt*. Only after Herzl's death in 1907 did Buber return to the world which he had glimpsed as a child when his scholarly grandfather took him to visit with Hasidic groups in Polish Galicia. One day Buber opened a little book called *Zvaat Habesht*— that is, The Testament of Rabbi Israel Baal Shem Tov . . . and the words flashed toward him, "He takes unto himself the quality of fervor. He arises from his sleep with fervor, for he is sanctified and has become another man and is worthy to create, and imitate God by forming his world." It was then, writes Buber, that he was overpowered in an instant by the Hasidic soul. Judaism as religiousness, as "piety," as Hasidut, opened up before him. Buber then withdrew from Zionist activities for five years and devoted himself to research and writing about Hasidism.

Hasidism à la Buber

Before Buber, the pietistic folk movement which later came to be known as Hasidism quickened little positive reaction on the part of enlightened Western observers. The nineteenth century German-Jewish historian Graetz was almost apoplectic in his reaction to the "new Essenism." He thought it disgusting that in an age when Moses Mendelssohn declared "rationalistic thought to be the essence of Judaism . . . another banner was unfurled, the adherents of which announced grossest superstition to be the fundamental principle of Judaism." The American-Jewish scholar, Solomon Schechter, was more judicious in seeing the movement as the revolt of an "emotional but uneducated people against the excessive casuistry of the contemporary Rabbis." Schechter found genuine spirituality and beauty in some of its legends, but pointed to its later degeneration into superstition as evidence that it was short-lived as "an active force for good."

It was left for Martin Buber, who saw Hasidism as a world of "legendary reality," to present its message in terms which could attract the Western mind. Its chronicles, he said, were the products of "fervent human beings who set down their recollections of what they saw or thought they saw, in their fervor, and this means that they included many things which were apparent only to the gaze of fervor." The *tzaddikim,* Buber asserted, were religious personalities "of a vitality, spiritual strength and manifold originality such as has never, to my knowledge, appeared together in so short a time span in the history of religion."

Buber concedes that there is little extant material, of the kind which historians call primary, about its founder, Israel, the son of Eliezer, who was born about 1700 in the small Ukrainian village of Ukob, to a family undistinguished either for learning or social position. From the beginning, there was strenuous disagreement as to Israel's scholarly attainments. As a child, he is supposed to have shown a greater predilection for lone sojourns in the forest than for formal lessons in the House of Instruction. For some time he was employed as a teacher's aide who conducted children to and from school. He is described as stocky, addicted to a stubby pipe, and usually dressed in rough clothes, a sheepskin cloak tied about with a rough belt. When he married, his brother-in-law, a Rabbi Gershon, was ashamed of his apparently ignorant and coarse new relative, even urging his sister to divorce her husband. But Israel's wife was loyal and the couple moved to a remote village in the Carpathian mountains, where Israel earned his living by digging clay or driving a wagon. Some time later, there seems to have been a reconciliation with his wife's family, and they moved to a larger town in the Ukraine where they ran an inn. Here Israel revealed himself as a baal shem, a title used by local Jews to describe individuals who achieve a reputation not only for mystical powers but as folk healers and seers. According to tradition, Israel began to be called the Baal Shem Tov, the master of the good name, when he was thirty-six years old, a pregnant number in Judaism, for it is twice eighteen—the numerical equivalent of the Hebrew word for life. It is also a reference to thirty-six hidden saints whose righteousness sustains the world. His active spiritual leadership continued to his death in May, 1760.

On this rather bare frame of supposed fact, the rapidly spreading Hasidic movement soon wove a semilegendary image of its founder. Although it is impossible to say where fact ends and the "exalted imagination" of the people enters, it seems clear that the stories about the Baal Shem reflect a rebellion against the "status forms" stifling eighteenth-century East European Jewish society. In particular, they questioned the assumption that Talmudic learning and distinguished intellectual ancestry are the main criteria for recognition in the eyes of both God and man. But the message of the Baal Shem Tov and his followers went far beyond an expression of resentment at the domination of the rabbis and their Talmudic academies. It was also an effort to combat the mood of despair which had fallen on the East European Jewish world after the year *Tach,* 1648. According to kabbalistic dreamers, that was the year when the Messiah would come; instead, bands of Cossacks, under Hetman Chmelnitski, decimated hundreds of Jewish communities.

Exhausted by the struggle to keep alive in poverty-stricken circumstances, chastised by their leaders for not devoting more time to the study of the sacred books, and bleeding from pogroms, the East European Jewish world was beset by a mood of black bitterness—*mora schora*. It was this mass melancholia the Baal Shem undertook to change. He began preaching that life should be filled with joy and high purpose, and, within a very few years, his disciples had triggered a current of enthusiasm which spilled over into five generations and resulted in a religious movement whose vitality can still be sensed in our day.

One reason, Buber suggests, for the success of the Baal Shem's struggle against despair was his teaching that the body be granted its elemental rights—those rights which were being labeled as gross, sensual, and therefore sinful. The biblical injunction, "hide thyself not from thine own flesh," was interpreted by the Baal Shem as a commandment to stop inflicting pain and deprivation upon one's own body. He himself enjoyed simple pleasures—a piece of herring, a drop of liquor, and the companionship of his wife, whose death, he said, caused him to give up his hopes of hastening the arrival of the Messiah, because he had become only "half."

A good illustration of the Baal Shem's antiascetic attitudes is the story of his meeting with Rabbi Jacob Joseph, a scholar given to frequent spells of depression. One day this rabbi had gone to the synagogue for the evening prayer and found it locked. The caretaker, he discovered, was in the marketplace with a crowd of men who were listening to a stranger—it was the Baal Shem Tov—telling stories. Angrily the rabbi summoned the stranger who was delaying the prayers of his community. When the Baal Shem Tov came before him, the words of chastisement that Jacob Joseph had prepared stuck in his throat, at which point the Baal Shem said:

"One day a peasant was driving three horses across the country and not one of them would neigh. He pulled the reins harder and harder, but they did not neigh, they only choked. Finally, he slackened the reins, and they neighed. The peasant knew what to do," said the Baal Shem Tov. "The peasant gave good advice. Do you understand? The peasant knew what to do."

"I understand," answered Rabbi Jacob Joseph, and became one of the Baal Shem Tov's disciples.

Another version of Jacob Joseph's conversion has it that the Baal Shem simply gave him a good bed and commanded him to sleep in it. When Jacob Joseph, who had never allowed himself the pleasure of a full night's sleep, awoke late the next morning, the world was brighter, his prayers sweeter, and he became a Hasid.

The suggestion to "slacken the reins" was interpreted by the opponents of the Hasidic movement as implying a cavalier attitude toward the Law, an accusation which the Hasidim angrily denied. But Hasidim did take it upon themselves to remind the scholars that the precept, "God desires the heart," was also an element of the Law. They proudly acknowledged that Eliezer, the father of the Baal Shem Tov, was not a learned man. His main spiritual virtue was that although he lived far away from the centers of Jewish life, he never forgot his prayers, a virtue accessible even to the poorest and most ignorant Jew. This claim, that every Jew, no matter how ignorant, could offer prayers acceptable to God, was the key teaching of the Baal Shem Tov, who was said to have cherished the prayer of an illiterate shepherd:

> *Dear God, though I keep cattle and sheep for others for pay*
> *For you I would keep them for nothing*
> *Because I love you.*

The important thing about a prayer, said the Baal Shem, was its *kavannah*. In the Kabbala *kavannah* was associated with esoteric knowledge about the dynamics of the *sefirot;* the Baal Shem did not deny this meaning but expanded it to include any sincere movement of the heart. To illustrate this, he used to tell a story about a man who bursts into tears just before blowing the shofar on the High Holy days, because he has forgotten the mystical formulae which were so carefully rehearsed with him by the rebbe. The rebbe, or spiritual master, assured him, however, that his tears were more effective in opening the gates of heaven than the secret *kavannot* that he had forgotten.

Another version of the story has the poor shofar blower crying, not because he has forgotten the *kavannot,* but because he is afraid to lose his job in the synagogue and will therefore be unable to support his wife and five unmarried daughters. This, too, is accepted by the rebbe as being at least as effective as mystical formulae in carrying the prayers of the congregation up to heaven. Without proper *kavannah,* however, prayers remain on the ground of the synagogue like "birds with broken wings."

Probably the most famous of these tales stressing the importance of inner intent over outer form is the story of the shepherd boy who cannot read the prayers but nevertheless insists on attending the High Holy Day services. In the midst of the service, moved by the religious atmosphere, the little boy takes out the pipe he uses in the field and blows it. All are shocked. His father boxes the boy's ear and sends him out of the synagogue. The Baal Shem Tov, however, goes on with his prayers, only "more quickly and happily." Later he says, "the boy made things easier for me."

That the divine presence of God, the *shekina,* will not rest where sadness or despair prevails, was another cardinal teaching of Judaism stressed by the Baal Shem Tov. One must never say about events in life that they are bad, although one is permitted to say of some things that they are bitter, since sometimes "the doctor prescribes sweet herbs, and sometimes bitter ones." Nor should a person become depressed by his sins, for this is Satan's device for separating us even further from God. The holy sparks of God are hidden everywhere, even in sinful situations; how else could there be any pleasure in sin? Instead of despairing, a sinner must "lift the holy sparks" out of their uncongenial surroundings and into a place where their joy-giving qualities can be more fully released.

Along with the Spanish or Sephardic style of prayerbook, Hasidism adopted many ideas of the kabbalistic circle of the Holy Ari in Safed. We have already seen how the doctrine that holy sparks were to be found everywhere, even in the lowest regions, was used by the followers of Shabbatai Zevi and Jacob Frank with anarchistic results. Memories of these heresies were still vivid and served to strengthen the objections of the Misnagdim, as opponents of the new sect were called. The latter were also appalled by the indecorous behavior of the Hasidim during prayer, for the Baal Shem's followers felt that they ought literally to fulfill the psalmist's cry, "All my bones shall praise the Lord," and their shouting, clapping, and turning of somersaults in the synagogue scandalized the religious authorities.

The most important theological objection raised against the Hasidim was their extremist interpretation of the rabbinic teaching, "There is no place empty of Him." To say that He was present, or was even to be identified, with that which was obviously polluted, was nothing but pantheism, claimed the Vilna Gaon. This revered Talmudic authority issued a series of excommunication bans in an attempt to prohibit the Orthodox community from having any kind of traffic with the new sect. These bans went to the extent of forbidding intermarriage between the two groups, and the resulting bitterness lasted for generations. Only today has the historic cycle made a full swing, and the movement which was once denounced as heretical seems to have itself become the standard bearer of extreme, unbending Orthodoxy.

Despite the opposition of the Misnagdim, the movement launched by the Baal Shem Tov spread with amazing rapidity. Within a few years, it had attracted thousands of followers, who were divided into dozens of Hasidic dynasties all over Eastern Europe. The Nazi scythe decimated these communities, but there are still thousands who claim to follow the way of the Baal Shem Tov, and the present popularity of Hasidic stories and legends has convinced many that the Baal Shem's death-bed commandment to "let the waters of your wellsprings spread outward" is in the process of being successfully carried out by his followers.

Scholem's Critique

Some observers would give the non-Hasid Martin Buber the largest share of credit for the current interest of the Western world in Hasidism.

Both the Orthodox Hasidim and a scholar such as Scholem, however, complain that Buber's version is highly subjective. Hasidism is not, Scholem insists, an example of a religious faith that wishes to turn man to the demand of the "here and now." Buber's error arises from paying too much attention to its legends and too little attention to the kabbalistic ideas expressed in its theoretical literature.

The Hasidic masters did, indeed, teach that man meets God in the concreteness of his activity within the world and tried to give a moral, often humanistic interpretation to kabbalistic doctrines. The phrase from Proverbs, "In all thy ways shall you know Him," was interpreted to mean that man can meet God in every circumstance of life. Man can perform the "deepest meditations and acts of unification even through his most earthly actions, such as eating, drinking, sexual intercourse, and business transactions."

With all this Scholem agrees. His main point, however, is that Hasidim did not exhort their followers to find "joy in the world as it is, in life as it is, in every hour of life in this world as that hour is." The method which Hasidism used for finding joy and meaning was "to extract, I may even say distill, the perpetual life of God out of life as it is. This extracting must be an act of abstraction. It is not the fleeting here and now that is to be enjoyed, but the everlasting unity and presence of Transcendence. Of course, it is precisely this notion of abstraction in and joy in the uplifting of the sparks to which Buber's interpretation of Hasidism takes exception."

What Buber fails to notice, Scholem complains, is the element of destruction involved in draining the vital life force out of the "here and now."

The fact is, says Scholem, that "Buber is a religious anarchist (a term that is not meant to disparage him); I am an anarchist myself, though not one of Buber's persuasion." This leads Buber to present a type of Hasidism which "does not acknowledge any teaching about what should be done but puts the whole emphasis on intensity, on how whatever one does, is done. Therefore, references to the Torah and the commandments, which to the Hasidim still meant everything, become extremely nebulous in Buber's presentation."

Buber, however, vigorously defends his subjective approach to the Hasidic reality. Since his purpose is "to recapture a sense of the power that once gave it the capacity to take hold of and vitalize the life of diverse classes of people," this requires "a selection of those manifestations in which its vital and vitalizing element was embodied. And this in turn requires an act of judgment. I have never pretended to tell more about Hasidic truth than what I heard." Buber's principle of selection represents "an evaluation of what is the central truth of Judaism and Hasidism. Having achieved the maturity of this insight, I have not made use of a filter. I am the filter." Buber stoutly denies that Hasidism's doctrine of the sparks negates reality, quoting a rebbe's answer to the disciple who asks him what had been most important to his teacher: "Whatever he happened to be doing at the moment." The Hasid accepts and dedicates to God whatever is happening in the here and now.

Since specialists are still debating the nature of Hasidism, it would be presumptuous for an amateur to offer an opinion as to whether Scholem or Buber are closer to a correct interpretation. S. Z. Setzer, for example, has pointed out that no Hasidic doctrine was new to Judaism. Joy, clinging to God, enthusiasm, the values of simple faith and the inner intent—all these prescriptions for life can be found in classical Jewish sources. The same is true of customs such as the *tisch*—the communal meal shared with the rebbe; or the petitions and bequests which the rebbe, as an intermediary, was asked to convey to God; or the mystic significance of the dance and the song. Although Hasidism offered no new doctrine, Setzer acknowledges its contribution in rearranging the priority of the old teachings, placing the heart, joy, and prayer at the head of the Jewish ladder of values. Anybody who wants to discover the real ideology of Hasidism, he feels, can sense it in the following classical Hasidic texts:

A king once decided to test the love of his people. Being skilled in the art of optical illusion, he built a palace, in the center of which he placed his throne room. Along the hallways leading to the throne room, he built rooms which he filled with jewels, clothes and food. Outside the palace he erected a high wall and surrounded the wall with a moat. The moat was surrounded by great fires. Legions of fierce soldiers guarded all the entrances.

When he had finished building the palace, he issued an edict commanding all his subjects to express their love by coming to his Throne room. From far and wide, people came to answer the call of their beloved king. But most of them, when they saw the obstacles about the palace—the fires and water and high wall and soldiers—turned away. Of those who persisted and entered, some were distracted by the chambers of sparkling goods which lined the corridors. Only a few remembered the king's commandment and trusted in their sovereign's mercy. Confronting the barriers of fire, water, high walls and fierce guards, they knew not how to proceed, but in their love and eagerness to see the king, called, "Our father, our king—help us to come to you." And for these, all the obstacles without and all the temptations within immediately disappeared, and they found themselves in the presence of the king.

This parable would seem to support Scholem's insistence that the *tzaddik* urged his followers to detach themselves from concrete realities. But as his second illustration of classical Hasidic doctrine, Setzer offers us the teaching of the Baal Shem: "When one sees a beautiful woman, or hears a lovely melody, one need not say that it is not beautiful or lovely. One should, however, think: but this creature or this creation, does it not draw its beauty and loveliness from the Source of all beauty and all joy? Why should I not go to the Source?"

What shall we conclude from these illustrations? That Hasidism destroys reality by turning it into that nothingness which the mystic identifies with the deepest reality, or that it enhances reality by rooting it in something deeper? Or is it both—a "going" and a "returning," as the kabbalists say?

One thing is certain. The picture of Hasidism and the image of the Baal Shem Tov which has become so acceptable to modern secular minds needs a correction. The Baal Shem was not just an affirmer of life, a champion of the poor and unlettered, and an advocate of a religion which could be fully expressed by love of one's fellowman. He was a mystic, even an ecstatic, whose religious seizures might be diagnosed in our day as psychotic. Like all Jewish mystics, he emphasized the hidden truths over the revealed aspects of Torah. Like the kabbalists of old, he tried to effect unities through the use of sacred names and played the alphabet and letter game. But in his case and that of his immediate followers, this emphasis on the hidden went beyond a knowledge of abstract secrets and was transmuted into behavior which changed the life tone of society in a direction set by his own life-affirming personality. Previously, the emphasis on hiddenness usually led to asceticism. But the Baal Shem argued that if innerness were so important, why make so much fuss about secret formulations or outer forms of ritual and prayer? Indeed, why so much concern about giving the body either pain or pleasure? Shouldn't there be, rather, an increase of indifference to all outer phenomena? That is how one should interpret the biblical commandment, "I placed the Lord before me always." The Hebrew word *shiviti,* I placed, comes from the root *shaveh,* which implies equality. he person who placed the Lord always before him will be able to see outer circumstances—illness or health, poverty or wealth, insult or praise—as equal in importance. A person should neither flee from nor toward life's beauty or pleasures; the important thing is always to penetrate beneath the surface and see, as Buber phrases it, "that the beating of the heart of the Universe is 'holy joy.'"

Buber's claim that Hasidim, by and large, were able to see life with this kind of vision would seem to be supported by evidence and

is of far more practical relevance than arguments about the precise
definition of Hasidism. Nevertheless, those who are looking for what
Buber saw in Hasidism will be in for a shock when meeting flesh
and blood representatives of this movement today. There is no point
in hiding the difficulty which confronts any searcher for holy sparks
in our day who goes from Buber's books to the real Hasidic world.
The problem may as well be presented immediately and in its sharpest
form—as I myself experienced it—by way of a contrast between a
meeting with Buber himself and a meeting with the Beltzer Hasidim.

Buber—the "Antimystic"

It was never difficult to arrange an appointment with Buber.
Over the years I had simply called him on the telephone, and a clear
German voice would answer, "Buber." There would be a pause to
allow for examination of the datebook, then a day and time would be
set. During one of my visits, I asked Buber how he could make
himself accessible to passing visitors and still manage to get his work
done. He answered me by repeating a story which he had also told in
a book describing his "way" in Hasidism. One day, Buber said,
when he was still a young man, he had been sitting in his home in
Vienna, immersed in the mystic aura of his studies, when he was
interrupted by the ring of his doorbell. It was a stranger. He had no
appointment, but he wanted to speak with Buber. The scholar had
answered the visitor's questions politely, but he did not "answer the
questions which were not asked" and told the man to make an appointment for a fuller visit. A short time later, Buber heard about
the man's death, probably a suicide. After this, he decided that the
demand of the "here and now" was more important than any abstract
study; it was this incident which helped to turn him away from the
mysticism that had previously attracted him.

Not all analysts of Buber's writings agree that he has eliminated
mysticism from his philosophy. S. H. Bergmann, his lifelong friend
and a former teacher of philosophy at the Hebrew University, argues
that the philosophy of the I and Thou is rooted in mystic premises.
When I was in Jerusalem a year before Buber's death, I decided to discuss this question with him.

It was winter, and the weather was cold and rainy that evening. I saw Buber in his study, and it was clear that he was just recovering from a siege of illness; his face was pale and splotched with red marks. He wore a sweater underneath his brown heavy jacket, and the room was overheated by a small kerosene stove.

"I know you, do I not?" he asked, looking at me closely.

I was surprised at the question and told him we had met several times in this room. He asked me to sit down near a small table, while he brought up a chair for himself and placed it in a position where we could look at each other directly. I asked him how he was feeling.

"Better. But for illnesses at my age, one needs good doses not only of antibiotics but of faith and humor." He spoke as if to himself. "Yes, faith is difficult, which is why one needs humor. And humor has something to do with a sense of the moment that is passing, floating." He paused, as if thinking. "But, also, I believe in eternity."

"What is eternity?"

"Eternity is not infinity. What it is I cannot understand. I cannot understand infinite numbers either. But I believe in them. All I know is that nothing is more certain than death. I do not believe in immortality. But I do believe in eternity. With death I enter into eternity. Do you understand? That is faith."

I really didn't understand, but wanted to turn the conversation to the subject of mysticism.

"We must know," Buber said slowly, "what we are talking about when we use the word *mysticism*. There is in Judaism no *unio deo* [union with God]—only the unity of God and the *shekina*, the presence of God."

I asked whether there were not some expressions of Jewish mysticism which did stress the unity of the individual soul with God, and finally mentioned the name of Scholem.

"Ah, my friend Scholem. He has made a science of the Kabbala. I respect it, but I am not interested in the technical phases of the subject. But as to your question—why am I not in favor of mysticism? It is because the term itself means a leaving of the here and now. A leaving and a coming back. I am against the leaving of the here and now, even for a while. Do you understand? Please ask if you do not."

I asked Buber what he was writing these days. He was trying to record, he replied, some of the crucial moments in his life. But his writing, he said, was really like talking. He tried to visualize the person to whom he was speaking as he wrote.

"You know," the old man mused as if speaking to himself, "I wasn't always like this. I don't like my early books, the ones I wrote until the age of twenty-five or so." He was still for a moment. The only sound in the room was the slight hiss of the kerosene stove. "Actually, I didn't become a person till late, almost forty."

I could see that he was tired and did not want to press him with further questions. When I rose, he accompanied me to the foyer, where he shook hands warmly.

Buber died the next winter. For me, as for multitudes in the Western world, he had been a gate through which we thought we were able to glimpse what he called the "most powerful and unique phenomenon which the diaspora has produced." But the question of the resemblance, past or present, between the phenomenon Buber described and the Hasidic reality has lingered with me during years of visits to various Hasidic courts. Nowhere was it more sharply posed than during my exposure to the Hasidim of Belz.

Buber and Belz

Martin Buber and the Hasidic dynasty of Belz were first placed in juxtaposition in 1947, a few days after my first conversation with Buber. I had come to him while studying at the Hebrew University and asked how I could meet the Hasidic world he had described in his books. He offered a number of suggestions, one of them being a visit to the summer residence of the Belzer rebbe, which was then located in Bet ha-Kerem, a Jerusalem suburb not far from my residence. Buber suggested that I visit this court Saturday evening, the time which is set aside for the third meal.

I prepared myself for this initial venture into Hasidic reality by reading Buber's description of the third meal. This was the time, he had written, when "the spiritual leader becomes the focus of strength in which the blaze of the community-soul is gathered, and from which this blaze is borne aloft, fused with the flames of his own soul. . . . And the meal itself! We can approach an understanding of its tension and bliss only when we realize that all—each giving himself utterly—are united into an elated whole, such as can form only around an elated center."

Most Hasidim begin their third meal early Saturday evening at the end of the Sabbath. But Belzer Hasidim, I learned, feel that on the Sabbath "time is annulled." Therefore, they begin the morning prayers late and extend them into the afternoon; the afternoon prayers extend into the night, and the conclusion of the Sabbath, which for other Jews takes place shortly after sunset, is celebrated about midnight.

The headquarters of the Belzer court in Jerusalem was a dilapidated stone structure whose porch, windows, and interior were badly in need of repairs. Inside a large room, bare except for some long benches and wooden tables on which a few books lay scattered, several dozen young boys and men were either dozing, walking about, or talking. Some of the men wore the long, yellow robes that were favored by native-born Jerusalem Jews. Many wore the fur-trimmed *shtreiml* on their heads. The men had beards and about their waists was a black silken ribbon called a *gartel,* which symbolically separated the higher from the lower parts of the body. Some of the young boys had curled earlocks that literally reached down to their shoulders.

No one paid any attention to me when I entered and sat down alongside one of the tables. Everyone was evidently waiting for something to happen. Shortly before midnight, the expected event was upon us. Nothing was said, but suddenly the indolent atmosphere was shattered. As if impelled by an invisible charge, the Hasidim dashed to the sides of the room and strained their backs against the wall. The silence was broken by the slow tap of footsteps in the hallway. After a moment, a short man with long, unkempt gray beard and fiery little eyes entered the room. Directly behind him, carrying a chair that was covered with white satin, was a young man whose sidelocks fell in long curls that reached below his shoulders. The Hasidim, still pressed against the wall, watched their rebbe with intent, frightened expressions. The rebbe did not look at them but made his way very slowly to a long table at the far end of the room. Placing his hands over a cloth-covered plate, he remained standing for about five minutes, soundlessly mouthing the special mystic intentions, incantations that precede the act of prayer or blessing. He took a few pieces of bread from the plate and put them in his mouth. Some crumbs spilled over onto the straggly hair of his beard. "Reb Chaim!" he called in a thin voice. From a far corner of the room, a man ran swiftly to the rebbe's table. Back bent in gratitude, the Hasid took a piece of bread from the spoon proffered him by the rebbe, stuffed it into his mouth and ran back to his place. Three or four other Hasidim were honored with a similar invitation to partake of the *shiraim* (as the precious leftovers of what the rebbe has eaten are called). Then, the rebbe took a morsel of fish from the same plate, ate it, and pushed the plate aside. Immediately, there was bedlam. The Hasidim, who a moment before had been frozen against the wall, sprang toward the plate and struggled over it like a pack of famished animals. After it had been picked clean, they retired to their positions against the wall. A second plate of food was passed into the room by a woman stationed in the corridor and carried by one of the Hasidim to the rebbe's table. Now the ceremony began again—from the calling of the honored guests to the rush for the plate. There was a third plate, and a fourth. Each time the same order of ritual was followed. Finally, one of the men who had been standing against the wall crossed to a small prayer stand in the corner of the room and in a rapid, almost perfunctory manner began reciting the evening prayers that close the Sabbath. The third meal had come to an end.

I was rather stunned by the whole affair, so different from what I had been led to expect by Buber's lyrical description. If one assumed that Buber was right in insisting that Hasidism contained a spiritual kernel of rare force and beauty, all one could say was that this vital core was enclosed within a "shell" that would repel most outsiders. Could the kernel be extracted from the shell and still retain its identity? Or was this shell—the laws, customs, behavior, and dress that struck visitors as so peculiar—not only indispensable but the very essence of the Hasidic secret?

In one form or another, this question was to accompany my visits to various chambers of the Hasidic world. But just as my visit to Belz for the third meal produced the first formulation of the problem, a second encounter with Belz for a wedding eighteen years later brought it to a head.

Wedding in B'nai Brak

My second engagement with Belz, in the winter of 1965, took place in the town of B'nai Brak, a religiously oriented community not far from Tel Aviv. The occasion was an affair that aroused great interest throughout the Hasidic world. Sorele, the granddaughter of the Vishnitzer rebbe, was to marry Berele, the future rebbe of Belz, and about thirty thousand guests were expected from all parts of the world, among them dozens of rebbes representing other Hasidic dynasties. Invitations, it was said, had even been sent to a hundred rebbes who were already in the heavenly garden of Eden. I, however, did not have an invitation and sought help from a Jerusalem friend who was close to Hasidic circles.

Our conversation began with a discussion of a problem which has both intrigued and troubled historians of Hasidism. Why do Hasidim place so much emphasis on the genealogy of their rebbes? Scholars have pointed out that the son of the Baal Shem Tov, despite his illustrious father, did not become a rebbe. Evidently, in the early stages of the movement, physical relationship was not a decisive element in the choice of a spiritual leader. Later generations, however, strongly emphasized the biological relationship. This, say some scholars, led to *tzaddikism* and a degeneracy of the movement. My friend tried to offer an explanation: Not only Hasidism but traditional orthodox Judaism holds that spiritual characteristics were affected by "breeding." And Jewish history, with its long chains of intellectually and spiritually gifted families, would seem to substantiate this claim. Of course, the product of this genetic approach to the spirit was not guaranteed. That was why the future rebbes were educated and carefully observed by their fathers for signs of proper character endowments. One of the Lubavitcher chain of rebbes has described the training to which he was subjected. His hours of study, his behavior, his prayer, all had been under tremendous pressure. One day his father had asked him to remember his dreams and tell him about them. A week later he had told his father of a dream in which three famous *tzaddikim*, former rebbes, had appeared at the same table.

"What did they say?" his father had asked.

The young boy repeated what each of the rebbes had said in his dream. His father had nodded approvingly, satisfied that subconscious and conscious were being knit together as harmoniously as they were supposed to be in a rebbe. This linkage between genes and soul was not modern doctrine, my friend granted. But historically, a good case could be made for the supposition which underlay the interest of Hasidim in this coming marriage between the descendants of their illustrious Hasidic families.

"But let's be practical," my friend smiled. "Do you know what you are getting into at this wedding? Maybe I ought to prepare you with a brief lesson on the 'laws of pushing.' " I agreed to be his student in that recondite area of Hasidic folk-lore.

"Well first, you have to realize that the purpose of this pushing is not to get any place. It is a *mitzvah* in itself. No real Hasid stands aside nonchalantly when he sees a group of his comrades pushing. One wants to be where the pushing is most intense for the same reason that Hillary wanted to climb Mt. Everest—because it's there. Secondly," my instructor went on, "you must enter into the fray realizing that you will emerge minus a sleeve or, if you are lucky, a few buttons. And you must use *chochma,* wisdom. That means you have to know when to conserve your energy and when to spend it. While within the crowd, simply sway with it, letting them support you. But when you see an opening, you quickly move forward. After you have attained your new position, then comes the difficult task of holding it against all other attackers." He showed me how to anchor the body on one foot while letting other limbs move with the pressure of the crowd.

I interrupted the demonstration to remind my friend that without a ticket I could not even get within pushing range.

"No problem," he answered. "Why don't you call up Shmuel ha-Cohen Avidor, your editor friend?"

The suggestion seemed excellent. Editor of a first-rate Israeli religious magazine, Avidor was at home in the Hasidic world, yet enough outside of it to be a good guide. Besides, he was well over two hundred twenty pounds. This combination of avoirdupois and knowledge seemed ideal for the challenge at hand. I called Avidor who told me he had a special red pass guaranteed to open all the gates, "even the gates of heaven." Of course, there was no guarantee that any passes would be honored, but, he promised, wherever he went, I would go.

So it was that on the day of the wedding, I joined a long line of Hasidim jostling for seats on the buses which went from Jerusalem to Tel Aviv. Eventually, I got into a bus and during the trip read a newspaper article about the wedding, which I later discovered had been written by Avidor himself. The article related how, with two young comrades, the founder of the House of Belz had fasted and studied Torah at night in order to receive a mystic revelation of Elijah. The two comrades could not stay awake for the thousand nights which were required for this experience, but the wife of Rabbi Sholem had helped him by staying up with her husband all those nights and holding a candle so that he could study Torah. On the thousandth and one night, Elijah appeared to Rabbi Sholem and began to teach him the mysteries of Torah. The wife was not able to hear the voice of Elijah the Prophet, but received the promise that one day her offspring would light up the world like those candles she had used to make light for her husband.

It is with this legend, according to its followers, that the story of the House of Belz begins. Before Rabbi Sholem died, it was not unusual for five thousand Hasidim to travel to Belz in order to spend the holidays with him. His successors made trips to Hungary, Rumania, Czechoslovakia and other lands, and many more Hasidim joined themselves to the House of Belz.

The fourth rebbe was Arele, a man of fragile health, who spent most of his time alone studying Torah; it was in his time that the Nazi holocaust burst upon the Jewish world. The relatively passive Hasidim were slaughtered by the hundreds of thousands. When the Nazis came to Poland, it was learned that at the head of the list, scheduled for deportation and murder, was Arele, the Rabbi of Belz. But the Hasidim hid him in a nearby village, and one of their number, who resembled the rebbe, volunteered to sit in his house and to wait for the murderers.

When the Germans came to the house, they seized this man and, thinking that he was the rebbe, tortured and killed him. Later,

someone revealed to the Nazis that the Belzer was still alive, and
they began hunting for him. The Hasidim gathered a large sum of
money, bribed some officers, and managed to smuggle their rebbe over
the border and into Budapest. Here, his younger brother joined him.
The wives and children of both men were left behind and soon killed
by the Nazis. The two brothers resolved never to part from each other.
Dressed as Rumanian peasants, their beards shaven, they were both
smuggled across more borders and finally reached Syria; from there
they entered Palestine.

When the Palestinian followers of Belz heard that their rebbe
had arrived, a large group of them came to meet him, bringing with
them the silken black gown and fur *shtreiml* of Hasidic garb. It is
said that at first the rebbe did not want to put them on, saying that it
was all "too late." But his Hasidim cried and implored until he agreed
once more to act as their rebbe, but he insisted on taking up residence
in Tel Aviv, rather than in Jerusalem. The younger brother of the
rebbe married a second time, and a son was born to him. The joy in
the court of Belz was immense. "The chain continues," but the joy
was soon followed by sorrow, for the father of the infant died of a
heart attack. The Hasidim then came to the mother and told her that
the child had to receive the education of one who was destined for
Hasidic royalty. The mother resisted, for she didn't want to be
separated from her infant son. A compromise was arranged whereby
the child would live at home with the mother but would study Torah
from Hasidim. Thereafter the residents of Yehudah Halevi Street in
Tel Aviv became accustomed to seeing a young boy wearing white
stockings, with a gilded little hat on his head, walking through the
streets to school, accompanied by an honor guard of Hasidim. After
school, he would return home, change his clothes, and play with the
children of the neighborhood. The Belzer rebbe died when the child
reached the age of eight, and the Hasidim would no longer be put off.
The mother finally agreed to let her child study in the Belzer Yeshiva in Jerusalem. Succeeding years saw the child more and more
separated from his mother, but the Hasidim rejoiced, for it was becoming clear that they had found in this boy a future rebbe. They called
him the Yanuka, a term used for a spiritual child prodigy to whom

even elder Hasidim would come in order to hear words of Torah
and receive a blessing.

When the young boy became thirteen years old, after his bar
mitzvah, the Hasidim began talking about his marriage. There were
many "offerings" from other Hasidic dynasties, but the Belzer elders
took their time. Then word came from the Rabbi of Vishnitz regarding
his granddaughter Sorele and negotiations began in earnest. The
mother of the Yanuka visited the bride and gave her approval; the
next day the young man visited the court of Vishnitz in B'nai Brak
and met with the grandfather of his future bride. Of course, he did
not meet Sorele. The first meeting of the bride and groom, a brief
encounter consisting of a traditional dance in which they were mo-
mentarily united by a handkerchief, took place three days before the
wedding. "But tonight," the article concluded, "a few hours after the
wedding ceremony, the pair will again dance. The bride will hold
the edges of the bridegroom's long cloak, and they will dance about
for a few moments while the crowd claps and sings."

I came to Shmuel Avidor's home about five P.M. There was
some time before the wedding and I listened while my host drew
from a seemingly bottomless reservoir of anecdotes and information
about the House of Belz. He showed me the words of a song beginning "when the morning stars sang together . . ." which the Hasidim
would sing at dawn the next morning, when bride and groom were
supposed to be joined in conjugal union.

Our conversation was interrupted by the visit of a bearded young
man who was going to the wedding but had stopped by to ask my
editor friend if he had any pictures of Reb Arele, the founder of a
Hasidic group centered in Jerusalem.

"You are his grandson," Shmuel Avidor asked, "by his son?"

"Yes," said the young man, and I caught Shmuel Avidor's wink.

He asked the young man how things were going with his
father.

"Good—and it could be better, if only they would let us live,"
answered the young boy in cryptic reference to the rivalry within his
grandfather's house.

This kind of bitter split within a particular Hasidic dynasty had occurred frequently in earlier generations. Its basis was usually a difference of opinion about whether a rebbe received his authority by virtue of physical descent or through his own talent. The Baal Shem Tov deliberately skipped over his own son in choosing successors, but this was an exception.

It was important to the Belzer Hasidim that their Yanuka be properly descended and possess the "virtues of the father," but this meant that he had to be given intensive intellectual and spiritual training by a specially appointed Belzer Hasid. It was also the reason why three more years would pass before he was proclaimed a rebbe. The Hasidim wanted to be sure that he had the needed talent and character; after all, once he became rebbe, they subjected their total lives to his command. Although the crowning ceremony would have to wait for three more years, the younger Hasidim were already infringing the rules by asking the Yanuka for his blessing. In fact, Avidor explained, the Yanuka had accepted many of these requests for special prayers by virtue of a temporary dispensation which allowed him to act as a rebbe and mediate such requests to heaven on the eve of his wedding.

We arrived at the outskirts of B'nai Brak after dark and immediately saw evidence of the elaborate arrangements that had been made to handle the crowds. There were male ushers with fur-trimmed hats and silken caftan coats; on one of their sleeves they wore a band marked *sadran,* arranger. There were also female "arrangers" whose numbers were supplemented by a crew of young policewomen in attractive blue and white uniforms; after all, one could not expect pious women to ask directions of strange men.

We passed six ambulances ready for any emergency. The field where the wedding was to take place was enclosed by a fence and already surrounded by several thousand people. The women stood on one side, the men on the other. All eyes were centered on the wedding canopy which had been erected on a hillock in the center of the field. Below this canopy was an arbor decorated with cedar and myrtle branches. On it were signs carrying biblical quotations such as, "This is the gate of the Lord, the righteous shall enter therein." A loudspeaker system was broadcasting music played by a uniformed brass band stationed on the roof of a house within the fence. Occasionally the music was interrupted by announcements.

We headed toward the main synagogue where the Yanuka was to be received before the ceremony. The entrance was closed off by a temporary fence, in front of which several dozen Hasidim were pushing each other without getting anyplace. Shmuel Avidor caught the eye of an usher and received a go-ahead signal. "Hold on," he said, grabbing my hand, and we plunged into the crowd. I followed in his wake, and we got to the fence. There we were stopped. The usher had seen me and was balking about letting me into the synagogue.

"Without him I don't go," shouted Shmuel Avidor, but it was too late. We had hesitated, lost momentum, and a moment later were back on the outskirts of the milling crowd.

"This way," said Shmuel and pointed to an open gate with a sign above marked, "For rabbis, newsmen, and foreign visitors." I had with me a press badge used the previous year for a somewhat different occasion—the visit of Pope Paul. Shmuel suggested that I put it on. A few minutes later we were inside the fence near the steps of a large synagogue.

Inside there were hundreds of people. On one side, various groups were engaged in different stages of the evening prayer service. On the other, bright-eyed, bearded Hasidim were standing on a platform passing out cake, wine, and liquor. Against the east wall, several dozen elderly men were sitting around a long table, and in a corner to the side of the ark were the most distinguished guests of the evening, about a dozen, white-bearded rebbes with their attendants.

I wandered about the room, gathering impressions on the physical characteristics of the various Hasidic groups who were present. Obvious differences declared their separate origins, whether from the Ukraine, Lithuania, or Hungary. Why religious Jews so concerned with "pure" physical ancestry should so clearly reflect the genes of their Slavic neighbors is a problem whose solution would probably confront us with tragic historic episodes of pogroms and rape, but the evidence is clearly there. As for Belzer Hasidim, one had only to look around at the broad shoulders and ruddy faces to see evidence of healthy peasant stock, but it should be recalled that an earthy physical appearance coupled with vital spirituality is a favored Jewish combination. The Talmud says that the Egyptian pharaoh once sent his artists to draw a picture of Moses, whose face "shone with rays of light." To his surprise, they returned with what seemed to be the picture of a highwayman. The Baal Shem Tov, too, had this kind of rough peasant exterior. Yet there was something besides earthiness in these Belzer faces, something in the eyes of the smile. Hasidim would call it evidence of *hizdakkut,* a process whereby matter is somewhat refined and transmuted by spirit. That, precisely, had been the aim of Hasidism—not to despise or to leave the body, but so to refine it that an inner light could show through.

As for the rebbes, they appeared to average about five feet in height. I wondered if this was a result of inbreeding or of days and nights enclosed in the *yeshiva.* The future Belzer rebbe was also short and delicate in appearance. But Sorele, judging from her newspaper photograph, seemed to have the makings of the proverbial woman of valor. She was broad of body and face, and even had, I had been told, the hint of a mustache above her lips. That was good, for strong women are part of the Belzer tradition.

In addition to such unscientific impressions, I gathered more solid statistical data. For example, one man estimated that ten thousand chickens had given up their lives in honor of the wedding. Another offered me some realistic estimates of the numbers of Hasidim involved in this union. There were, he said, about five thousand Belzer and five thousand Vishnitzer Hasidic families. In Europe, these dynasties had numbered hundreds of thousands but had been totally defenseless before the Nazi scythe. Since the death of its last rebbe, however, the Belzer house of Hasidism had grown in numbers, principally because of its rigid opposition to birth control.

Avidor interrupted my research to announce that the band was playing the march which traditionally announces the arrival of the bridegroom. We went on out to the steps of the synagogue where we had an excellent view of his path. From the other side of the courtyard in front of us, a small swirling crowd of men with fur *shtreimlich* were approaching. The "arrangers" stiffened their linked arms, but as soon as the crowd reached the stairs, the line of defense collapsed into a whirling funnel of fur hats and black capotes. Somewhere underneath it all was the Yanuka. The mass of *shtreimlich* went past us, and we heard violent banging at some closed doors of the synagogue. The door to the side, which had been left open for the Yanuka's entrance, was completely ignored. Finally, the Yanuka was inside the synagogue.

We went toward the wedding canopy in order to prepare our positions for the next phase of the wedding. Shmuel caught sight of a gate which led to the roof from which the entire operation was being directed. He pulled me along and waved to a bearded man wearing an army chaplain's uniform, evidently the chief "arranger," and soon we were on the roof of the Vishnitzer rebbe's house. Now we had a perfect view of the whole operation. It was a bit noisy, for directly in back of us was the orchestra, led by a tall, thin Vishnitzer Hasid with a pointed beard and a huge white handkerchief flowing out of the side pocket of his capote. The orchestra leader was all aglow, explaining to those about him that each song being played had behind it years of tradition. At one point, he announced a song which he himself had composed in honor of the wedding.

To my side, several young army soldiers operated walkie-talkie radios which connected them with units on the far side of the crowd. Near the *hupah,* another arranger was trying to keep headquarters on the roof informed of the situation immediately around the wedding canopy. He had an electric bull amplifier but was evidently too excited to use it, and his voice had become completely hoarse. Between the music of the orchestra and the loud-speaker orders, I caught snatches of a running conversation between Shmuel Avidor and an army general, who had brought two young soldiers, one of them his son, to see the wedding.

"Do you hear that melody?" I heard Shmuel say. "That's the holy melody of the Baal Shem himself."

A few moments later, I heard a Hasid politely differ with a comment which Shmuel had made about a particular Belzer custom. Shmuel bristled.

"Can you recite, in five minutes, the whole chain of descent from the first Belzer rebbe till now?"

The Hasid grinned and tried to take up the challenge. Somewhere around the third generation his memory as to who was married

to whom began to falter and Shmuel took over triumphantly, effec-
tively silencing his competition for the rest of the evening.

One of the young men with the general whispered a question
—something to do with the problems of the connubial union which
was going to take place early the next morning. The bridegroom had
been fasting since the evening before and besides, as a sixteen-year-old
who had been raised in an atmosphere of utter holiness and purity,
wouldn't he be having some troubles?

Shmuel reassured him.

"In general, it is the bride who is told about these things. She is
the active one."

Detecting the young man's line of interest, Shmuel regaled him
with other tidbits of folklore about the intricacies of a Hasidic
wedding night. Since, from the mystic perspective as has been seen,
the secrets of sexual intercourse are linked with divine mysteries,
the students of the wise have always been curious about the behavior of
their teacher in the privacy of the bedchamber. The Talmud even
records the questions disciples of Rabbi Akiba put to his wife, requesting information about the behavior of the great sage during the act
of sexual intercourse. Amongst Hasidim, this curiosity could become so
intense as to make it necessary to inspect the wedding chamber, so as
to make sure that no avid student of these inner mysteries had hidden
himself there.

This interesting discourse was broken up by the music announcing the approach of the actual wedding ceremony. One path
leading to the wedding canopy led from the house below us; the other
came from the synagogue, in the opposite direction. Now, the arrangers took their place alongside the ropes which marked off both
paths. As the band played, honored guests and family, including
women, appeared on the paths, climbing the small hillock on which
the wedding canopy had been built. Some of the men held candles.
Surrounding the wedding canopy, they completely blocked the view
of the thousands who had come to witness the ceremony. The band
struck up another march and from the direction of the synagogue,
the swirling fur-hatted group of men that I had seen an hour earlier
came rushing down the path. Presumably, the bridegroom was in
their midst. Finally from the house beneath us came the bride, accom-

panied by her mother and sisters. She was dressed in white and wearing a white hood so thick that she had to lift it up in order to see where she was stepping. Last to walk up the path was the Vishnitzer rebbe. He was very ill and had just left his sick bed in order to say the seven traditional blessings over the couple. Behind him walked a young boy with a garden chair. At the bottom of the hillock, the old man sat in the chair and rested for a few minutes. Then he walked up to the wedding canopy, and the band stopped its music. The crowd remained hushed. We could hear nothing, but everyone understood that the old rebbe was reciting the wedding blessings.

Behind me, Shmuel Avidor was whispering to the general, "If I close my eyes now, I can see behind this moment so much illness, so much suffering—a whole world that has gone, shattered."

Then it was over. The bride and groom descended and each, surrounded by their attendants, walked separately toward our house. Below, some young Hasidim formed a circle and began to sing and dance. Everyone shook hands and said, *"mazal tou, simmon tov*—good luck and a good omen." At my side one of the bearded arrangers clenched his fists and looked skyward with shining eyes.

"At last it's happened, what an accomplishment!" Was he referring to the wedding arrangements or was he, too, thinking of the men who had sacrificed themselves to the Nazis in place of the rebbe; the fathers and mothers who had gone to the death chambers assuring their little children that all God's ways were good though mysterious; the rebbes who had been struggling with demonic forces above even while the *tzaddikim* were carrying on the battle below. Now they had succeeded; the chain would continue.

The bride and bridegroom had entered into the house below us through separate doors, and there was nothing more to see. We turned to Shmuel for a description of what was happening within. The bride and groom, he told us, would be led into a room and there left alone a few moments for the first time, in symbolic *yichud,* unification. Then, the men and women would sit down at separate tables for a meal which would have doves on its menu as a symbol of peace and purity. This meal would continue for several hours after which the bride and groom would go to a platform in a large community hall where the thousands of guests could pass by and wish them *mazal tov.*

Nothing much would be happening after that for the public to see, and it was doubtful whether we could get into the dining hall of the rebbe's house where the singing and dancing would continue. He suggested that we return to Tel Aviv and come back later in the morning. We drove to Tel Aviv where I decided to leave the rest of the Belzer wedding to other observers.

Early the next morning, I called upon Shmuel to thank him for his guidance. Red-eyed, his hair mussed, his shirt crumpled, he had not slept, but had returned to the wedding about three o'clock in the morning. For an hour he had remained in the crowd about the building where the bride and groom were having their wedding feast, but there was nothing to see. He was about to return home when he came upon an open window; after squeezing through it, he had found himself directly in back of the Yanuka's chair.

"What I saw there made the whole evening worthwhile." Still moved by his experience, Shmuel tried to describe the scene. Using some books on his desk, he outlined the shape of a large hall which was divided in the center by a semitransparent glass partition. On one side of the glass, almost a thousand Hasidim were crowded around the large table at which the Yanuka and special guests were seated. On the other side of the glass partition were the women. Since there was some visibility through the glass partition, the bride sat with her back to the groom and the men.

For hours the hundreds of men shuffled about the table chanting and clapping hands. Shmuel Avidor imitated the contorted faces of the dancers as they moved about, repeating *mazal tov, simmon tov;* it was as if they were trying by physical effort to push the upper spheres into a position which would propitiously match the union taking place below. In one corner of the room, a reporter from *Time,* his hand wrapped in a handkerchief because he had cut it while entering through another window, lay on the floor drinking a bottle of beer.

"It was like an African folk dance—ecstatic," said Shmuel. "And there was a *badchan,* a wedding jester, who stood on the table and carried on for hours."

Wearing a Mexican sombrero, putting on and taking off a false nose, this *badchan* entertained the guests with rhymes parodying modern Hasidic life. These rhymes were offered in the *akdomus* chant which was used on Shavuot. At one time, the *badchan* started imitating the manner in which Hasidic women walked through the streets in their high heels, but the crowd, though laughing, made him stop by clapping loudly. Then, holding a large sack in one hand, he called out the gifts which the newly married couple was receiving.

"And the rebbe from Boston gives a silver snuff box," Shmuel Avidor imitated him. And the silver box was thrown into a large sack which soon contained gold-headed canes, silver goblets, menorahs, and bundles of cash.

Then Shmuel described to me the strangest part of all: the silent orchestra. This orchestra was made up of seven or eight instruments including a violin, a double bass, a trumpet, saxophone, even a drum—all wooden dummies carefully constructed to look like the real thing. Shmuel imitated the Hasidim conducting their pantomime orchestra, blowing the saxophone, fiddling, beating a drum, all without a sound. Shmuel did not know the origin of this custom but hoped to find out.

I thanked Shmuel Avidor and went off to Jerusalem; later that week I asked some Belzer Hasidim, including one who had worked for weeks in constructing the dummy instruments, about the origin of the silent orchestra. They shrugged; it was done as a *shpitz* for fun. It was an old tradition; that's all they could say about it.

I never was able to learn if there was any profound significance to the Belzer silent orchestra. Somehow, though, it assumed significance for my own efforts to understand Hasidism. Perhaps it was the association—or the lack of association—between Hasidism à la Martin Buber and Hasidism at a Belzer wedding. More than eighteen years had passed since I had first encountered Hasidism in just this juxtaposition—Buber and Belz. Ever since that time I had been wondering what it was that separated Buber's version of Hasidism from Hasidic reality. Now, in the absurd concept of a silent orchestra, I thought I had a key. For that was precisely what Buber and other modern interpreters of this movement had tried to filter out of Hasidism, its absurdity. Yet was it not precisely these elements, more than any system of ideas, that gave Hasidism its characteristic flavor? Was it not these things, rather than alleged theoretical heresies, that out-

raged the Misnagdim, the "opponents" of the movement. They were
appalled by people who literally turned somersaults in the synagogue
to fulfill the psalmist's injunction to praise the Lord with all one's bones.
It was ridiculous, they thought, for people to enlist trees and flowers
in their prayers or to worship God by playing melodies on flutes. It
was silly of a Hasidic rebbe to take out his watch and place it on
the table when he said "Hear, O Israel," because he wanted a tangible
reminder of this time-bound world to pull him back from the timeless realms into which his proclamations of God's unity would lead
him. It was grotesque and undignified for grown-up, pious Jews of
East European villages to greet their rebbe by riding backwards on
their horses, their beards tucked in their blouses, pretending they were
cossacks; for Belzer Hasidim to walk around with the upper buttons
of their shirt undone so as "to expose the heart." And it was absurd
to believe what Hasidim believed about their wonder-working rebbes.
Yes, this world was absurd, as absurd as the Chagall paintings of
floating green skies and fiddlers playing on house roofs.

But was it any more absurd than the claim that one must dance
and sing and rejoice because God was everywhere, even in the midst
of evil and pollution? Of course, classical Judaism had always asserted
that "no place is empty of Him," and that man must "worship the
Lord with joy for His mercies are over all His work." This is all
good Jewish doctrine, but in accepting it so completely Hasidism becomes an exercise in the absurd. Or, if you will, Hasidism is Judaism
with its most childlike, dreamlike, and fantastic elements acted out
in a kind of pantomime—like a silent orchestra playing music that
only the heart can hear.

But I am anticipating. Belz is an example of Hasidism which
poses the mystery of the kernel and the shell in extreme form. It has
served us as an example of the shock which awaits anyone who walks
from the atmosphere of Buber's writings into the reality of Hasidic
life. Not all contemporary Hasidism, however, will subject us to this
kind of trauma. There are chambers within the Hasidic world of our
day which can soften this kind of trial, or at least offer a chamber of
transition. There is, for example, a school of Hasidism which prides
itself on being *au courant* with the most advanced scientific and philo-

sophic thought of our age. Its rebbe even studied at the Sorbonne. Without doubt, the gate most accessible to probers of the contemporary Hasidic scene can be found in Brooklyn, at the headquarters of the Lubavitcher movement.

6

THE LUBAVITCHER MOVEMENT

One day in the summer of 1896, my father took me for a walk in the fields. The crops were ripening, a light breeze moved through the sheaves, ears of corn nodded and whispered to each other.

My father said to me:

"See, my son—Divinity! Each movement of every ear of corn, and of every tuft of grass, was anticipated in the primal thought of the first Adam, who could foresee the future of all the generations."

We had gone into the forest, and I, absorbed in our conversation, stirred by the sound of my father's voice and the purity of his words, had distractedly broken off a leaf from a tree and was holding it in my hand, tearing it to bits and dropping the pieces to the ground.

My father said:

"The Holy Ari used to say, apart from the fact that every leaf of a tree is a creature that has in it divine life, and was created by the Name, Blessed be He, for some predesigned purpose—there is also contained in every leaf a spark of some soul that has descended to this world in order to be redeemed.

"And now, regard how careful a man must be in this world, whether awake or asleep. For in what way is he who is awake different from the man who sleeps? In inner powers and feelings. Every person who sleeps has outer powers, but his inner powers are blurred. Is that not why one can in a dream see a thing and its opposite at the same time? And how do we know whether a person is awake or asleep? See, even now, as we were speaking about Divine Providence, you absentmindedly plucked a leaf, held it in your hand, tore it into little pieces, and scattered the pieces to the ground. Should one regard the creations of the Holy One, Blessed be He, so lightly? The Creator, Blessed be He, wrought this creation too for some purpose, there is divine life in it. Within its own body is contained its own life. In what way is the 'I' of the leaf less than your 'I'?

"Yes, there is a great difference. The leaf is in the category of the vegetative world, and you in the category of the 'human.' But everything created has its own end, and its Divine obligation to accomplish something in the world."

—From reminiscences of RABBI JOSEPH ISAAC SCHNEERSOHN,
the sixth Lubavitcher rebbe

The heavy wooden door of the red brick house at 770 Eastern Parkway has a gothic trim that is carried over into the stained glass windows. The building, both within and without, must have been very impressive at one time. Old residents of the neighborhood recall, with a touch of malice, that it was formerly owned by a doctor about whose practice there had been some lifted eyebrows. People who now see young bearded men in their black hats and coats going in and out are aware that the structure now houses some kind of Jewish religious group, but there cannot be many passersby who know what is really going on, that here is the headquarters of a unique spiritual realm whose authority extends into many lands and whose ruling head exercises an almost absolute control over the lives of tens of thousands of followers. Menachem Mendel Schneersohn is the name of the man whose office is to the left of the entrance, behind some windows whose shades are always drawn. He is the present Lubavitcher rebbe and a direct descendant in the seventh generation of Schneur Zalman, the original founder of this Hasidic dynasty. He is also the son-in-law of the previous rebbe.

To 770 Eastern Parkway have come thousands of visitors, curiosity-seekers, and "fellow travelers," such as Zalman Shazar, the president of Israel, and Jacques Lipshitz, the sculptor. There are also many who come to beseech the rebbe's intercession for their troubles, for though Menachem Mendel Schneersohn is a man who has studied at the Sorbonne and speaks a dozen languages, he is also a *tzaddik*, looked upon by some of his followers as a miracle worker. Stories of miracles are readily to be heard at 770 Eastern Parkway, but they are of a peculiar Lubavitch flavor, that is, with a rational explanation. An example is the story of the American soldier in Korea who one day wandered off from his squad looking for a stream in which to wash his hands before opening his can of C rations. A shell struck the squad's position, killing every one of his comrades. Today the young veteran vows he owes his life to a visit he had made, just before shipping out to Korea, to the rebbe of the Lubavitcher movement. The latter had counseled the young man to observe, even while in combat, as much as he could of the Jewish Law, including the commandment to wash one's hands before eating.

There are hundreds of other examples, but the rebbe and his

followers do not like their movement talked about as if it were only a source of miracle tales. The plain facts of the history of the movement, they point out, are more wonderful than all the stories about the powers of the Lubavitcher rebbes. Founded about two hundred years ago in northern Russia, it has since been active in many other countries and is today in some ways stronger and more influential than when it first began. Though mysticism lies at its core, the Lubavitcher movement has been blessed with a flair for organization and public relations that has enabled it to strike firm roots in environments as diverse as communist Russia, North Africa, and the United States. As in the past, thousands of Lubavitcher followers continue to accept the rebbe's word as authoritative, not only in questions of ritual, but in matters of health, livelihood, and, if it comes to it, life itself.

The first of my many visits to Lubavitcher headquarters took place in 1955. I found an office where several men were typing, chatting, or using the telephone. The one girl working in the office had on a plain long-sleeved dress. The steel filing cabinet, the telephones studded with interoffice buttons, the quiet activity, all created a businesslike atmosphere, hardly what I had expected to find at the headquarters of a sect of mystics. I asked where I could find a Rabbi Weinberg who, I had been advised, would be a good initial contact.

"Rabbi Weinberg, of course—the globetrotter we call him," one of the men grinned. "I think he's home now between trips, and you can call him for an appointment."

As for an appointment with the rebbe himself, I was directed to Rabbi Hodakov, the rebbe's personal secretary, a thin, fair man, who at the moment was using one of the several phones on his desk at the other side of the office. "Incidentally," my informant added, "Rabbi Hodakov was a member of the Latvian government before our rebbe's predecessor made him his secretary."

When Rabbi Hodakov had finished his phone conversation and disposed of two bearded young men who had been waiting to speak to him, I walked over to his desk. He extended a limp hand and asked if I spoke Yiddish. There was a quizzical but good-natured expression in his light blue eyes as I indicated my purpose in seeking an audience with the rebbe. Rabbi Hodakov turned the pages of a little black book and murmured that the rebbe's calendar was filled for the next six months but he would see what he could do for me. The rebbe received people only three times a week, beginning at eight o'clock in the evening.

I asked how long these evening sessions lasted.

"Oh, sometimes till three, sometimes till five o'clock in the morning," he smiled. His smile, charming and rather bashful, showed a trace of pride when he mentioned the rebbe.

I asked if the rebbe slept during the day after these meetings.

Rabbi Hodakov raised his brows. "During the day the rebbe is busy directing the activities of the Lubavitcher movement in every part of the world."

"When does he sleep?"

The answer was another slightly mysterious smile and a shrug. Then he made a note in his black book and told me that I could see the rebbe four weeks hence at ten o'clock in the evening. "Anybody can get to see him, but, of course, there have to be priorities, and," the bashful smile appeared again, "sometimes people have to wait a long time."

"Incidentally," I asked, "how many followers of the Lubavitcher movement are there in the world?"

"How many Jews are there in the world?" answered Rabbi Hodakov good-naturedly.

Later I learned that Rabbi Hodakov's reply had not been altogether facetious. Lubavitcher Hasidim regard the rebbe not only as their own leader but also as the spiritual shepherd of all Israel in his generation. "He is to us," one of his closest disciples explained, "what Moses was to Israel in his time. Not that the rebbe is to be compared to Moses, 'like whom there has been none other since.' But the rebbe is like a little Moses, like 'a picture whose size has been reduced.' " That is the difference, my informant went on to say, between the Lubavitcher Hasidim and other Hasidic sects. The other rebbes are interested mainly in their own Hasidim, while the Lubavitcher rebbe considers himself responsible for the spiritual and bodily welfare of every Jew, no matter where he lives or what he believes. In this respect he follows the first Lubavitcher rebbe, who taught that "Israel is really one soul with different bodies."

The following week I called Rabbi Weinberg. The genial personality of the globetrotter came through even on the phone, but when I met him, it was still surprising to find such a young man; despite his beard, he did not seem much more than thirty years old. My visit had been arranged for the early evening, and all his children were asleep except for a five-year-old whose head (covered by a yarmelke) kept popping out of the window above while his father and I conversed on the small porch below. *"Gei shlofen, yingele*—Go to bed, little boy," Rabbi Weinberg called out to him, and the little head darted in, only to reappear a few seconds later. Rabbi Weinberg's English was touched by the slightest of accents, and I asked him if he always used Yiddish with his children. He told me that Yiddish was still the basic language of the Lubavitcher movement, though his children spoke English. The rebbe delivered his discourses in Yiddish but was fluent in a great many languages. "He studied science, you know, at the Sorbonne, before being chosen rebbe."

Rabbi Weinberg began to supply me with stories about people who had been helped by the rebbe. A girl from Brazil, for example, had been advised by her doctors to undergo a serious brain operation, but the rebbe had disagreed. " 'They make their living by cutting; I make my living by not cutting,' the rebbe likes to say." His opinion had finally been upheld by a brain specialist, and the child was now well.

How could such powers be explained? Rabbi Weinberg admitted it would be hard for someone who had not seen the evidence with his own eyes to believe. Basically, the rebbe had unusual powers because he was a holy man, that is, every limb of his body was sanctified by pure living and by the total observance of God's commandments. This was not an idea peculiar to Hasidism; even Maimonides, the philosopher and rationalist, had asserted that the spirit of prophecy might descend upon anyone who had completely purified his heart and tongue and limbs. In addition, the rebbe, being a direct descendant of Schneur Zalman, the founder of the Lubavitcher movement, had inherited the accrued merit of his ancestry. Of course, to Rabbi Weinberg it was quite clear that the movement represented the main branch of the Hasidic movement inaugurated by the Baal Shem Tov.

I asked him how Lubavitcher Hasidism had been able to escape the degeneration of spirit which had marked other Hasidic sects.

"Mesiras nefesh," he replied quickly, "the willingness to sacrifice oneself. Our rebbes set us an example; they showed us that if something is very important, it can be done. If something matters very much—as much as life itself—you find a way to do it."

Besides, Lubavitch believed that no Jew was ever wholly lost to God. The Alter Rebbe, Schneur Zalman, had taught that within every Jew there was a point of authentic religious faith, an element of pure Jewishness, *"dos pintele Yid."* One had to remember that "the soul itself was so much deeper than what appeared to the eye," and hence surface appearances ought never to discourage one from attempting to tap a man's inner capacity for faith in and love for Judaism. It was this principle that gave the movement its missionary spirit.

Before I left, Rabbi Weinberg told me that if I wanted to see Lubavitch in action, I could do no better than be present in two weeks' time at the *farbrengung.* This festival was the annual celebration of the release of Rabbi Joseph Isaac (predecessor of the present rebbe) from the Spalerno prison in Leningrad, where he had been held by the communists. Hasidim would be coming from all parts of the world for the occasion, and I would have a chance to hear the rebbe "give Torah."

I spent the next two weeks trying to learn more about the Lubavitcher movement in order to be better prepared for the *farbrengung.* Understanding could not grow without an acquaintance with the movement's history. Fortunately, Lubavitcher Hasidim are constantly publishing collections of anecdotes out of the lives of previous rebbes. Families who trace their genealogy back to favorites in earlier Hasidic courts also tend to keep full records; even the songs sung by other generations of Hasidism have been carefully compiled and published.

The central name in all these chronicles is Schneersohn, a name derived from the founder of the movement, Schneur Zalman of Ladi, a small town in White Russia. He is the Alter Rebbe, sometimes called simply "the author of the Tanya," after a collection of essays and letters which is studied by every Hasid almost as reverently as the bible itself.

Schneur Zalman (1745–1812) was born in a part of White

Russia that was under the spiritual influence of the "Jerusalem" of its day, Vilna in Lithuania. It was in Vilna that the traditional rabbinic exaltation of Talmudic scholarship reached its apex and found its apotheosis in Elijah the Gaon (1720–1797). The natural course of events for Schneur Zalman, whose brilliance as a Talmudist was recognized when he was still a boy, would have been to go to Vilna and study in one of the schools dominated by the spirit of the great master, but Schneur Zalman chose Mezritch in the Ukraine, where Dov Baer, the holy Magid, or Preacher, and immediate successor of the Baal Shem, held forth. In the house of this teacher, Schneur Zalman said later, "We drew up the Holy Spirit by the bucketful, and miracles lay around under the benches, only no one had time to pick them up."

The teachings of Dov Baer, as they were copied by his pupils, provided much of the ideological framework of Hasidism. One of his favorite ideas was based on the kabbalistic doctrine of the *eyin,* the great Nothing which in Kabbala became a synonym for the *ein sof,* the infinite potential of all existence. All creation had to pass through this stage of nothingness, through a moment "when the egg is no more and the chick is not yet." This was the moment, the Magid claimed, of contact with the *sefira* of *chochma,* the profoundest level of creation that precedes all differentiation and is therefore beyond comprehension. Hence the temporary turning of something into nothing had to precede every great moment of self-renewal. Another favored comparison of the Magid was that of the kabbalistic teaching of *tzimzum,* the contraction of God's light, with the action of a father who pretends to keep away from his little son in order to train him to walk on his own power.

Dov Baer encouraged his Lithuanian disciple to produce a new Code of Law which would supplement the seventeenth-century work of Joseph Karo, which was then widely in use as a guide to religious and ritual life. The Magid also urged him not to follow those Hasidim who abandoned themselves to purely emotional expressions of religious devotion, but to combine the heart with the mind. Schneur Zalman followed his teacher's direction, since it was also the inclination of his soul. Although "he could burn with the fiery flame" of love for God and tremble in ecstasy, he also strove for precision and control in his thoughts and language. The result was a clear, carefully organized system of thought, called *chabad,* after the first letters of the Hebrew words for wisdom (*chochma*), understanding (*bina*), and knowledge (*daat*).

Chabad

Chabad philosophy argues that the feelings of the heart, however important, are often ephemeral, they need to be stimulated, controlled, and fixed by the powers of the mind. This implies respect for scholarship and a touch of contempt for a piety which would "burst the vessels" of rational control. Other Hasidic groups might argue that *chabad* does not comprehend the *hitlahavut,* fiery enthusiasm, of the real Hasid, but Schneur Zalman is certainly not offering a cool, rational religious system. *Chabad* is actually a systematized mystical philosophy, based almost completely on the Zohar and later kabbalistic thinkers. Wisdom, understanding, and knowledge refer to the upper triad of *sefirot,* which precede the lower triads of feeling and of action. This upper triad must dominate the lower because, in the kabbalistic scheme of cosmic creation, the intellectual impulses are the progenitors of the feelings. After all, the Gaon of Vilna was himself a kabbalist, as well as the leading Talmudic authority of the day. Instead of effecting reconciliation, however, Zalman became the victim and symbol of a conflict which tore communities and families apart and brought Hasidim and their opponents, the Misnagdim, to the point of forbidding intermarriage with each other. A few sentences from the ban of excommunication hurled at the Hasidim by the Vilna Gaon in 1796 shows the temper of the struggle that raged for generations: "Woe unto the evil renegades who have brought forth a new law and religion . . . Let no one pity them. Be vengeful for the Lord. Let the sparks fly from your feet and flames from your mouth, and let the sword avenge . . ."

The Alter Rebbe tried to visit the Gaon to explain that Hasidism was not a "new religion" and that the Hasidic emphasis on the Talmudic teaching, "There is no place empty of Him," was neither pantheistic nor contrary to rabbinic theology. His efforts were of no avail: "When we arrived at the Gaon's house, twice he shut the door in our face."

The Hasidic leader tried to comfort his followers, assuring them that in time the hatred and bitterness against Hasidism would pass away.

Not all Hasidim were so tolerant, however, and, on the day of the Gaon's death, groups of Hasidim were accused of dancing in the streets of a Vilna suburb. The followers of the Gaon swore vengeance and they carried out their threat. Twice Schneur Zalman was denounced to the Russian government for heresy and subversion by Jewish opponents, and both times he was sent to prison. But after his second release, in 1801, it was apparent even to the Misnagdim that the Hasidic movement was firmly established.

The most surprising aspect of Schneur Zalman's turbulent life was the time he found in it for constructive organizational work. Some claim that this organization, rather than the Tanya's ideas, accounts for the dynamic history of Lubavitch. Most of the other Hasidic sects survived for a generation or two on the memory of their founder's inspiration and then decayed. But in line with his conviction that "inspiration" could only be preserved in the vessels of the mind— wisdom, understanding, and knowledge—Schneur Zalman set up an effective school system. He believed also, with the Baal Shem, that "a hole in the body makes an even greater hole in the soul," and concerned himself with economic and social projects in behalf of destitute Jews. He took a particular interest in the welfare of Jews who lived in out-of-the-way communities and always sent his disciples to such areas to teach and guide.

These three fields of endeavor—educational, economic, and missionary—continued to be the main concerns of all the Lubavitcher rebbes who succeeded the Tanya. When the sixth rebbe, Rabbi Joseph Isaac (1880–1949), came to America, he immediately began working along similar lines.

One of the pictures of Rabbi Joseph Isaac shows a man with a full beard streaked with gold and gray, sitting at a table and holding a pencil over a blank piece of paper. The most impressive part of Joseph Isaac's face are his stern, commanding eyes, which are in sharp contrast with his white, almost effeminate hands. It is a face that radiates what the Hasidim call *malchus,* the visage of royalty and command. Joseph Isaac's life seemed in some respects prefigured by the career of his ancestor, and, like his great forefather, he had to face charges brought against him by fellow Jews. The now defunct Yevsektsia, the Jewish section of the Russian Communist party, accused him of subverting the regime by propagating the Jewish religion in an underground network of religious schools throughout the Soviet Union.

He was arrested by the secret police and condemned to death, but again the first rebbe's destiny seemed reenacted in his life. Prominent foreign statesmen intervened on his behalf with the Soviet authorities, and he was released from prison on his birthday, the 12th of Tammuz, 1927. He was able to leave Russia and settle first in Latvia, then in Warsaw. He lived through the German bombardment of Warsaw and, again through high diplomatic influence, escaped. In 1940, he arrived in New York, a sick and broken man. Nevertheless, in the remaining ten years of his life he was able to establish his movement firmly in the New World.

The talents of this European rebbe, who spoke little English, seemed peculiarly well adapted for America. Perhaps his powerful will could have imposed itself on any environment, but there was something American in his flair for practical activities. He organized Torah Missions to spread religious literature among Jewish farmers, who were amazed to find bearded young men knocking at their doors and professing an interest in their souls. Lubavitcher *yeshiva* buses began rolling through the streets of cities and towns all over America, carrying Jewish boys and girls to newly founded all-day Hebrew schools. A publication society was established, and religious textbooks, in English as well as Hebrew, began to make their appearance. Joseph Isaac proved again that "nothing can stand before the will," and the movement born in Lithuania spread to every part of the United States, South America, Israel, and Australia. Before his death, Joseph Isaac saw a new and promising field for Jewish proselytizing in North Africa, and the Lubavitcher network of schools began to function there.

The Farbrengung

I had been warned to come early to the *farbrengung* if I wanted a seat, but the wooden tables and benches set up in the courtyard adjoining the building were already filled when I arrived. At one end of the courtyard was a long table covered with a white cloth and mounted on a platform. Most of the seats on the dais were still empty, but a row of chairs behind the central table was already occupied by bearded dignitaries of the movement. A microphone had been set up at the center of the table and hooked to loudspeakers at the other end of the courtyard. I saw a few inches of space on one of the rear benches and, following the example of others, climbed from table to table over the backs of the seated people to reach it—the tables and benches had been packed so closely together there was no aisle space left. It was a humid summer evening, and there were beads of sweat on the faces of many of the Hasidim, who wore full jackets or long black coats along with large-brimmed hats. But nobody seemed to mind the heat, and the crowded courtyard was only further proof to the Hasidim of the greatness of their rebbe.

The person next to me was dressed in a neat business suit and conventional gray hat. He was a Conservative rabbi in Brooklyn who had been raised in the Lubavitcher movement and "would never cut his ties to them." He tried to attend every "gathering" and, despite his own strayings from strict Orthodoxy, was an admirer of the rebbe. I asked him how he felt about the powers which the Hasidim attributed to the rebbe. "Listen," he answered, "I know only this—nobody is more concerned with the fate of Jews—every Jew—than the rebbe, and that is what attracts me to him." He indicated a man with a black beard sitting near us. "He was raised in Russia in the Lubavitch 'underground.' If you ask him how he was able to maintain his religion at the risk of death, he will tell you it was the inspiration of the rebbe."

My neighbor pointed out some of the important personages in the courtyard. Directly to the right of the rebbe's chair was a red-bearded man, Rabbi Mintlik, who was head of the Eastern Parkway Yeshiva. Seated at one end of the table on the dais was Rabbi Gur Aryeh, the brother-in-law of the rebbe. I tried to get a look at him, for we had already spoken on the phone and arranged an interview. Joseph Isaac had had no sons, but he did have two daughters, and Gur Aryeh had married one of them. But it was the other son-in-law, Menachem Mendel, who had been chosen as rebbe after Joseph Isaac's death. I wondered on what grounds the choice had been made.

At about nine-thirty the yard suddenly became quiet. There was the sound of the scraping of chairs and benches as people tried to stand, and all eyes turned to the door which led from the courtyard into the main building. Into the yard with quick step walked the seventh rebbe of the Lubavitcher movement, son-in-law of Joseph Isaac and a direct descendant on his father's side of the Alter Rebbe.

Rabbi Menachem Mendel turned out to be a man of average height and build. The most striking feature of his well-formed face was his deep, gentle blue eyes, in which there was little of the *malchus* —imperial sternness—of his predecessor. His complexion was pale, contrasting with his short black beard in which streaks of gray were beginning to appear. His frock coat, hat, and tie were all black and neatly tailored. The brim of the hat was just a bit larger than a conventional brim, but smaller than that of the Orthodox Hasid. I had heard that when Rabbi Menachem Mendel was studying in Paris, he had refused to wear the long black coat which was customary in Hasidic circles. Now he alludes jokingly to his former habit of dress as a device that gave him more hours for study— "Hasidim didn't come to me when I wore a short coat."

There must have been considerable discussion when the question of elevating Menachem Mendel to the spiritual throne of Lubavitch arose; Lubavitcher rebbes had never approved of secular studies, and some of the elders of the movement must have wondered whether a Paris gentleman could ever be a rebbe. Nevertheless, it was apparent to all who knew him that Menachem Mendel was suited by birth, by marriage, and by his own intellectual and spiritual gifts to be the leader of the Lubavitcher movement. For his part Menachem Mendel was genuinely reluctant to assume the leadership. He had taken courses in electrical engineering in Paris, while his wife was studying architecture, and they had planned to earn their living in these professions. It required two years to persuade him to accept the position of rebbe.

All this, however, was past. As he mounted the dais now and took his chair, Rabbi Menachem Mendel seemed very much at ease in his role. The audience rose when he entered and remained standing until he sat down. Once seated, he turned to receive a bottle of whiskey which he passed over the table to some outstretched hands below. As if by prearranged signal, little paper cups and bottles of whiskey appeared on all tables in the yard.

The students on the bench in front began clapping hands and swaying back and forth in rhythmic accompaniment to a song. Everyone, including the rebbe, participated in the singing. In the middle of one particularly animated melody, the rebbe leaned forward and began beating out the rhythm on the table with his fists, at which the singing of the Hasidim immediately mounted in volume and intensity. The rebbe, a slight smile on his lips, began to sway from side to side and rose from his chair. An almost physical current of excitement ran through the audience and the singing reached a fever pitch. Near a fan in the back of the courtyard a man wearing a hat which came down to his ears was jumping up and down, clapping his hands, his eyes closed as if hypnotized. Behind the rebbe, an elderly man with a long white beard was hopping from leg to leg, waving his arms about. Then the rebbe sat down, and at once the current of excitement subsided.

Rabbi Menachem Mendel cleared his throat and reached for the microphone. The courtyard grew quiet as the rebbe called out several names. One of those called was sitting near me. He leaped to his feet, his face flushed and his hands trembling as he raised his cup to the rebbe and said, *"L'chayim,* to life!" The rebbe, with a faint smile, vigorously nodded his head in return and moved his lips in an answering *"L'chayim."* After all those he had singled out by name had offered toasts in this fashion, others in the room began to rise from their seats, and as soon as they had succeeded in catching the rebbe's eye they too called out, "To life!" Near me, a youngster was unable to hide a grimace of distaste as he downed his cup of strong liquor. These exchanges between the rebbe and his Hasidim continued for about an hour, and then they began singing a slow melody with Yiddish words that sounded like *"Essen est zich, shlofen shloft zich, ober davenin davent zich nisht"* ("Eating and drinking take care of themselves, but not prayer").

Only one person in the room seemed not to be singing, and that was the red-bearded rabbi standing at the rebbe's right. He stood immobilized, staring fixedly at a spot on the table before the rebbe. I was told that this was Rabbi Mintlik who had the honor of being the rabbi's cup-bearer; his feeling for the rebbe was so intense that it had reached the level of *hitbatlut,* self-extinction. The act of extinguishing oneself before the will and personality of the rebbe was evidently considered one of the summits of Hasidic devotion.

After the singing was over, the rebbe reached for the microphone and cleared his throat with a nervous little cough. As one, the *farbrengung* rose, and my neighbor informed me that we were about to be instructed in Torah.

According to the mystic tradition, the words of the bible have a revealed meaning, the *p'shat,* which serves to mask a deeper, mystical significance. These hidden meanings can be found by various modes of interpretation. There is *d'rush,* the allegorical reading of biblical stories in which characters such as Sarah and Abraham and the events of their lives are understood as illustrations of simple moral teachings; then there is *remez,* literally, the hint, which points to profound doctrines and ideas dealing not only with the moral relations of man to man but with the mystic connection of man and God. The most difficult level of hidden meaning is *sod,* the secret. This is concerned with cosmological and theosophical speculation. It is a realm of discourse which can be understood only by a student already familiar with the technical concepts of the Kabbala, and must be heard standing, in a state of "awe and trembling."

As soon as he began speaking, it was apparent that the rebbe's discourse was in the realm of *sod,* and it was also obvious that very few of the Hasidim present could follow his words; after fifteen minutes or so had passed, I noticed that eyes were closing all around me, and not in mystical ecstasy.

"The reason the Hasidim must stand while the rebbe 'gives Torah,'" my neighbor whispered to me, "is that they might fall asleep if they were to sit down."

For about a half hour, the rebbe continued to discourse on the secrets of the "upper and lower waters" and the "smaller and larger visages." When he concluded, we all took our seats, the singing started again, and gradually vivacity and life seemed to surge back into the gathering. There was another round of toasts, following which the rebbe once more took the microphone.

This time no heads nodded and everyone followed his discourse.

It was, in essence, a repetition of his first talk, only now brought
down from *sod* to *d'rush*. He spoke in simple Yiddish, expressing his
ideas clearly and carefully. The theme of the *d'rush* was that Abraham
had actually been a missionary. He quoted the rabbinic commentary
on God's commandment to Abraham, "Get thee out of thy land and
thy birthplace," wherein the rabbis compare Abraham to a vial of
incense that must be moved about if its fragrance is to be felt. Similarly, said the rebbe, the descendants of Abraham must never be
content to remain in a place where they feel completely at home;
they too must "get out of their land." Isaac also was inspired with a
sense of mission, for what else is the inner meaning of the story which
tells how Isaac redug the wells of his father? These wells are the
symbol of the living waters within the soul of every Jew, which, like
the wells in the bible, can be stopped up. But the descendants of
Isaac must not be discouraged. They must try again and again to lift
the stones from the wells and to free the fountain of living waters.

I found myself rather disappointed in the rebbe's discourse. It
seemed to me as though the ideas had been deprived of their complexity, perhaps their profundity. But I remembered having been
told that this was the secret of Lubavitch, its capacity to "make obvious
the hidden." Of course, the rebbe was also trying to achieve a practical
objective in his talk. In his audience were Lubavitcher Hasidim from
New Haven or Melbourne or North Africa who longed to be close
to their rebbe but who in a few hours would have to return to lonely
places where they were trying to "create an environment." And I
soon discovered that there was another reason for the rebbe's missionary theme. In a few weeks, several dozen students from the Yeshiva
were to set out in pairs to visit almost every state in the union in an
attempt to "remove the stones from the Jewish wells of spirit."

Taking just enough money to cover their expenses, along with
matzoh and canned foods for towns where strictly kosher food was
not available, these young men journeyed forth every year before the
High Holidays. Often they came to communities in the South or
the West where they had no contacts at all. The problem in such
towns was not the puzzled stares which people cast at these bearded
rabbinical students, but that their efforts were so rarely rewarded.

In former days, when Schneur Zalman had sent emissaries to

the isolated communities of the Caucasus, they had been received gratefully, and usually they succeeded in leaving behind them a reinspired congregation or a new school. The young men today had to be satisfied with less. They tried to dispose of a few pieces of literature or to give encouragement to some elderly person who was trying to maintain a kosher diet under difficult circumstances.

The rebbe then delivered another discourse on the subject of youth, after which there was more singing, and then the cycle of discourse and song began again, continuing for several hours. It would have become very tiresome except for the fact that the rebbe seemed to be arranging his talks so that they became shorter and lighter in tone as the hours went by. One of them, for example, was about the current craze for vacations in the country. It reminded him, said the rebbe, of the person who had been ordered by his doctor to spend an hour every day in the fresh air of the woods. Unfortunately he lived three hours from the woods and in order to observe the doctor's prescription he ran to the woods at night after work, then ran back exhausted, but he obeyed the doctor's prescription. So it was, the rebbe smiled, with many of us who feel we must go to the country in the summertime. The food is worse, and the train schedules are difficult. But we fulfill the commandment "to vacation in the country."

Several hours had passed, and I decided to relieve the pressure of the hard bench by taking a little walk during the next interval of song. Outside in the courtyard some young people were selling literature and large photographs of the Lubavitcher rebbes. Near the entrance, some fifteen or twenty women had been standing all the evening. Several of them held young children in their arms, and most of them wore long-sleeved dresses and kerchiefs that covered their heads in Orthodox fashion. A few were dressed quite stylishly and used make-up. I wondered if they did not resent the custom which forbade their sitting with the men or participating in the exchange of toasts with the rebbe. The week before, I had raised this question in the home of a Lubavitcher Hasid. But both the Hasid and his wife had assured me that there was much more married happiness within the movement than in the "outside" world.

Of course, they said, most of the marriages took place within

Lubavitch itself. But once in a while, the wife added with a smile, "there is an intermarriage—somebody from Lubavitch will marry somebody from the Satmer rebbe—but even that works out." Besides, the rebbe was quite accessible to women when it came to interviews. I had asked them about the rebbe's family life. There was an awkward pause, and both of them dropped their heads as they informed me that the rebbe had no children. For some reason the Master of the Universe had withheld this blessing from the man who reputedly had the power of bestowing it on others.

The rebbe was just beginning to speak again when I returned from my stroll. The essential purpose of the evening, he said, was to attach ourselves in spirit to the Tzaddik, his father-in-law, Rabbi Joseph Isaac. Such attachment was not made more difficult by the fact that the Tzaddik was now dead. In a way it was easier, for there were no limitations now to his spirit: the body no longer stood in the way of his essence. But how could we attach ourselves to a man's essence? The answer was by educating others in his ways. Therefore, the rebbe urged, let everyone participate in this attachment and write his own name and the name of his mother on a piece of paper (so that the rebbe might mention them in his prayers) and offer his contribution to the educational ideals and institutions of Rabbi Joseph Isaac, former Lubavitcher rebbe.

As the papers and envelopes were being passed up to the dais, the rebbe's humor broke out again: "Let's introduce a new custom in America—the custom of giving money joyously and with a song." His request was immediately granted.

At about two A.M. I left the *farbrengung,* which showed no signs of ending, and walked toward my car trying to sum up my feelings. It had been an interesting evening, and yet frustrating. There was no question about the genuineness of faith in that courtyard, but it was a faith that seemed completely beyond the comprehension of most people in the twentieth century.

Perhaps the rebbe, who, I recalled, had studied science at the Sorbonne, would be able to resolve some of the questions I still had.

Alone with the Rebbe

I arrived for my appointment with the rebbe at 10 P.M. one evening the following week but was still waiting after midnight when a

The Lubavitcher Movement   157

young student ran into the outer office to announce that the "case"
from California, a man who had flown in to consult with the Lubavitcher rebbe about a business problem, had just left. That meant it
was my turn, and clutching my notebook, I hurried past several
people in the hallways whose appointments with the rebbe would be
even later. Remembering that there are thousands who depend on
the rebbe for major, and even many minor decisions in their lives,
and that a worldwide spiritual network, including schools and chari-
ties and publications, waited on the personal attention of this one
man, I made a resolution not to stay long.

Rabbi Menachem Mendel Schneersohn, the seventh Lubavitcher
rebbe, was folding some papers at a desk in the far corner of a large,
rather bare room. His fedora hat, neatly tailored frock coat, and
carefully arranged tie, all black, set off the pallor of his face. The
brim of his hat was bent, casting a shadow over his deep blue eyes,
which looked up with a direct but good-humored expression. I extended my hand, forgetting for the moment that the Hasidim do
not offer their hands to the rebbe, who is to them a holy vessel and
not to be touched casually. But Rabbi Menachem Mendel didn't
seem to mind the impropriety; he shook my hand and motioned
gently toward the chair by his desk, suggesting in a soft voice that I
address him in English, although he would reply in Yiddish.

Before I could begin my inquiries, he asked me what kind of
work I was engaged in and what I had studied. My notebook with
its proposed questions remained closed, and I found myself chatting
freely about matters I had not expected to discuss. The rebbe listened,
nodding his head from time to time to indicate understanding, and
gradually the sense of urgent haste I had felt in the hallway began
to ebb away. We spoke about religious leaders in Israel, particularly
the former chief rabbi, Abraham Isaac Kook, at the mention of whose
name the rebbe nodded slightly without saying a word. I sensed that
his silence was a way of expressing disapproval without transgressing
the commandment, "Thou shalt not speak evil," and asked if he did
not share my admiration for Rabbi Kook.

The Rabbi shook his head gently. "He tried to mix too much
together. Philosophy, law, mysticism—there were too many paradoxes
in his teachings. A leader should not confuse the mind too much."

Suddenly a buzzer sounded, a signal from Rabbi Hodakov,

the rebbe's secretary, that almost a full hour had passed since my interview began. Hastily I turned to my prepared questions and asked how Lubavitcher Hasidism, a mystical movement, had become so skillful in worldly matters like public relations and methods of business efficiency. The rebbe folded his hands on his desk and in a measured voice outlined his answer, which was punctuated by an occasional mild cough.

Lubavitch's interest in public relations was simply a practical extension of its special interpretation of the oneness of God. God was in everything, and therefore evil had no real existence. But it must *appear* to have real existence, so that man might have freedom of choice. It might seem to us an evil thing for one man to cut another with a knife, yet there were occasions, as for example a medical operation, when a good and not an evil purpose was served by the cutting of a man. So also, what appeared evil in *our* sight was, in the light of a higher wisdom, really good. To believe otherwise, to believe that evil has a positive existence, was to be driven in the end to the conviction that there are two divine powers rather than one. The oneness of God implied that everything was ultimately justified; in this way, the rebbe concluded, "We try to understand Hitler and similar matters."

Again the buzzer sounded, but the rebbe indicated that I needn't hurry. I turned to my central question: how could the rebbe assume responsibility for giving advice to his Hasidim not only on religious matters, but on medical problems or business affairs, especially when he knew that his advice was binding?

Menachem Mendel did not seem offended. "To begin with, it is always pleasant to run away from responsibility. But what if running might destroy the congregation, and suppose"—the good-humored smile in the rebbe's eyes grew stronger—"they put the key into your pocket and walk away? What can you do then—permit the books to be stolen?"

I was surprised to hear him hint at the well-known fact that it had taken the Hasidim more than a year to persuade Rabbi Menachem Mendel to become the seventh Rebbe of the Lubavitcher movement. But this wasn't the answer to my question, which I tried to press by leafing through a copy of the Tanya (a collection of the writings of the first Lubavitcher rebbe, Schneur Zalman) to find a letter in which the Alter Rebbe tells his Hasidim that they must not ask him for help in nonspiritual matters. The rebbe interrupted my search to say that I was probably looking for Letter 22. "That letter," he pointed out quietly, "was printed after Schneur Zalman's death, and besides," he smiled, "despite the letter, he did give advice in material matters."

Sensing after a moment that his explanation did not satisfy me, the rebbe cleared his throat and continued. "When a man comes with a problem, there are only two alternatives—either send him away, or try to help him. A man knows his own problem best, so one must try to unite oneself with him and become *batel,* as dissociated as possible from one's own ego. Then, in concert with the other person, one tries to understand the rule of divine Providence in this particular case. And, of course, if the man who comes to you shares your ideas and faith, there is immediate empathy" (he used the English word).

But didn't the power of the Lubavitcher movement stem directly from this faith of the Hasid in his rebbe? Rabbi Menachem Mendel demurred gently, "I'm not so sure."

The buzzer rang again, and I looked at the rebbe to see if my interview was over. Instead of sending me away, however, he began talking about Conservative and Reform Judaism. His voice remained soft, but the opinions were firm. "The great fault of Conservative and Reform Judaism is not that they compromise, but that they sanctify the compromise, still the conscience, and leave no possibility for return." The rebbe went on to explain that though the Lubavitcher movement encouraged every Jew to observe as many of the commandments as he could, even if only a few, it insisted that the Jewish religion as such should be identified exclusively with the Orthodox tradition; otherwise, a repentant Jew who wanted to "return" would not know what there was to return to.

When the buzzer rang once again, I rose to leave, but Rabbi Menachem Mendel stopped me: "Wait—now I would like to ask you a question," he said, and I sat down again. "How is it that you are not Orthodox?" Surprised, I offered something about not being able to believe that the whole of the Torah was given by God.

"Yet you believe in the oneness of God," the rebbe pressed. "And if you follow out the implication of that belief logically, then you must come to the *mitzvot,* the commandments, as surely as theorems follow from axioms." Again the rebbe used English words. I remained silent, and after a moment he leaned back in his chair and spoke as if answering himself, "But I guess in America people don't feel the need for a full logical *shitah,* system of belief, as they do in Europe."

For the fifth time the buzzer rang and, disturbed at the thought of all those people waiting outside, I made a determined effort to leave. But as I stood up the rebbe stopped me again. "You haven't asked, but probably you'd like to know, what Hasidim think about miracles?" I remained standing while Rabbi Menachem Mendel asserted that even science recognized all "laws" as mere probabilities and that there was no way to fortell every event in nature with certainty. He cited the throwing of dice as an example, a strange *mashal* (illustration) I thought to myself, for a Hasid to use.

After he had finished expounding the Hasidic view of miracles, I asked him if it would be possible to see him again when I had become more familiar with the Lubavitcher movement. "Gladly," he smiled, "but not until after the High Holy days" which were only a month away.

Actually, my first meeting with the rebbe had brought me no closer to understanding what it was that made a Lubavitcher Hasid. I knew now that Rabbi Menachem Mendel was a warm and sincere leader, a man who, though in absolute control of a large and influential organization, lived modestly and devoted every minute of his waking hours to the advancement of Torah and the needs of other human beings. That such a man could arouse love and admiration in his followers was not at all surprising, but this alone could not be the explanation of the amazing vitality of the movement.

I knew that I had not yet begun to understand the inner dynamic of Lubavitch, and the next day I asked Rabbi Hodakov for permission to spend some time at the Yeshiva speaking and even studying a bit with the "boys." To my surprise he hesitated. "You know," he said, with a rather bashful smile, "even in medicine everything depends on the quantity—a little may do good, and a lot, harm. . . ."

However, he finally agreed to my request, and the following morning I spoke to Rabbi Mentlik, who supervises, under the guidance of the rebbe, the High Yeshiva at 770 Eastern Parkway. I recognized him by his red beard and silver-rimmed spectacles as the cup bearer who had stood all night by the rebbe's side during the *farbrengung* without participating in the singing and without even so much as moving. When I informed him that Rabbi Hodakov had given me permission to study, he spoke to a few boys who, in singsong voice, were discussing a passage in the Talmud, and they made room for me on the bench.

I found myself sitting next to an eighteen-year-old lad with long fuzzy earlocks. He mentioned to me that he had been born in Russia and raised there in the educational underground once maintained by the Lubavitcher movement under the Soviet regime. Though we began studying a problem in Talmud together, it was soon clear that our minds were elsewhere. I was interested in asking him about his experiences in Russia, and his curiosity was aroused by the phenomenon of a Reform Jew wandering about the halls of Lubavitch. Whenever we came to a break in the Talmudic discussion, we would immediately exchange questions. He told me how his father had been sent to Siberia after being denounced to the secret police for his religious activities, and how the rest of the family had finally escaped to southern Russia. Then he wanted to know how a rabbi could accept one part of the bible as holy but reject the commandments ordained in some other section; did not the bible declare itself to be entirely inspired? He could understand, he admitted earnestly, that a rabbi might want to hold a pulpit in a Reform synagogue, to make a better living or for social convenience, but the logic of the Reform position was beyond him.

I had resolved not to enter into any religious disputations at the Yeshiva, but it was hard to put the young Hasid off. The next night he brought up the subject again. When he saw that I was determined not to enter into a serious discussion, he sighed, lifting up his hands in a weary gesture of resignation, "What can be the *tachlis,* after all—

the purpose of anything—if not to fulfill the word of God? In forty or sixty years, everything passes away. What meaning can it all have if not to obey God's commandments?" I was struck by this youngster's easy dismissal of forty or sixty years of life. A few days later he caught me in the hallway and again questioned the logic of the liberal religious position. A bit irritated, I asked if the fact that so many intelligent people were unable to see the logic of Orthodoxy did not make him wonder about the absolute certainty of his own convictions. My young friend was delighted that I had risen to the debate and his reply came swiftly. "Ah-hah—but Abraham too was alone—yet he had the truth. And we know now from the atom bomb how much power there is in the 'little.'" Again I had the feeling which often came to me while speaking to the students at the Yeshiva: a sense of walking along together and coming suddenly to a door of the mind through which only a Hasid could pass, while others were left outside, bewildered.

Once I confessed this sense of frustration to a gray-bearded elder, who was walking around the study hall while the boys were busy at their lessons. He was a specialist in the ideology of *chabad*, and his main task was to convey the *lechut*, the inner marrow or mood, of mystic doctrines to the students. He brought his red-rimmed eyes close to my face and asked whether I put on phylacteries every morning. "Once," he said, "I had shoes that were too tight, and I got a pain in my head." He tugged at my sleeves to emphasize his point. "The shoes can affect the head, do you understand? If you want to understand Hasidism, you must observe the commandments. What you do will help you understand."

This was good *chabad* doctrine, for Lubavitch strongly believes that one's physical life has a direct effect on the mind. Our food and speech and deeds have the power to open or close the "vessels of the spirit." In the Tanya, Schneur Zalman frequently associates qualities of the soul with specific parts of the body ("The evil spirit is in the left ventricle of the heart, and the love of God flames in the right ventricle"). *Shekina*, the divine presence, is of course at home in the brain, from which base it can cause the love of God to flame up, high enough at times to completely overwhelm the powers of darkness on the "other side."

Similarly, the study of the Torah was not looked upon merely as a means of acquiring knowledge. "Torah, Israel, and the Holy One, Blessed be He, are One," says the Zohar. That means that the Torah is not just an instrument for conveying the will of God, but *is* the divine corpus, the *ein sof,* in a form which permits Israel to become one with it. It is like a person who becomes one with an object which he contemplates; indeed, in the case of Torah the identification is more complete. By merging himself with thoughts of Torah, by pronouncing its words and by causing his limbs to be "clothed" in the actions it commands, the Jew can achieve his *unio mystica.*

The notion that the capacity of the mind to understand the mysteries of religion is dependent on actual physical performance of the commandments, explains the bargain which another man, whom I had heard described as a *typishe* Lubavitcher Hasid, tried to make with me when I asked him to help me study the Tanya. He demanded payment, which was to consist of my agreement to observe one more of the 613 commandments.

I don't think we ever formalized our covenant, but for several months I enjoyed visiting this Hasid, who served as a rabbi in a community not far from New York. Like most Hasidim, he would have preferred to live closer to the rebbe, but the rebbe had insisted that he go out into the world and "create an environment." The process of creation was difficult; the members of his congregation wanted him to shorten the prayers and include more English in the services, so that the young people would be attracted. He, on the other hand, felt that young people would remain in the synagogue only if real Orthodoxy were shown to them—a joyful Judaism with a living soul and not just the "dry bones." This difference of opinion made for problems. But, my *typishe* Hasid would always remind himself with a smile, "One must have *bitachon,* faith." Besides, the rebbe and the *chevra,* the "boys," were only an hour's trip away, and when "I get into New York, all the problems immediately roll off my shoulders."

And there were other Hasidic devices for overcoming one's troubles. One could lift the soul by humming a Hasidic melody, or one could comfort oneself by pressing Hasidic doctrine into practical use. "All I have to do," the Hasid laughed, "is to look at the president of my synagogue sitting on the other side of the pulpit and say to myself, 'No—he's not really there—not really—only one reality is really there, and of that reality I needn't be afraid.' "

My friend was alluding to the central idea of Hasidism that "there is no place empty of Him"; since God is everywhere, we need only penetrate the veil of appearances to behold the underlying reality. In *chabad* Hasidism this doctrine is intricately elaborated. God's "light" assumes "garments" so that it may be perceived by fleshly eyes. In this form, it is called "the light that clothes itself," to distinguish it from "the light that surrounds," which is the infinite light pervading all creation that never assumes visible form.

In the Tanya and in other *chabad* literature, the theme of the hidden or clothed light is repeated with endless variations. It is this outer clothing which often prevents us from recognizing God's goodness. The clothing is necessary, for the bare light is too much for us to behold. Yet it can appear to us as cruel, just as a son may so interpret his father's loving, but firm, acts of instruction. Only as the son's wisdom grows is he able to recognize that the restrictions or reproofs which his father inflicted upon him were really acts of love. In the same way, man's perception of the mercy and love which are hidden in suffering depends on the profundity of his insight. Hence the highest level to which a human being can reach, says the Tanya, is the condition of the saint, "for whom everything is good." The saint is able to "receive his sufferings in love," because he really doesn't see them as sufferings. He sees all apparent evil as a hidden form of good. Indeed, the more hidden, the higher the good, since the closer we come to the source of the good, the more incomprehensible it is to our limited perception.

Of course, a doctrine like this is dangerous when applied literally in all situations. It can be used to blur all distinction between good and evil. It can be used to say, as did the Frankists, that even sin is a hidden form of good. Hasidism did not go that far, but essentially it did insist that evil was basically an illusion. What else could it be, if "there is no place empty of Him"?

It is this pantheistic element in Hasidism that was vigorously attacked by the Gaon of Vilna. The Talmudic dictum, "There is no place empty of Him," insisted the Gaon, meant only that His providence extends over all creation; it did not mean that God is coextensive with creation. "It is sinful to say that we know anything about God's essence," the Gaon argued, "and particularly sinful to suggest that polluted and evil things can be synonymous with God."

During the pauses in our conversation, my Lubavitcher friend had a habit of humming, and the warm good humor of his voice helped soften the harshness of even his most rigid Orthodox opinions. With a smile, he confessed his suspicion that Jewish children whose mothers did not observe the laws of ritual purity were physically as well as spiritually maimed. With the same smile, he defended his belief in the power of the rebbe, "whose mouth has never said a lie and whose limbs have never committed a sin." The rebbe was such a man and therefore able to bestow blessings.

Often childless families came to the rebbe to ask his blessing—yet he was childless: did this not affect the faith of Hasidim? My friend looked pained, and I apologized for my question. But no, I had misunderstood his reaction, my friend explained. It was not that Hasidim doubted the power of the rebbe, but they were the "branches and he the root" and they simply shared in his pain.

The major effort of the Lubavitcher Hasidim is the construction and expansion of their school system. The rebbe directs this activity, as he does every activity of the movement, but it is Rabbi Gourary, the rebbe's brother-in-law, who is immediately concerned with the educational program and particularly with its financial aspects. His office is located in the Lubavitcher Yeshiva on Bedford Avenue in Brooklyn, and I arrived there one day during the noon-hour recess to find the streets around the large brick building filled with little Hasidim playing ball and chasing one another up and down. Some were dueling with ash-can covers as shields and sticks of wood as swords. All of them of course wore hats or head-coverings of some kind and the older boys had long earlocks, but apart from this they were indistinguishable from any group of children who had been released for lunch-hour games. I stopped one of the ash-can warriors long enough to learn that Rabbi Gourary could be found on the third floor of the building.

The rebbe's brother-in-law, a small Panatella cigar in his mouth, was seated behind a desk opening some letters when I entered his office. On the desk there was a tray containing the remnants of a sandwich and a half-finished glass of tea. Rabbi Gourary was a pleasant-looking man with perceptive blue eyes; his hair and beard, though gray, had obviously once been blond. He extended a limp hand in greeting and continued to open his letters, occasionally finding a check which he would place on a separate pile.

On the wall I noticed a picture of Rabbi Joseph Isaac, the present rabbi's predecessor and father-in-law who was also Rabbi Gourary's father-in-law. I asked Gourary by what method a new rebbe was chosen in the Lubavitcher movement when the deceased rebbe had no sons, as was the case with Rabbi Joseph Isaac. He and Menachem Mendel, being Joseph Isaac's two sons-in-law, had been the obvious candidates for the office, and I had often wondered on what basis Menachem Mendel had been chosen. Gourary looked at me sharply for a moment. "If the rebbe leaves a will," he answered briefly, "his instructions are followed. Otherwise, the elders of the movement decide."

What about the stories that people told about the powers of the rebbe? He waved his cigar impatiently. "I'm not responsible for all the stories people tell." As for the rebbe's advising on medical problems, "The rebbe can send them to a good doctor. Of course," he added quickly, "Hasidim believe in the rebbe's blessing. A Hasid believes in higher destiny—what you call luck. But what is luck, after all, but higher destiny? Hasidim believe in the power of the rebbe to influence that destiny."

I asked Rabbi Gourary what made Lubavitch so much more successful than other Hasidic groups. His reply was quick: Lubavitch had taken the inner spirit of Hasidism and expressed it in forms you could "get your hands on."

Asking me if I'd like to see the school, Rabbi Gourary pressed a buzzer. A moment later, a young man with the inevitable beard appeared and was instructed to take me on a tour of the school. *"Gei gesunterheit,* go in health," Rabbi Gourary said, offering his hand as I arose.

My guide led me down a flight of stairs and we visited several classrooms where the boys sat in pairs behind rickety desks. Here and there a pair swayed back and forth in unison as the two children chanted their lessons in Hebrew and Yiddish. My guide explained that the younger pupils studied Jewish subjects from nine in the morning until one-thirty in the afternoon, after which they followed the public school curriculum required of all parochial and private schools by the New York Board of Education. The upper grades went on with religious studies until two-thirty in the afternoon, and only then did their secular lessons, while the oldest boys, old enough to be free of control by the Board of Education, studied Talmud and Hasidic teachings until as late as seven o'clock in the evening.

In one of the classes we visited, a tall young teacher, wearing a felt hat that rested far back on his head, asked if we would like to hear the children recite. Several dozen hands shot up waving wildly in the air. His eyes gleaming proudly behind his spectacles, the teacher glanced around the room for a minute, and then called out, "Moishele." A chubby boy of about eight whose heavy winter cap had come undone, leaving an ear-flap hanging down, immediately drew back his hand, embarrassed at having been chosen. He walked hesitatingly to the front of the room and stood tongue-tied while the children, sensing that he would not deliver, began to wave their hands again. The teacher ignored this renewed supplication, and encouraged Moishele by quoting the first few words of the portion they had been studying in the bible. Moishele took courage and recited the rest of the passage.

It was the section that dealt with Jacob's meeting with Esau upon returning from his sojourn with his father-in-law: "And with Laban did I live." Moishele chanted Jacob's words in Hebrew, translated them into Yiddish, and then added in a singsong voice the eleventh-century commentary of Rashi, "And the 613 commandments did I keep." The teacher pointed out the letters of the Hebrew word *garti* ("did I live") could be rearranged to spell *taryag,* which means 613. This was why Rashi had suggested that when Jacob said, "And with Laban did I live," he was also indicating that though he had resided outside his own "environment," he had maintained the 613 commandments of the Law. Whatever scholarly critics may say about this manner of interpreting the bible, its pedagogic effect is clear. To Moishele and the boys at the Lubavitcher Yeshiva, Jacob was no stranger. He covered his head, wore earlocks, and like any Lubavitcher Hasid, was concerned with the never ending challenge of a foreign "environment."

Later that afternoon I returned to 770 Eastern Parkway just in time to see the older boys coming back from their assignments as teachers in the "released-time hour"—that period which is set aside once a week in New York State public schools for religious instruction according to denomination. Many Jewish organizations object to the released-time hour system. But Lubavitch would not dream of neglecting the opportunity to send its boys out to stimulate that element of pure Jewishness, that *habad* Hasidim believe exists, however deeply buried, in every Jew. Now, home from their pedagogic labors, the young students were beginning to study *hasidut,* the term they use to describe the mystic "inner" studies. They gathered in pairs or small groups around their texts, but the transition from the outer to the inner world took a while. "Come on, Herb," I heard one boy calling out good-humoredly to a companion whose mind was clearly wandering, "you'll lose your portion in the world-to-come."

Dusk was approaching, and some older men began to drift into the study hall to wait for the day's-end prayers. One of them stood by the pulpit and bound his waist with a *gartel*—that cord which a Hasid wears to remind him of the distinction between the "higher" and "lower" parts of man.

This practice suggests that Hasidism is not as positive in its attitude toward the body as some of its modern interpreters seem to think. Man's lower, animal soul, his vegetative impulses and needs, must be controlled and often fought by his higher soul, which is part of the divine soul. The body, said the author of the Tanya, is like a city over which the power of light and the power of darkness continually struggle. There are some *tzaddikim,* saintly ones, who have utterly banished the evil force within them. But most people are in a condition of *benoni,* in-between, who must use their intellectual powers to make sure that the right side prevails. This battle between higher and lower is continuous in this world. Only at certain times, during study and prayer, does the struggle dissolve under the influence of the unities being effected in the world of the *sefirot.*

In the study hall, everyone was now waiting quietly for the

important moment when the soul was going to strive for contact with its source. As if at a silent signal, they moved to one side of the hall; almost immediately the rebbe entered with quick steps and walked to a large chair facing the congregation. He took his seat without looking around, at which point the man with the *gartel* began reciting the prayers.

Lubavitch has always emphasized the importance of clinging as accurately as possible to the musical tradition which has come down with each prayer, and the leader of the service chanted the familiar melodies in a sweet, low voice. When the *Sh'monah Esrei,* Eighteen Benedictions, was reached, the whole congregation rose, and the murmur of prayer gave way to complete silence, in accordance with traditional usage. As they began to read the prayer to themselves, the Hasidim inclined their knees slightly at the words "Blessed be Thou" so that the silence was broken continually by the creaking of the floor. Here and there, also, someone sighed softly as he pressed his fists against his chest and asked for forgiveness. There are times when, despite all efforts, the light of God does not flow into the soul. In this case, Hasidim follow the advice of the holy Zohar: "A wooden beam that will not catch fire should be splintered. . . . A body into which the light of the soul does not penetrate should be stamped underfoot." But this element of self-chastisement in *chabad* Hasidism is carefully tempered lest it lead to the sadness and despair which are Satan's chief weapons. Hence the sigh of regret is also close to joy, since the sadness is already a sign that the "other side" is being broken; as the psalmist says, "A broken and contrite heart, O God, Thou wilt not despise."

The stillness in the room deepened as everyone strove to bind higher and lower together, hoping to break through the private barriers that still separated them from the light of the divine presence.

That night I arranged with Rabbi Hodakov for my second appointment with the rebbe. It was more than a year now that I had been trying to "understand" Lubavitch—the faith and loyalty of its Hasidim, the success and continued vitality of its organization, its resistance to the degeneration common to hereditary spiritual dynasties. The obvious explanations did not really satisfy. After all, other religious groups had offered the same escape from personal responsibility, the same feeling of historic mission, the same sense of community.

The Lubavitcher Hasidim themselves had a ready explanation: "We have had great rebbes." But I was beginning to believe that part of the "secret" might be precisely that Lubavitch depended less on its rebbes than did other sects. That warm mystic mood of Hasidism, that sense of God's spirit pulsating through all creation, the inner marrow or *lechut,* as they called it, was not entrusted for communication to the personal powers of a single man. Other Hasidic leaders in Schneur Zalman's day had been as great; there was the saintly Levi Yitzchak of Berditchev (d. 1804), for example, and the gifted Nachman of Bratzlav (d. 1810), but their sects had remained vital for only as long as the founders were vividly remembered. Schneur Zalman, however, had constructed a system whereby the delicate and ephemeral grasp of the unworldly could be captured in "vessels" of rational formulation— vessels which could on demand be made to pour forth their supply of "living waters." The meticulous concern for organized study, for well-edited textbooks, for public relations and good business proce- dure, all so apparently incongruous in a sect of mystics, was actually a key to Lubavitch's special history. These vessels of thought and or- ganization had made of Hasidism something "you could get your hands on."

Yet to the Lubavitcher Hasid, the secret still lies in the great- ness of his rebbe, and it is true that without this faith of the Hasid in his rebbe, there would be no Lubavitcher movement. But can one understand how such a faith operates without sharing in it? I thought not, and brought to my second meeting with the rebbe an eagerness to identify, if only for a moment, with the Hasid's faith. I also brought with me a cold and a slight fever, which I now suspect had something to do with my experiences that evening.

The Second "Aloneness" with the Rebbe

My appointment was again for ten P.M. I came on time, though knowing by now that with respect to appointments, Lubavitch fol- lowed the dictum of another rebbe, the Kotsker, who maintained, "Where there is a soul, there cannot be a clock." On arrival, I found a group of Hasidim in the study hall, listening to one of their com- rades who reputedly had a gift for remembering every word of the rebbe's discourses. Several weeks ago the rebbe had spoken Torah, and since then the Hasidim had been gathering to hear this man with the photographic memory "repeat the Torah."

Noticing that the phones in the office were quiet, I approached Rabbi Hodakov's desk, and requested a few minutes of his time. The rebbe's secretary shrugged his thin shoulders and invited me to take a seat. "Rabbi Hodakov," I asked, "could you tell me briefly what Lubavitch offers people?"

Rabbi Hodakov sat straight in his chair and his eyes brightened. Then he spoke so forcefully that a student standing over in a corner of the office looked up in surprise. "I can tell you in one word—*leben,* life." He paused for a moment. "There are other kinds of death besides the one of the grave. What is life for one creature on earth need not be life for another. A monkey may act like a man, and I don't know how he feels then—but if a man acts like a monkey, he stops being a man—he stops living.

"What is it that makes life?" Rabbi Hodakov's voice grew even stronger as he continued to speak. "It is the fulfillment of a mission and a purpose. In nature, we have different classes—mineral, vegetable, animal, and then man. Within the class of man, there is a species called the Jew. The Jew has his purpose like every other species, but what is this purpose?"

A few more students had entered the office and were now listening openly to our discussion.

Rabbi Hodakov went on passionately. "We would not have known the purpose if God had not done us a *chesed,* a gracious favor. He gave us a Torah."

The room had become quiet. The boys edged close, and I think Rabbi Hodakov was aware that he had an audience. I too felt self-conscious. All were waiting for my next question. Through the slight haze of my fever, an appalling thought suddenly penetrated to my mind. This was not just a conversation. It was going to become a *vikuach,* a religious disputation similar to those held in the Middle Ages between the "believer" and the "heretic." I, of course, was cast in the role of the heretic, and the boys in the room who had gathered to listen were convinced that, like all heretics, I was about to be annihilated by the logic and spiritual power of the truth. But dabbing my watery eyes and running nose with a handkerchief, and feeling somewhat like a lamb stretching out its neck to the knife, I offered the question that I knew was expected of me. "But how do we know that God gave us the Torah?"

Rabbi Hodakov's eyes glinted; the knife was lifted. "When was the Constitution written?"

I mumbled a date, hoping that it was correct.

But Rabbi Hodakov was not interested in my knowledge of American history. "How do you know?" he demanded.

Witnesses and correlating documents, I ventured, adding a protest to the effect that the Constitution did not purport to be more than a human document. I remember using the word "witnesses" deliberately because I felt that he would want to seize on it in answering me.

"Ah-ha," Rabbi Hodakov sat up in his chair to deliver the *coup de grâce*. "If witnesses are to be believed about a human document, then how much more difficult would it be to find real witnesses for a divine document? Wouldn't it be even more difficult to forge such testimony?"

Actually, I wasn't sure that I followed his logic, but I blamed that on myself, or on the fever which was blurring my mind. Besides, I had come across the same line of argument before; it was made use of in the twelfth century by Judah Halevi in his *Sefer ha-Kuzari*. Six hundred thousand witnesses, says Judah Halevi, saw the Torah given by God to Moses. The event has been related by father to son in an unbroken chain of testimony. How could the claim that a whole generation had witnessed the giving of the Torah possibly have been invented in some later age? The elders would deny having heard of the event from their fathers and the claim would fall to the ground. Consequently, concludes Judah Halevi, revelation must be as credible a fact as any recorded event in history.

This argument had never impressed me before, but it now occurred to my feverish mind that it was very sensible, and I wondered why I hadn't understood it on other occasions. I was reaching for my handkerchief again when the buzzer rang. The rebbe was waiting. I grabbed my notebook and escaped into the hallway.

The quiet of the rebbe's office and his soft-spoken greeting were like balm after the "disputation."

"*Shalom aleichem,* Rabbi Weiner," Rabbi Menachem Mendel smiled, extending his hand.

I protested that, after a year of visiting 770 Eastern Parkway, I knew that a good Hasid should not take the Rebbe's hand.

"We don't have to begin that way," he said, beckoning me toward a chair. He looked a bit paler than when I had first seen him a year ago and there was more gray in his black beard, but the same grave smile played in his deep blue eyes.

I opened my notebook and sat back in the chair, again conscious of how comfortable and relaxing it was in the rebbe's office. Then I remembered that this was my last chance and resolved to ask even the most embarrassing questions in an effort to solve the enigma of Lubavitch. I explained to the rebbe that more than a year had passed since I began trying to understand the movement, and that I had come to him now with a confession: I did not understand. Would he mind if I started this interview by asking him about the character of a Hasid?

Rabbi Menachem Mendel smiled and told me to go ahead; as before I could speak English but he would answer in Yiddish.

"Isn't the fact that Hasidim turn to the rebbe for almost every decision in their lives—isn't this a sign of weakness, a repudiation of the very thing that makes a man human, his *b'chirah,* freedom of will?"

The rebbe's answer came without hesitation, as if he had dealt with the question before. "A weak person is usually overcome by the environment in which he finds himself. But our Hasidim can be sent into any environment, no matter how strange or hostile, and they maintain themselves within it. So how can we say that it is weakness which characterizes a Hasid?"

I pressed my question from another angle and told him that I sensed a desire in *chabad* to oversimplify, to strip ideas of their complexity merely for the sake of a superficial clarity. As a matter of fact, I blurted out, all his Hasidim seemed to have one thing in common: a sort of open and naive look in their eyes that a sympathetic observer might call *t'mimut* (purity) but that might less kindly be interpreted as emptiness or simple-mindedness, the absence of inner struggle.

I found myself taken aback by my own boldness, but the rebbe showed no resentment. He leaned forward. "What you see missing from their eyes is a *kera!*"

"A what?" I asked.

"Yes, a *kera,*" he repeated quietly, "a split." The rebbe hesitated for a moment. "I hope you will not take offense, but something tells me you don't sleep well at night, and this is not good for 'length of days.' Perhaps if you had been raised wholly in one world or in another, it might be different. But this split is what comes from trying to live in two worlds."

The rebbe's *ad hominem* answer encouraged me to be personal in return. "But you too have studied in two worlds, and your Hasidim are rather proud of the fact that you once attended the Sorbonne. Why then do you discourage them from studying in the 'other world'?"

"Precisely because I have studied, and I know what the value of that study is," the rebbe replied quickly. "I recognized its usefulness. If there are people who think they can help God sustain the world, I have no objection. We need engineers and chemists, but engineering and chemistry are not the most important things. Besides, to study does not mean only to learn facts. It means exposure to certain circles and activities which conflict with a believer's values and faith. It's like taking a person from a warm environment and throwing him into a cold water shock-treatment several times a day. How long can he stand it? In addition, studies in college take place at an age when a man's character is not yet crystallized, usually before the age of thirty. Exposure then is dangerous."

There was a slight pause, and then I asked the rebbe if he would object to being questioned about himself. He shrugged smilingly. Well, then, I said: the boys at 770 Eastern Parkway claimed that the rebbe was able to see things they could not see and that he was not mere flesh and blood. He himself, in our last interview, had given me a rather more rational explanation of the powers of the rebbe, saying that they were a matter of empathy. But I wanted to know whether he regarded himself and his six predecessors as mere flesh and blood.

For the first time he hesitated over his answer. "Are you asking me to tell you about myself?" he smiled. "I don't think you should write about me and my beliefs. But I can tell you what the position of the rebbe is in Hasidism. We are, of course, all of us only flesh and blood, and I'm not responsible for all the stories you may hear. But you must approach the facts of the case without preconceived theories. Science, after all, means the willingness to observe facts and follow them to whatever conclusions they will lead, not to try to push the facts into a desired pattern."

"Do you believe, then, that the rebbe has special insight and can see things and know things beyond the comprehension of ordinary people?" I still wanted a clear answer.

"Yes," said the rebbe.

"And is this power given only to the rebbe, or to other men also?"

"As a believer," replied the rebbe, "I am convinced that it can only be given to a 'keeper of Torah and *mitzvot*.'"

At that moment, a question I had not planned to ask came to my lips. "What is a *b'rachah*?"

"What?" asked the rebbe, slightly startled.

"What does it mean when somebody comes to ask you for a blessing?"

"Are you asking me what I mean by a *b'rachah*?" the rebbe deflected the question. "Better that I tell you what Hasidism means by it. A man is affected by many levels, higher and lower. It is possible for the *tsaddik*, the rebbe, to awaken powers slumbering within a man. It is also possible to bring him into contact with a higher level of powers outside his own soul. A person lives on one floor of a building and needs help from the floor above; if he can't walk up himself, someone else must help him get that help."

"Does that mean that the rebbe can help a man up to a higher spiritual plane?"

"That's the hardest way," answered the rebbe. "The easier way is to bring these powers down upon him."

I asked about miracles, and this time the rebbe replied immediately. "To believe in the creator, and to believe that there is a continuous relationship between the creator and the creation, is necessarily to believe that the creator can do anything with His creation."

We spoke about religious faith and I suggested that many people would like to believe but found it hard. Rabbi Menachem Mendel disagreed. "It's not so hard for people to believe. There are millions who believed in Gandhi and millions who believe in the Pope, and even atheists when pressed to a corner come up with belief."

When I protested that in most cases doubt seemed to overwhelm faith, the rebbe nodded. "There can be doubts. To question God, however, is the first indication that one believes in something. You have to know something about God even to question Him. But we must try to overcome doubts by a constant feeding of the spirit. Just as a body that has been kept healthy can overcome a crisis, so a soul can defeat its crises and its doubts if it is constantly kept healthy."

"In that case, why are there so many without faith?"

The rebbe looked at me directly. "They are afraid of their faith. They are afraid of following out the consequences of the faith which they would arrive at by honest observation of the facts. They are afraid that they might have to abandon some of their comfort or give up cherished ideas. They are afraid of changing their lives."

I brought up another problem. Several weeks before I had heard him say that America, rather than Israel, was the place where Jewish life could flourish best. How did he reconcile this attitude with the commandment to leave the *galut,* the diaspora?

"What is *galut? Galut* means the estrangement of a person from his essential self. If a person moves from an environment where he observed the commandments and had a Jewish soul and comes to America where he forsakes the Torah while growing rich, free, and comfortable, he has nevertheless gone into exile, because he has left himself. It's not just assimilation, it's worse, it's what we call in English an *inferiority complex.* It is the admission that one's own values are inferior to the values of those around one. In Israel, too, it may be possible to go into *galut,* to forsake the Torah and lose the spirit which is our essential nature, to be 'like unto all the nations.' In addition," the rebbe said quietly, "America has not only the largest Jewish population in the world, but great material resources. Even as the spiritual can affect the material, so with material resources one can do things for the spirit."

The buzzer at the rebbe's desk sounded. Rabbi Hodakov was reminding us that others were waiting. I decided to ask a final question. "Many Jews today are searching," I said to the rebbe, "they want to return. What would you say to them to help them find their way?"

The rebbe paused for a moment. "I would say that the most important thing is 'no compromise.' I would send to them the words spoken by the prophet Elijah: *'How long halt ye between two opinions? If the Lord be God, follow Him; but if Baal, follow him.'* Compromise is dangerous, because it sickens both the body and the soul. A compromiser who tries to mediate between religion and the environment is unable to go in either direction and unable to distinguish the truth."

But would not people reject such rigid alternatives?

"This is the contribution of *chabad* Hasidism," the rebbe pointed out. "It's important to know that one must do everything, but at the same time we welcome the doing of even a part. If all we can accomplish is to save only one limb, we save that. Then we worry about saving another."

The buzzer rang again, and I arose, but the rebbe motioned for me to wait. To my surprise, he informed me that he had carefully read some articles about religion in Israel which I had published in *Commentary* (July and August, 1955). Another hour passed as Menachem Mendel Schneersohn gently but firmly offered his criticism of the pieces. It was after three o'clock in the morning when I left the rebbe's office and guiltily passed a bearded young man who was still waiting for his appointment. The secretary's office was closed, but from the street through a window I could see that Rabbi Hodakov was bent over his desk, his head buried in his arms.

The next morning when I returned to retrieve a briefcase I had left in the office, Rabbi Hodakov was still at his desk. His eyes were red and the phylacteries were on his head and arm. While he recited the morning prayers, one of the boys attended to his busy telephone. Two of the older students came up to me as I was leaving the office. They had heard that I had spent almost three hours with the rebbe early that morning, and they wanted to know what I thought now about their rebbe. Their eyes shone with pride as they awaited my reply. I remembered that the rebbe had said that the open look in a Hasid's eyes was not naiveté but the absence of a *kera,* a split.

Indeed, I thought, there is no split at Lubavitch. It offered its followers a world in which the mind was never confused by contradictions; where life was not compartmentalized; where the tensions between heart and mind, flesh and soul, God and His creation were all dissolved in the unity of a higher plan. Within this plan the leather strip of the phylacteries and the gas chambers of Hitler both serve their function, for "there is no place empty of Him." And any doubt or confusion that arose might be clarified by making oneself "as nothing" before the rebbe, who in turn made himself "as nothing" before the will of God.

No, there was no *kera* in the eyes of the Hasidim who awaited my answer. They nodded their heads enthusiastically as I expressed my admiration for their rebbe. I confessed to them that before leaving early that morning, I had asked the rebbe for his personal blessing. What was more, my cold of last night was much better. They shook my hand as if I were paying them a personal compliment, for, after all, in this respect too there is no split in Lubavitch, where the Hasidim "are only the branches and the rebbe is the root."

There is something immensely attractive in a "way" which provides answers for all questions, whether they be details of personal life or problems of cosmic significance. It is reassuring to have a logical explanation for chaos and to learn that God is most revealed where He seems to be most absent. It is heartening to believe that what seems like meaningless accident is actually the revelation of God's most hidden essence and that pain is the chastisement of love; but not all souls are able to turn darkness into light with the help of such a clear system. There are many individuals whose struggle with darkness is more agonized and torturous, because they themselves are deeply touched and at times almost overcome by this darkness. Such individuals may be drawn to another rabbi who called himself a "moon man," one whose strength and even faith was subject to periods of waxing and waning.

7

BRATZLAV—The Dead Hasidim

Master of all the worlds, Fountainhead of all happiness . . .
Help me to immerse my meditations and all the impulses of my
*   heart, and the depths of my thought in the mysteries of joy . . .*
And grant, O my creator,
That I believe with complete faith that all fires of suffering
And all the nine measures of destitution and illness and pain, and
*   the heaps of trouble in this world, and punishment in the next*
*   world, and*
All the deaths—
That they are as nothing:
As absolutely nothing
As absolutely nothing
Against the wondrous joy of clinging to Thy Godliness,
And the sweetness of the Torah . . .
Therefore does my prayer stretch itself before Thee,
My Father in Heaven,
Save me and help me from this moment to be alone in the fields
*   every night . . .*
To cry out to Thee from the depths of my heart . . .
To set forth all the burdens and negations that remove me from
*   Thee,*
Light of Life.
And give strength to strengthen myself in spite of everything—
To strengthen myself with great happiness,
With happiness that has no end,
Until my heart lifts up my hands to clap, to clap, to clap, and my
*   legs to dance until the soul swoons, swoons, swoons.*
And help me ever to make a new beginning and to be a flowering
*   well of Torah and Prayer,*
To work always with quickened spirit,
And to stand with powerful strength against the scoffers and mock-
*   ers,*
Who go about in our days—days of double darkness . . .
But oh, against all the troubles and burdens,
Thy joys, and Thy delights, are strong and powerful . . .
Oh our great Father, home of delights and wellspring of joy.

—Prayer of RABBI NACHMAN *of Bratzlav*

Nachman, the son of Feige, was a great grandson of the Baal Shem Tov. He was born in 1772 in Medzibozh, the town in the Ukraine where his famous grandfather was buried. When a child, he would prostrate himself in prayer for hours on the grave of the Baal Shem. In an age when asceticism was not rare, Nachman's fasts were so stern as to occasion astonishment. At one time, he tried gulping his food in a way which would avoid giving him the pleasure of taste. He often expressed a desire to wander about as a beggar from door to door. This yearning for self-deprivation seemed to carry over into his later life and may help to explain why after months of difficult voyaging to the Holy Land, dreamland of his soul, one hour after touching its soil he decided to return to the boat and Europe. The delegation which had come to meet him persuaded him to stay for a year, after which he went back and settled first in Bratzlav and then in Uman, towns in the Ukraine. He died at the age of thirty-eight, saying, "My light will glow till the days of the Messiah." His disciples interpreted this statement to mean that they would never need another spiritual leader to take his place. Consequently, today, more than one hundred and fifty years later, the Hasidim of Rabbi Nachman of Bratzlav still speak in the present tense of their rebbe and are therefore known in other Hasidic circles as the "dead Hasidim."

A Hasid without a live rebbe is almost a contradiction in terms, but the Bratzlav brand of Hasidism thrives on paradox. Rabbi Nachman preached the virtues of a naive faith, but was himself a complicated personality strongly attracted to "forbidden" literature. His constant cry was, "Don't despair!" but he had to fight frequent seizures of melancholy, calling himself a "moon man," fated to alternate between periods of light and darkness. Bratzlav is completely ethnocentered, inclined toward medieval ideas about Satan and sex, and contemptuous of worldly wisdom. Its literature, however, has attracted sophisticated minds and been translated into many languages.

That Bratzlav exercised a strange fascination for individuals who came from utterly different environments, I knew from personal experience. I had made many visits to the chief Bratzlaver synagogue in the Orthodox quarter of Jerusalem, Meah She'arim, where one can see Rabbi Nachman's intricately carved wooden chair, which had been broken into small pieces, smuggled over the Russian border, and reassembled in Israel. On Sabbath mornings, I had listened to weekly readings from Rabbi Nachman's thirteen stories, which Bratzlaver Hasidim study all their lives, and I had participated in the quiet dance with which they close every prayer session. I had seen a white-bearded convert from Russia, who sat in a corner vigorously chanting, "May I cast out the *goy* from within me." A bearded Hasid, who was a graduate of Brown University, explained that the Bratzlaver way "was especially suitable for those who had to struggle with deep despair."

Despite this evidence of Rabbi Nachman's appeal, I found it difficult to believe that in the 1960s a group of American-born young people living in New York, most of them college-educated and from nonreligious homes, declared themselves to be devout followers of Rabbi Nachman. One day, however, I received a telephone call from a Rabbi Wasilski in New York, who told me that his wife, "a Hunter College graduate," had read what I had written about Bratzlaver Hasidim and suggested that we meet at the Brooklyn Yeshiva where he was teaching.

Bratzlav in Brooklyn

Rabbi Wasilski turned out to be a younger man than his voice over the phone had led me to expect. He was in his early forties, with a thin, sallow face and small black beard. "Not an American type, you see," he said with a smile. He wore the wide-brimmed black hat and long, loose-fitting black jacket of the *yeshiva* rabbi, but, he quickly told me, he was not a rabbi, only a teacher of elementary grades.

"When you teach the *aleph-bet,* it is easier to be completely honest—after all, an *aleph* is an *aleph.* . . ." He supported seven children on his meager salary as Hebrew teacher, but was not complaining. "After all, I'm working now on my second million—with my first million, I didn't make out so good." He showed me through the Yeshiva, a terribly run-down structure with scuffed floors and splintered wooden furniture. It was empty because all the boys were studying at summer camps, but we came across one blond lad seated alone at a desk over a large folio of the Talmud.

"He is a *masmid,* a student who studies day and night, and also a *tzaddik,* a saint," said Wasilski, within the hearing of the embarrassed boy, whose face turned red and who did not look up from his text. We left the student alone and went to the room where Wasilski conducted his classes. He insisted that I sit at the teacher's table while he sat behind one of the old wooden pupil's desks. I asked him to tell me about his own connections with the Bratzlaver Hasidim; perhaps he could begin by telling me exactly what a Bratzlaver Hasid was. He asked me to bear in mind that he was not an authority on Bratzlaver Hasidim, "That is not so simple." He smiled hesitatingly. "The way I see it, when the Messiah comes, we will all be Bratzlaver Hasidim, but perhaps I can tell you how I came to it. I was born in Lithuania, a Litvak—they are not Hasidim, you know. They stress mainly the study of Torah, rather than the hidden teachings. It was when they sent me to study at the Branover Yeshiva, after my bar mitzvah, that I first met some Bratzlaver Hasidim."

It was hard to say exactly what attracted him, Wasilski reflected. "Maybe there was some *gilgul,* some reincarnation, in me that attracted me to their stories. Maybe their way of prayer. You know something about the way Bratzlaver pray, yes? They try to spend at least an hour alone every day talking with God. 'A man who does not have an hour alone to himself is not a man,' said the rebbe." The best time for this prayer was at midnight, but, of course, this was difficult in some circumstances. But, once up, you could stay up to fulfill a custom which the Talmud ascribes to the *vatikin,* the first ones, who were careful to time the saying of their prayers with the first rays of sunrise. In addition, a Hasidic Jew had to put on two sets of phylacteries before his morning prayers. Usually this second set, donned according to the ritual of the tenth-century Rabbenu Tam, was not put on until the man was married.

"That is because it is forbidden to have 'strange thoughts'— you know what I mean—especially when you are wearing the phylacteries. It's easier to avoid these thoughts when you are married."

Wasilski told me that he had visited Jerusalem, where his friend was the Rosh Bayit, the head of the household, as Bratzlaver call the man who, though not a rebbe, is regarded as a spiritual leader. Wasilski had spent five years with him in Siberia and in Tashkent during the war. Only last week he had sent him a *qvitel,* a note that Hasidim send to their rabbi, requesting a prayer of intervention and offering a monetary contribution. The Rosh Bayit was accepting the donation and offering the prayer, but with the understanding that it was being offered not in his own name but in the name of the "true *tzaddiḳim*." The *qvitel* had been sent, Wasilski said, after he had recovered from a jaw infection which had prevented him from speaking or eating for five days.

"When, for the first time, I could open my mouth, I understood again what it means to pray. What does a man want to say when he is suddenly given life after thinking he is finished? What are the first words, but praise and thanks to God? If one could always have that kind of awareness, he would never sin."

Wasilski apologized for his sermonizing and asked permission to relate another personal ancedote. Some years ago, his little son, who was just learning to talk, had come to him in the living room of their house and said, *"Tate"* (father).

"What do you want, my child?" Wasilski had asked, but the child did not say what he wanted. He had only repeated the word *tate* in a tone "which almost made me cry—as if he were trying to say something. I kept on asking, What is it, *mein ḳind?* till I suddenly realized that he was not asking. He was saying something. He was saying, *'Tate,* I know you are there if I need you; I know you will take care of me if I'm hungry, if I'm sad.' He was telling me that he trusted me, that he was glad I was there. I forgot all about it until Rosh Hashanah, when I was praying here. I pray in a corner in the synagogue, and the prayers of the congregation are nice. They were nice and yet something was wrong—with my own prayers. I thought to myself, here I am after so many years, of trying to pray and learn but my prayers are on a lower level than they were when I was a child in the yeshiva. I felt worse and worse, and my prayers grew more and more weak until suddenly I thought of my son. I turned to the corner and started saying over and over again, *'Tate, Tate.'* Just that over and over again. I don't remember what happened except that when I looked down, the floor was wet with tears, and I knew I had been praying."

But didn't all Hasidic groups agree with this emphasis of prayer, I asked?

Wasilski shrugged. He was no expert, but thought that some of them, like the Lubavitcher movement, stressed *chakira,* intellectual effort and logic. Bratzlaver, on the contrary, wanted utter simplicity and warmth of feeling. It was this kind of warmth and enthusiasm that he tried to instill in his young students by telling them the stories of Rabbi Nachman. "Why not—the stories are holy Torah, but the rebbe himself, when he gave permission to his Hasidim to print them, said that 'in any case, they are nice stories.'

"You know them? The first story, for example, about the daughter of the King?"

Wasilski proceeded to refresh my memory. A king has an only daughter whom he loves dearly, but one day, in a moment of anger, he says, "May the No-Good-One take you." The next day, the princess is missing. The king is brokenhearted, for it was only a thoughtless word that had come to his lips, and he mourns for his lost daughter. The second-to-the-king, as he is called in the story, promises to find her and sets out on his quest. After years of wandering in the desert, he comes to a palace and meets her. She tells him he can take her back if he will fast for a year and on the last day of the year neither sleep nor eat. But when the last day comes, the second-to-the-king forgets his promises, eats some fruit from a tree, and falls asleep. The chance to rescue the princess is lost. But he receives a message that he can find her in a "pearl palace on top of a golden mountain." Again he begins looking, but nobody has ever heard of such a place. But he persists. Finally he comes to a wild man. "A kind of Tarzan," Wasilski describes him to the children. This "Tarzan" is in charge of all the wild creatures. He too tells the man that there is no such place as a pearl palace on top of a golden mountain. He has undoubtedly been fooled, says the Tarzan. But since the seeker persists, he refers him to his brother, who is in charge of the birds. The latter also insists that there is no such place, but he calls together the birds, who affirm that in their travels they have never seen a pearl palace on top of a golden mountain.

The seeker is finally referred to the third brother, who is in charge of all the winds. This brother also discourages him but agrees to call together the winds and ask them. The winds report that they too have never seen anything resembling the sought-for palace, but then one wind arrives late, explaining that it had to bring a princess to a pearl palace on top of a mountain. What do they hold precious in that place, asks the third brother?

"Everything is precious there," replies the wind, and the second-to-the-king sets out for the mountain, where he finally succeeds in rescuing the princess.

"But I have spoiled the story," Wasilski said, shaking his head. "It should be told exactly as it is written, and important to the story are not only the words, but the gestures, even the sighs of the teller."

He appeared a bit crestfallen, and I understood what he meant. The usual Bratzlaver reading of Rabbi Nachman's stories is interspersed with admiring sighs, shakings of the head, and an occasional suggestion of deeper implications. Although Bratzlaver Hasidim are urged to read the stories without too much analysis, in practice teachers are given a few hints of their underlying meaning. Thus, the lost princess in the story Wasilski summarized is understood to be the *shekina,* the presence of God, and second-to-the-king is Israel trying to restore the kingdom of God to its original harmony. The pearl palace on the gold mountain is the hope and dream that there is a place where "everything is precious—everything," not only what the world recognizes as important, but the tear that nobody saw, the life apparently wasted. As for the stubborn insistence that what one seeks is really there, this is the meaning of religious faith, and sleep, which the Talmud calls a sixtieth part of death, is always, for Nachman, the symbol of chaos and waste. By sleep he meant any form of existence which diminished consciousness—involvement with the vanities of the world, mindless pursuit of physical pleasure, or sleep in a simple bodily sense. Hence, it was only natural for Wasilski to want to introduce me to his suitcase of books, although it was already almost midnight. I told him it was rather late.

"Of course," he said, "we are accustomed to begin at midnight." He contented himself with showing me a few pictures which he had taken in Jerusalem the year before. He let me examine a photograph of the wooden chair of the rebbe in the corner near the small curtained ark. Above were the fluorescent lights with their black painted inscriptions of donors. There was a picture of the Rosh Bayit, the gray-bearded man with the thick eyeglasses who read the rebbe's stories every Sabbath morning. Then I saw a snapshot of a young lad with

a conical black hat, friendly dark eyes, and long earlocks. I recognized
him as the Arele who some years ago had appointed himself as my
guide into the world of Bratzlaver Hasidism. He had cheerfully regaled me with frightening tales about the whippings and torture which
the sinful soul endures the first few days after death. Arele had taken
me home to meet his father, a Rabbi Cheshin, whose large blue eyes
had widened when I told him that most American women did not
keep the monthly law of ritual immersion. "But then the children are
born with a *p'gam,* a defect," he had exclaimed.

I apologized for lingering over the photographs. Wasilski
walked me to my car and offered to introduce me next time to a
Rabbi Rosenfeld, who, he said, was converting American youngsters
into Bratzlaver Hasidism against the will of their parents.

"He himself is almost American-born, and he uses all the modern
methods, even tape-recordings."

Before we parted, Rabbi Wasilski gave me several copies of a
small paper-bound booklet called *Tikkun-Klali, a General Reparation,*
containing ten psalms which the rebbe had urged his followers to read
frequently. They were especially recommended as a repair for the "sin
of the covenant," a euphemism which alluded specifically to an in-
voluntary seminal emission and the general category of sexual misde-
meanors.

The Converts

Several months passed before I could take advantage of Rabbi
Wasilski's invitation to meet the Brooklyn brand of Bratzlaver Hasidism. Several times I called without finding Wasilski in, which was understandable, since he taught from a quarter to nine in the morning
until three o'clock every day, then returned in the evening to teach until ten at night. Then I lost the card with his name and phone number.
The operator insisted that nobody in Williamsburg spelled his name
the way I was trying to spell it. After several attempts at alternative
spellings, I was about to give up on the theory that the powers "above"
were obviously not interested in seeing this meeting take place, but
my final attempt at spelling succeeded. When I told the rabbi of my
difficulties, he assured me that they were a sign that "those above" did
very much want us to meet. Bratzlaver followers believe that all good

things are surrounded by *mini'os* (obstacles). "If it's easy, it's a sign that it isn't good." We finally made our date for the next Sunday afternoon, which turned out to be another sign of divine favor, since it was a sweltering hot afternoon.

On the way to Rabbi Rosenfeld's house, Rabbi Wasilski good-humoredly discussed the problems of teaching a Bratzlaver brand of Hasidism in the United States. He was more interested in teaching a spirited Orthodox Judaism than the specific tenets of his own Hasidic school. In class, the rabbi tried to teach his children not only with words but by example. For instance, he would often take his *peyot* (earlocks), which he usually wore tucked behind his ears, and wear them hanging down before his ears. "Next time the child goes to a barber, he may ask the barber to leave his earlocks grow." The earlocks, the *tallis koton,* the beard—"It is all part of the outer guard," said Rabbi Wasilski, continuing his good-natured preaching. "After all, if we go dressed like this, there are certain places we can't go, and things we can't do. It's like, what do you call it, a safety belt in the car. It helps prevent accidents."

The rabbi told me about the group I was about to meet. Rabbi Rosenfeld had been brought to this country when he was one year old and, though he spoke Yiddish, was more comfortable in English. He was a teacher in a local Talmud Torah and had "converted" several dozens of young people, most of them from nonreligious homes, to a full-spirited Orthodox Judaism of the Bratzlaver variety. These conversions had often evoked the vigorous opposition of the children's families, some of whom had called in the police to protest Rabbi Rosenfeld's "kidnapping." Despite opposition, the rabbi enjoyed the devoted following of young people, who would let nothing, not even parental opposition, stand in the way of their faith. The young men in the group usually met Saturday evening, but I was going to meet a newly organized women's group. They were ladies who had become devoted followers of Rabbi Nachman, even though most of them came from nonreligious homes.

Rabbi Rosenfeld lived on the first floor of a brick apartment house. With his short-cropped hair and open-collar shirt, he was, as Rabbi Wasilski had said, an American-style rabbi in appearance. Very American style too were the women waiting for us in the foyer. I had expected to find some elderly ladies. Instead, I saw six or seven girls who appeared to be scarcely out of their teens. Some of them even wore the long black stockings currently in favor among young elements in suburbia or Greenwich Village. Their hairdos were also in the latest fashion. Most of them were married, and all of them had visited the grave of Rabbi Nachman in the Soviet Union, in Uman, last year. Two of the husbands, young bearded men, were also present. We walked into the small living room. The girls giggled when somebody complained that there was no *mechitza,* the traditional Orthodox barrier to divide men from women.

Rabbi Rosenfeld, seated in the center of the room, preceded the "lesson" with an apology for not having a more intriguing subject to present, but he wanted the instruction to proceed "in order." On Saturday evening, he explained to me, a group of young men met here and listened to a tape recording which Rabbi Rosenfeld had prepared in previous years. These recordings were all in English, with every kabbalistic and Hasidic term carefully explicated. There was some kabbalistic significance even in the fact that tape was being used to teach Hasidism. Tradition classified existence into four levels, ranging in order from top to bottom: "speaking" (referring to man); "living" (animals); "vegetating" (plants); and "silent" (inanimate matter). In the Kabbala of the Ari, when man ate *chai* (animal), he thereby lifted the holy sparks of that level upward. A *tzaddik* "like Rabbi Wasilski," here Rabbi Rosenfeld grinned at his friend, who waved back in mock gratitude, "can even lift the level of 'vegetation' up and thus skip a level. Through the tapes, we take 'silent' (inanimate matter) and bring it up to the level of 'speaking.' "

The discussion proceeded in this bantering yet utterly serious style. The stories in the Talmud or in the Bratzlaver tradition were to be listened to, even if at times boring, since stories contained "higher" truths than even the laws of the bible. They were the "clothing" of the Kabbala, and a person listening to them was thereby in touch with the very highest sphere, even if he was not conscious of the hidden truths he was imbibing.

The actual "subject" of the lesson concerned a "difficult" subject, namely, the spiritual level of a man's "second *zivvug,*" his second marriage.

"You know that according to tradition, a man must not be alone. Whether he likes it or not, he has to get married."

The girls exchanged giggles, and Rabbi Rosenfeld continued. "It is said that after God created Adam and Eve, He created Man, which is interpreted to mean that man was only complete after he had received his wife. An unmarried man is an incomplete man. The question here is, what is the spiritual status of a second marriage, in case a man becomes a widower or is divorced?"

It was clear, according to the rabbis, that the second marriage could not equal the spiritual level of the first. As an example of this point, the rabbi related a saying of the Baal Shem Tov to the effect that after his first wife died, he was "only half a man." If his first wife had lived, he, the Baal Shem, would have been able to have his *histalkut* (death) in the "market place." The point of this remark was a comparison with the *histalkut* of Elijah, which took place far from civilization (that is, Elijah had to first leave the physical behind in order to achieve a high spiritual level, whereas said the Baal Shem Tov, "I could have risen up even in the market place"). There were other involved comparisons, including a reference to Rabbi Nachman's second marriage. His wife was ill a great deal, and there were other problems. "But his second wife was so pure and holy that she consented to be Rabbi Nachman's wife even under the difficult conditions he laid down, namely, that they should not live together as man and wife in a physical sense. Imagine what purity and holiness it takes for a woman to accept a marriage under such conditions."

Yet, even with this kind of a second wife, and she had been the one mainly responsible for erecting the house marking the grave of Rabbi Nachman, he could not attain the spiritual level of the first *zivvug*. "The moral is that no matter how bitter your fate with your first wife, make the best of it." Rabbi Rosenfeld cast a glance of mock suffering in the direction of his wife, a buxom young woman, who smiled back in return. To my side, Rabbi Wasilski heaved a few deep groans.

The rabbi was about to continue his lesson, but I was unwilling to let the topic go by so easily. It seemed to me that the Bratzlaver school of Hasidism was unusually concerned with the Lilith aspects of the feminine element in the world. Rabbi Nachman's teachings were filled with warnings about the evil thoughts that women could arouse in a man. I also knew that Bratzlaver Hasidim, in Jerusalem at any rate, felt very strongly about not seeing women around the synagogue. "A reverse form of lewdness" was the way one woman visitor had characterized their attitude, but she might have been prejudiced by the fact that she was spat upon by a Hasid when she opened the door of the women's section to catch a glimpse of Rabbi Nachman's chair. Finding myself with what seemed a unique opportunity, I asked the young Bratzlaver ladies if they did not sense this antifemale, second-class status in their religion.

"Oh, no," they burst forth together.

I presented the arguments I had often heard from "emancipated" women when talking about the status of females in the Orthodox tradition—the menstrual taboos, the *mechitza* segregating sexes in the synagogue, the shaven heads and the wigs.

The "victims" of this male-dominated religion exchanged giggles and again denied that they were suffering. They certainly appeared to be quite happy with their lot. And—was it Satan's influence or just the high fashion of their very tasteful wigs? I found them quite feminine and attractive. One lady who was wearing long black stockings began to answer me, then hesitated. Rabbi Rosenfeld encouraged her to speak her mind.

"On the contrary," she burst forth with animation, "we feel sorry for the housewives who feel no purpose, whose daily accomplishment consists simply of buying more things from the supermarket. We have something important to do, no matter what our circumstances. Why, even an old Jew, sick in bed, if he is religious, feels that he has something important to do. He can study a few more minutes. He has a mission to carry out."

"Perhaps you would like to hear these girls tell you how they came here?" Rabbi Rosenfeld asked. "There are some interesting stories, for most of them came from nonreligious homes and with great sacrifice to themselves."

This was exactly what I wanted to hear, but the girls were reluctant to speak personally about their conversions. Finally, the girl with the black stockings told her story. It had started with a friend who lived in her apartment house, who had occasionally given her

advice and help. At first she didn't know that this advice had anything
to do with Bratzlav. But the *eytzos,* the advice, had worked. Only
later did she find out that this advice came from Rabbi Nachman,
and she began reading the books and ultimately joined the group
led by Rabbi Rosenfeld. Here she had met a young man who had
undergone a similar experience, and they were married. She had gone
last year to visit the rebbe's grave in Uman, and it had been the most
fulfilling experience of her life.

Exactly what were these *eytzos,* and how did she feel helped by
them, I asked.

"For example," she answered, *"hisbod'dus,* the practice of being
alone every day for a while and talking aloud with God." This could
be done by simply going into one's room and locking the door, then
not being ashamed even if others thought you were crazy when they
heard you talking this way. The result of this and other "advice" was
a sense of being closer to *ha-Shem,* the Name, and strength and joy.

"We haven't got a forest here for *hisbod'dus,* like Rabbi Nachman recommended," said Mrs. Rosenfeld.

"Nor a cliff," added her teen-age son who had joined the group
while we were talking. "You know the story about the rebbe who
walked over a cliff while he was in *hisbod'dus* and then walked back
without even noticing."

What are some other of these *eytzos,* I asked again.

"*Simcha* (joy), *hisbod'dus* (contemplation), and *hischazkus*
(strengthening)," Rabbi Rosenfeld took over now. "These are old
Jewish ideas, but with Rabbi Nachman the old became new again.
Hischazkus, especially, is the key. That means that a person should
never despair. 'Jews, don't despair,' was the constant cry of our rebbe,
may his memory be a blessing. Even if a Jew has been trying all his
life to reach a higher level but feels that he goes forward two steps
and back five, still he should not despair, for a Jew has in him the
divine spark which will always see him through."

But this is advice which can be found in many places, and the
Orthodoxy of Bratzlav is the Orthodoxy of any Hasidic group. "What
is it that draws these young people here?" I asked.

Mrs. Rosenfeld pointed her finger at her husband, smiling, and
the others nodded.

Rabbi Rosenfeld denied that he was the attraction. "Of course, Bratzlav is but part of the crown of Jewish Orthodoxy. But it is the purest jewel in that crown. Furthermore, you will find that our group, unlike some other Orthodox groups, do not attack. We do not feel it necessary to make others smaller, even though we know that our way is the best."

I was eager to get back to the "witnessing" and asked a young bearded man sitting at my side if he wanted to "testify."

"If you don't mind," he replied, "I would like to turn the tables and ask you why you are interested in us." In fact, he suspected the motives which had brought me there. After all, he knew that I was personally not Orthodox. Was my interest in the group anything more than the interest I might show in a Buddhist group? Didn't I suspect that he and the others in the room were "leaning upon crutches" with this kind of Orthodox faith?

The others were disturbed by the aggressive tone of my questioner. I tried to avoid a debate, saying that Rabbi Nachman had no confidence in the kind of truth that was attained through philosophic discussion or argument. "A simple, natural faith" was the ideal he held forth to his disciples.

The young man was not satisfied. He wanted to continue discussing my "sincerity," but Mrs. Rosenfeld told us it was time for supper.

"He had to endure a lot of violence," Rabbi Wasilski whispered to me, explaining the aggression of my attacker. "There were times when he came here with his head bandaged by blows from his father, who disapproved of his religious feelings. All the young people here had difficulties at home. The girls had to set up their own dishes and keep Sabbath, despite the wishes of their families. But in his case the reaction was really violent."

During supper, Rabbi Rosenfeld's five-year-old daughter regaled us with a number of Hebrew songs and a rendition of the blessings recited after meals. Rabbi Wasilski ran out of the room in mock horror at the child's liberal use of God's name for entertainment purposes, and the others laughed. Later, as we walked across the street to the synagogue for the evening prayers, my antagonist spoke to me more calmly about his preference for Bratzlaver over other brands of Hasidism.

"The others, for example, try to run away from their sadness and the work by a dance. But not us. We don't run away."

"What he means," added Rabbi Rosenfeld, "is that the Bratzlav way is to seek out the joy that is in the sadness—not to forget the sadness."

In the synagogue I was shown the classroom where Rabbi Rosenfeld had made most of his spiritual conquests. "The age of eleven and twelve is the best age for influencing young people," he said. "We have had some success too with college youngsters, but it is much more difficult."

We prayed quietly. Some boys took out a *gartel,* the black band worn by Hasidim during prayer, and wrapped it around their waists. Rabbi Wasilski recited the final *kaddish* prayer.

Following the service, everyone went to the house of another young disciple of Rabbi Rosenfeld. A party had been arranged here for another member of the group who had been married the night before. Rabbi Rosenfeld had not been invited to the wedding because the parents had still not forgiven him for "converting" their son into a Bratzlaver Hasid, but now the "gang" was together with their mentor. Most of the young men present were in their early twenties, clean-shaven and neatly dressed. Some of them were in college, others were married and working as Hebrew teachers. Their wives were gathered in another room of the small apartment. There was nothing about these young people in terms of external appearance to designate them as Bratzlaver Hasidim.

"They are as different from my kind of Bratzlaver as the moon to the sun," Rabbi Wasilski confided with a cheerful groan.

I could not stay for that part of the evening when each person was supposed to offer a word of Torah in honor of the young bridegroom. I drove Wasilski home, and he told me about the objections which some mothers raised when they saw their children becoming too religious. "Maybe they're afraid that they will grow up not to care enough about money." We started talking about the affinity which Bratzlaver Hasidim seem to have for poverty. In the stories of Rabbi Nachman, the heroes are usually beggars who turn out to be truly rich. Money is associated with Satan.

"It is not that we have anything against being well-off. But, evidently, when it comes to money, the *Baal Davar,* the 'Master of the Business'—Satan—takes a hand. He knows when to interfere, because Bratzlav is the real thing that he fears. So he makes it hard. But we're not against money."

I had found this out, I said, for one of the young girls had bashfully but firmly gotten me to contribute to the Bratzlaver Yeshiva and synagogue that were being built in Jerusalem's Meah She'arim.

"That was something else. But as far as personal needs—how much money does a person really need to get through this world? How many gallons of gas does your car need—ten, twelve? You don't put extra tanks here. Look, I don't complain because there are no mattresses in the car or it's too narrow for comfort. Soon I'll be home and then I'll have everything I need. Meanwhile, I'm just on the way."

I dropped Rabbi Wasilski off near his house and continued on my own way, trying to make some sense out of the vivid but jumbled impressions of the day. What was it about Bratzlav which could attract young people of the type I had just met? Why not a more normative Jewish Orthodox way? The answer I had received was *eytzos,* concrete personal guidance through the example and the teachings of a rebbe. But why a dead rabbi like Nachman of Bratzlav, rather than leaders of groups like the Lubavitcher, or the Gerer, or any of the dozen heads of Hasidic sects in Brooklyn or Israel? "Better a dead rebbe who is alive, than a live rebbe who is dead," Rabbi Rosenfeld had explained. Could it be that in some ways a dead rebbe can be more "present" and more responsive to the needs of a soul precisely because he is not alive and subject to the limitations of the human condition? Perhaps. But there was also something about this dead rebbe; Buber had used the word "strenuous" to describe the special quality of Nachman's seeking. Adin Steinsaltz in Jerusalem had suggested that the Bratzlaver way should be described as tortuous; its goal is an utterly simple faith, but this was pursued through twisted paths. Evidently there are souls who need help for their battle against the adversary, and no one is better qualified to offer such help than a man who has himself struggled with the adversary—struggled and fallen and risen, as it is written: "Seven times shall the *tzaddik,* the righteous man fall, yet also rise."

The Bratzlaver Concept of the Tzaddik

As we have seen, Hasidism, by definition as well as historic fact, stresses the importance of the righteous leader, the *tzaddik* or *rebbe*. Its opponents vigorously criticized this tendency to venerate men or think of them as intermediaries with God. But Hasidim were always able to quote biblical and Talmudic sources which asserted that there were indeed men, such as the prophets, who were endowed from above as well as appointed below to act as special vessels of blessing and power. Despite rivalries, however, Hasidim recognized that "every sun should have its own heaven," implying a tacit agreement that each of the various schools should stick to its own territory.

Nachman of Bratzlav got into considerable trouble during his lifetime because he disturbed this arrangement. There probably has been no Hasidic leader who felt so deeply about the importance and function of the *tzaddik,* whom Nachman sometimes called a master of prayer, or in one of his favorite images, the "master of the field."

> *There is a field*
> *Where trees and plants*
> *Of indescribable beauty grow,*
> *Ineffably precious.*
> *Fulfilled is the eye*
> *That has once glimpsed it.*
>
> *Trees, plants,*
> *Holy souls are they,*
> *Growing, becoming.*
>
> *Wait they must,*
> *For the master of the field.*
> *Only he can mend, replant.*
>
> *Some can be mended*
> *Only by another's death, another's deed.*
>
> *He who would become master of the blissful field*
> *Strong must be, a tzaddik, strong and wise,*
> *Capable of mounting to the highest. . . .*

Another image Rabbi Nachman used for the *tzaddik* was the "banker" who "exchanges" all bad qualities for good ones. He "finds the one point of light . . . the point of good and self-respect in each person which he must be conscious of in order to strengthen his belief in himself."

The true *tzaddik* could be recognized by several characteristics, according to Rabbi Nachman. For one thing, he must suffer great humiliations and must be able to accept these humiliations in silence, for only then can he be brought into contact with the "root of his repentance" which is the "mending power" of his life. The *tzaddik* has himself never sinned, but he is a constant *baal t'shuvah,* a penitent who begs forgiveness for not having yet attained a higher spiritual level than he has already reached. To remain on a given level, no matter how exalted, is a sin. Thus the *tzaddik's* life is one of perpetual restlessness and movement, demanding ever greater purity and holiness. But since it is only dissatisfaction with the place and condition in which he stands that tells him when a new effort is required, the "ascent" must always be preceded by a period of "falling" spirit. Every "descent" constitutes both a challenge and an opportunity.

But the "falls," the periods of "waning," cannot be utilized by a man who is chained by memories which remind him that his efforts to ascend in the past have failed. This sense of "oldness" is the prime instrument of Satan. It "deludes men into believing that everything goes on in the same order, and that a person is already old in his ways and cannot turn from them." The remedy for the sense of "oldness" comes through contact with the true "righteous leaders, who renew themselves like the phoenix, fulfilling the Scripture: 'And those who hope in the Lord renew strength.'" For if one will understand that he can meet the power and goodness of God in any place, he will then know that there is never any cause for despair. Indeed, when one feels most removed from God, one is at the point where contact can again be made. 'By feeling the pain and the longing, the yearning to be again face to face with his Holy Presence, one already creates a bond which raises him infinitely high. . . . It is thus that the very descent into hell and the abyss of evil can become the ascent to the highest."

Nachman's essential teaching was this repeated insistence that the troughs of life are to be used as preparations for new soarings of the spirit, and his conviction that in this effort we are united with the deepest will of the universe. Of course, the doctrine that "every ascent must be preceded by a descent" is a standard teaching of Judaism's hidden wisdom. What gave it freshness for Bratzlaver Hasidim was the emphasis that their rebbe, a "moon personality," placed on a constant struggle with "fallings." What antagonized other Hasidic groups, however, was Nachman's insistence that in every generation there was only one true *tzaddik*. And, Rabbi Nachman more than hinted, he was the Moses-Messiah figure of his time.

The record of the fierce debates aroused by Rabbi Nachman's personality in his day, which have been collected in a special volume called *Elim Trufoh,* help to explain why Bratzlaver Hasidim emphasizes *hitchazkus,* stubborn self-strengthening. Such strength was needed not only for the inner battle against the *Baal Davar* (Satan), but for outer battles with other Hasidic groups.

It is not easy, within the complex and highly interrelated world of Hasidism, to single out the characteristics of a specific school. The followers of Rabbi Nachman, however, point to the fact that groups of Bratzlaver Hasidim still make the difficult pilgrimage to the grave of their leader in the Russian city of Uman, print and circulate the extensive literary heritage of their movement, have built and continue to maintain an impressive new synagogue in Jerusalem—and all this is done though they have no real organization, no living leader or administrative institution, and no wealth. They are proud of the fact that an elderly Bratzlaver grandfather kidnapped his own grandchild and smuggled him out of Israel because the parents were planning to leave the country for Russia and deprive their child of an Orthodox education. I saw this grandfather one Sabbath in their synagogue, a very old, sick man, almost blind, and toothless. One would never have guessed, watching his quiet prayers, that his stubbornness was responsible for an international police hunt and a political controversy which shook the Israeli government.

Bratzlaver *hitchazkus* is not demonstrated by outer appearances but by reliance on that inner point that exists in every Jew and can never be broken. This was the explanation of a fragile young man who gave daily lessons in a building that Bratzlav called an academy of

higher learning. The only students at that time of day were four old
men and one twenty-year-old. Their teacher was the father of twelve
children, one of whom was paralyzed and another in an orphans' home.
His wife suffered from a mental illness that made it impossible for
her to take care of the house, and the father depended entirely on
charity. To say that this teacher was always overflowing with Hasidic
joy would not be correct; there were days when he was obviously
weary to the point of exhaustion. As he read and explained the writings of Rabbi Nachman, however, his voice grew strong and the light
in his heavily bespectacled eyes grew bright. What was the source of
such strength? Rabbi Steinsaltz suggested that such a strength came
out of weakness. Bratzlaver Hasidim had retreated from the real
world by the simple device of calling it an unreal world. "All of life
is a dream," Rabbi Nachman had taught, "from which a person can
be awakened by the stories of the *tzaddik*."

Whether or not Steinsaltz is right, there is no question that the
main source of Bratzlaver *hitchazkus* is their literary heritage. Those
modern psychological schools that recommend the use of poetry and
literature as a means of therapy could, if they knew about it, use
Rabbi Nachman's followers as living proof of their theory.

The Literary Heritage

In his small classic, *The Earth Is the Lord's,* A. J. Heschel relates the story of a Hasidic sage who once started to study a volume
of the Talmud. A day later, his disciples noticed that he was still on
the first page. Assuming that he had encountered a difficult passage
that he could not resolve, they said nothing. But when a few more
days passed and they saw that their rebbe was still on the same page,
they finally asked him why he did not proceed to the next page.

"But," replied the rebbe, "I feel so good here. Why should I go
elsewhere?"

As in many Hasidic tales, the point is made by hyperbole. But
there is no understanding of Judaism which does not include a comprehension of the fact that for traditional Jews, the study of Torah,
not only the knowledge acquired or even the deeds to which it leads,
but the act of learning in itself is life's peak experience. Hasidism inherited this perspective, while adding what it felt was a necessary

corrective to an excessively legalistic diet: prayer and *aggadah,* the last term referring to the more poetic and legendary aspects of Torah. Once Hasidism had taken the liberty to rearrange the components of traditional spirituality each Hasidic school was permitted to design a menu in response to its own needs. In Bratzlaver Hasidism, the emphasis is on its library of books, whose content consists principally of the aphorisms, parables, commentaries, stories, and life of Rabbi Nachman. This material is supplemented by a collection of prayers, letters, and reminiscences written by Nathan of Nemirov, the man who was originally responsible for collecting and publishing the Bratzlaver literary heritage.

A portion of this library has been translated and made available in popular form by Martin Buber, Meyer Levin, Elie Wiesel, and others. Quite naturally, it is the parables and stories, rather than the more abstruse Torah commentaries, that have attracted their interest, although Buber has produced a highly edited version of *The Journey of Rabbi Nachman* to the Holy Land. It is easy to understand the attraction which Nachman's brief parables might have for a modern reader. There is one, for example, which seems to anticipate twentieth century therapeutic techniques. A prince becomes mentally ill and feels that he has become a rooster. He insists on sitting "naked beneath the table to eat pieces of bread and bone." The king and his physicians despair of curing him, but a wise man comes along and offers to heal him. The latter takes off his own clothes and sits under the table with the prince. When the prince asks him what he is doing, the wise man says that he, too, is a rooster. "And they both sat together until they became used to each other." Finally, the wise man asks for a shirt, telling the prince, "You think that a rooster cannot wear a shirt? Even though he is a rooster, he can wear a shirt." And both of them put on shirts. After a while, he asks for pants and soon both of them are wearing pants. The same process is used to get the prince to eat regular food and, finally, to sit at the table. Nachman concludes his story by saying that every man who wishes to come closer to the worship of God is a "rooster, that is, enveloped in grossness." By the above technique, however, the *tzaddik* can gradually lift up the man, and bring him to the right way of serving God.

The tale resembles Kafka's "Metamorphosis," a story about a

man who feels he is turning into a cockroach, and there are critics who see a literary affinity between Kafka and the Hasidic rebbe. But Buber seems more perspicacious when he declares that Nachman's tales really form an entirely new literary genre. Like Kafka, he makes heavy use of symbolism, but it is a symbolism whose meaning can be largely resolved by familiarity with the kabbalistic and Hasidic imagery that fed the rebbe's imagination. Furthermore, most of Nachman's tales have a clear didactic function, offering a specific way and perspective on life. To be sure, as S. Z. Setzer suggests, there are times when the artist in Nachman gets the better of the preacher. In his early years, Nachman tried to suppress the artist in order to play the role of the religious leader who was expected to teach through traditional forms of discourse, but shortly after his return from the Holy Land, Rabbi Nachman declared, "Now I will begin to tell stories." In the few years left before his death, he began to relate the tales which make up the center of the Bratzlaver literature—the *Thirteen Tales*.

The Thirteen Tales

In his Yiddish translation of these stories, Setzer points out that the reader is offered an unusual opportunity, a glimpse of an artist in the very throes of creation. This was made possible because of the devotion of Nathan of Nemirov, who lived in a different city and would come to the town of his rebbe when he heard that Nachman was about to begin a new tale. Nathan not only recorded the story in the original Yiddish and later translated it into Hebrew, but he often described the circumstances which seemed to call forth the story.

Thus, Nathan records how a discussion about events "in the world" could cause Rabbi Nachman suddenly to say, "and all this has been told in a story . . . ," at which he would launch into his tale. One story about "A Master of Prayer" began while Rabbi Nachman was talking with his cantor and noticed that he was wearing a torn coat. "But you are a master of prayer," the rabbi said, "and through prayer life-feeding forces are made to descend. Why, then, shouldn't you at least have a whole coat?" And a few minutes later, he began, "There was once an incident wherein a master of prayer . . ."

On another Saturday night, Nathan reveals, Rabbi Nachman

was sitting at his holy table and chatting with his followers about how Napoleon had risen to such heights. The Hasidim asked how it was possible for an ordinary soldier like Napoleon to suddenly become an emperor. "Who knows," Rabbi Nachman had said to them, "what kind of a soul he had? Maybe it was exchanged, for there are heavenly chambers where occasionally a soul gets exchanged." Soon thereafter he began a story about two children, one, the son of a king, and the other, the daughter of a serving girl, who were mixed up and exchanged. . . ."

Most of Rabbi Nachman's tales were not, however, triggered by any obvious outer stimulus. They were started, and often continued for days, under the mood which Nathan describes as "and the spirit of the Lord rested upon him." They were spontaneous, yet amazingly compact and logically worked out, rich with multiple allusions. It was as if they had been prepared for years in the realm of the subconscious, a subconscious linked to the kabbalistic lore that he had absorbed all his life. The rebbe himself was aware of the fact that the images and events that he related were influenced by traditional mystic imagery: "Rabbi Simeon ben Yochai discussed the secrets of the Kabbala openly. But before this time, secrets were transmitted in veiled form—through stories." Rabbi Nachman let his followers know that in his stories "every phrase, every word is filled with holy mysteries"; they ought to be read, therefore, in fear and trembling. On the other hand, he added, they are also pleasant stories that can and should be read without elaborate interpretation. It is no surprise then that Bratzlaver Hasidim vacillate between these two approaches when they read the stories today.

The stories themselves, Setzer has pointed out, see reality through the mystic prism of a world in which distinctions between "the organic and the inorganic, life and death, have become blurred, and everything is included in one great life in which everything is of equal importance." The action in most of the stories stems from a predicament where something has been lost, stolen, or somehow taken out of its proper place. Two birds that should be mates live at opposite ends of the world; children who belong in a certain house and family have been interchanged at birth; a king's daughter, imprisoned in a mountain fortress, waits for rescue by her beloved. Everything is look-

ing for its *tikkun,* the repair that will restore the broken harmony and
bring together that which belongs together. There is also a similarity
in the characters. They are usually opposites, like the wise man and
the simpleton, the weak beggar and the powerful hero.

Nachman's most famous story is called "The Tale of the Seven
Beggars." A young boy and girl, lost in the forest, hungry and alone,
encounter, on seven different days, seven different beggars. The first
one is blind, the second one deaf, the third dumb, and so on. Each
of the beggars gives the children a blessing that "they might be as he
is." Later the beggars explain the true nature of their blessings. The
blind beggar, for example, is not really blind, but has "seen" the
source of all that is to be seen in this world, which the mystics call
ayin, nothingness—and is hence blind to lesser realities. The deaf
man is deaf only to the foolish sounds of the world. The beggar with
the crooked neck is crooked only because he refuses to stand straight
in a world which is not yet straight and pure, and so forth.

Within the "Tale of the Seven Beggars," which Nachman never
finishes, telling his Hasidim that the identity of the seventh beggar
cannot be known until the coming of the Messiah, there is a passage
in which the kabbalistic imagery that undergirds all the stories is
laid bare. A number of shipwrecked passengers while away the time
trying to recollect their earliest memories. The oldest remembers
when "the apple was cut from the branch." Another recalls when
"the fruit began to grow." Still younger men remember the taste
and the appearance of the fruit before they were embodied in the
fruit. The blind beggar who is telling the story reports: "And I
remember all the stories and remember nothing." The symbolism
here offers a poetic restatement of the *sefirot* structure ascending from
the lowest and most material (the oldest, which was first to emerge
from the "womb") to the highest, which contains everything but
in form so undifferentiated that it cannot be described.

Another example of Nachman's allusive technique, one that
specifically outlines the Bratzlaver way, is a charming tale about a
wise man and a simpleton. Two friends from the same village
choose different paths in life. One decides to leave home (the old
house of religious tradition) and seek fortune and wisdom in the
outside world. The other remains in his father's house, becoming

a simple and not too skillful shoemaker. His wife occasionally taunts him by pointing to other shoemakers who earn more, but he refuses to be drawn into comparisons. He does his job and insists on being "continually happy." At meals he tells his wife, "Pass me the aperitif," and she hands him a glass of water. "Marvelous liqueur," he says, sipping the water. "Now the golden soup," and again she serves him water. The play is carried on into the main courses where he orders all kinds of meat and vegetables, receiving each time a slice of black bread. "But," relates the tale, "he tasted all these flavors" in the water and bread. Meanwhile, the "wise man" who has studied the whole of science and philosophy has become so smart that he can talk to nobody. Knowing so much, he is always comparing his achievements with others, and this leaves him in a condition of permanent discontent. The tale goes through many cycles, and the two old friends are at last reunited (like the polarized kabbalistic *sefirot,* they attract each other). But the inquiring, analyzing, and skeptical mind of the clever one plunges him into ever deeper quagmires of depression from which he is finally rescued, "brought to dry land," by a *baal shem*. Nathan adds a postscript to the story:

"Understand well what has been told, that one can live out this life with bread and water and a piece of animal skin for covering and yet have a better, happier life than the most clever or most wealthy individuals for, as we can see, the latter are always filled with sorrows. . . ."

Nathan's injunction is central to Bratzlaver Hasidism, but it is also a basic teaching of Judaism itself. The Talmud says that the happy man is he that rejoices in his lot. As with all Hasidic teachings, the living example of the Teacher provides the essential force. In the case of Bratzlaver, which has no living rebbe, this force has to come from recollections of a man who died more than one hundred-fifty years ago. Since that force is still felt, its source, as Bratzlaver followers insist, must have been *gevaldig,* awesomely fierce. In fact, it can still be felt in the words spoken by Rabbi Nachman to his followers at a deathbed scene that has been imaginatively repeated by the Israeli writer, Eliezer Steinmann. The bed-ridden Nachman, wincing in pain, coughing up blood, sees the dark, concerned faces of his disciples:

Brothers, my companions, why do you stand in such black despair today? God is with you, cast anxiety out of your hearts. The creator, be blessed, is good, His name is good. Be happy and rejoice, and trust in the Lord. If you are troubled because of me, God forbid; did I not teach you to be strong? Jews must be strong, and believe in the good. It is forbidden for Jews to be melancholy. Why are your faces fallen, Bratzlaver? God forbid, have you forgotten in your hearts that we have a God, great, strong, and ancient of days. . . . [Rabbi Nachman, it is said, sang out the word "ancient" in a sweet melody.]

He, be blessed, looks down from above upon us, and leads us, and we must go after Him, we must set our feet in the path and go, and go, and go . . . to go and to go, this is the important thing [whispered the sick man]. He will show us the way, all ways lead to Him, be blessed, and the ways are many to Him, as it is written, "In all thy ways shall ye know Him." *We go toward Him in many ways—but not in the way of sadness. Brothers, comrades, why do you worry? God is with you—we have to be happy, to be happy. . . . Remember the high level of every Jew. A Jew with a wave of his hand here can move worlds over there, and if he waves his hand this way, he moves worlds that way. Blessed is man who is created in the Image and has been given control over all the worlds. He is greater even than the angels. If the eye could look into the mysteries of the body, of flesh and blood, it would see that upon every vein and muscle there hang worlds. . . . Why has the presence of joy fled from you? Are you Jews who worry about making a living, who sit and worry, God forbid, about how little money you have? I have always counselled you, Bratzlaver, not to carry in your hearts any fear about making a living. Make a living, or don't make a living—it is all the same. To make a living is good, but if not, it's better yet. And why do we need to care for making a living, when a piece of bread and onion can have the flavor of the Garden of Eden? Or do you fear lest you are not kosher Jews? I say to you that you are kosher Jews, all of you are pious and kosher, but you must be strong, you must be heroes for the battle with the evil impulse, you must hold your place, hold strong!*

The fierceness of the way Nachman bequeathed to his followers is not immediately evident to the casual visitor. A tourist visiting the Meah She'arim synagogue of the "dead Hasidim" in Jerusalem, is likely to be impressed first by the lack of esthetic concern characteristic of Hasidic synagogues, but if he lingers longer he will be struck by what must only be one of the most unusual of literary circles—drawn from poverty-stricken immigrants from Russia, native-born Israelis who are constantly visiting the graves of holy saints, college-educated men and women from America—all coming together daily to read and reread words of and about a man who has been long dead, but is "present" the moment they open their books.

If he stays still longer, the visitor may notice that there is something besides a common literary taste which brings such diverse types together. But how to describe it? Is the Brooklyn rebbe right, who referred to an emphasis on stubborn inner strengthening? Or should one agree with Adin Steinsaltz in seeing the Bratzlaver retreat into a world of poetic fancy as a sign of inner weakness? Or do both qualities, like the polarized characters in Nachman's stories, somehow come together?

In any case, it should be evident by now that the Bratzlaver path is not as simple and direct as it may at first appear. Such fierce demands for naive belief, warnings against despair, and desperate reaching out for joy would indicate that he whom they call the *Baal Davar* is a master in the art of raising obstacles. And none are more tempted by these obstacles than those who follow Rabbi Nachman. But, say Bratzlaver Hasidim, how can it be otherwise? The "obstructor" knows where the treasure lies hidden. Obviously, he will send his strongest agents, erect his most formidable barriers against those who are heading in the right direction. To be sure, this line of reasoning—whereby the "obstacles" are proof that one is approaching the treasure—may tempt a visitor to ask Bratzlaver Hasidim why they should not seek out a school where the outer shells are even more repellent, at least to an outsider. One will not have to go far to find such an Hasidic house—indeed, just across the street, to the synagogue of Reb Arele.

8
EXERCISES IN MODERN HASIDISM

And I believe with perfect faith that He sustains and feeds all the worlds, those above and those below and all the creatures above and below, from the horns of the rhinoceros to the eggs of insects. . . . I believe with perfect faith that no accidents happen which are not intended by Him. Furthermore, I believe that there is no creature above or below that can do good or harm, or act in anything, even the slightest movement, without power coming from Him, be He blessed, for all is provided for by the Owner of the will, the Leader who leads His world with kindness and mercy.

—*From* REB ARELE ROTH, *"The Great Affirmation of Faith"*

Our probing into the world of Hasidism has, so far, been rather cautious. We have gone where the outer shell seemed thin and the fruit easily accessible to a modern mind, we have looked at Hasidism as filtered through the esthetic sensitivities of a Martin Buber or the scholarly analysis of a Gershom Scholem. Even Bratzlav, despite its strange ways, is very conscious of the world it is trying to reject, and there is a great deal of sophistication in the apparently cowlike faith that Rabbi Nachman and his followers try to achieve. But our description of Hasidism must not spare us a visit to groups who appear to be truly "out of this world," even by the Hasidic standards so far encountered.

Reb Arele's followers can be visited not only as an example of Hasidism *in extremis* but because they represent an unusual phenomenon in the Hasidic world, a newly born Hasidic sect. Their late spiritual leader, Reb Arele, was not descended from rebbe stock. He had attracted disciples almost against his will and by virtue of a charisma that Professor Scholem claims was characteristic of the pneumatic personalities who originated the Hasidic movement. Following Reb Arele's death, his followers split between those who followed the son and a larger group who chose the son-in-law as their rebbe. The latter have their center in Meah She'arim, and today worship in a large, still unfinished, concrete structure. Before moving into this new synagogue, they prayed in a small dilapidated wooden building hidden within a courtyard opposite the Bratzlaver synagogue, and it was there that a friend took me one Friday afternoon. Our visit, he told me, would be particularly interesting because it was both Purim and the eve of the Sabbath. This meant that the Hasidim were confronted with a dilemma. On Purim, Jews are commanded to drink till they cannot distinguish between the words of the prayer, "Blessed be Mordecai and cursed be Haman"—an order these Hasidim would probably be careful to fulfill. But it was also Friday evening, the eve of the Sabbath. The Sabbath Queen had to be welcomed in a spirit of pious sobriety.

The dimensions of the problem were clear the moment we entered. Reb Arele's Hasidim had fulfilled the commandment of drinking on Purim to the letter. Some of them were stretched out snoring on wooden benches or under the table. Others were staggering about the rooms, humming snatches of melody, or just sitting stupefied in a corner. The rebbe sat at the head of a long wooden table, his head bowed and his eyes half-closed, watched intently by two or three Hasidim standing at his side. He was, in a manner of speaking, the fusion point of the community soul, as Buber had promised: he, too, was drunk. Nevertheless, he was a strikingly attractive man. "See," my companion insisted, "the long pale, thin face, the blue eyes, the long light hair—just as the *goyim,* the gentiles, picture Jesus."

A teenager with blonde earlocks reaching down to his shoulders wove his way in our direction and peered at me with contempt. "You are Jewish?" he asked in Yiddish. "Where is your beard—what is a Jewish face without a beard? Where is the 'image of God'?" He spat in disgust.

A white-bearded man with twinkling blue eyes came over. "I have a secret to tell you," he promised the aggressive teenager, pulling him away. In a corner of the room, alongside some shelves of books piled in utter disarray, another young man was drunkenly crying on the shoulder of a friend. Here and there, an elderly Hasid sat gazing blankly at an open book. Dozens of children were scampering about the room. When their shrieking became too loud, a squat, dark, muscular man shouted "Sha!" and twisted whatever little ears he could grasp. About five o'clock in the afternoon, as the bright light outside was beginning to dim, this man, evidently the *shamash,* as the synagogue's master factotum is called, came to the center of the table and slapped down a heavy hand.

"*Shabbos,*" he called out, "*muktzah,*" reminding everyone to make sure they were not carrying items on their person which might transgress the laws of the Sabbath.

Immediately the atmosphere began to change. Some of the bodies prostrate upon the floor began to stir; those who were still sleeping were nudged by comrades. The rebbe rose and hurried out of the room, the *shamash* clearing a way for him between the scampering children. Then minutes later the rebbe returned, his long earlocks wet. He had just immersed himself in the *mikveh,* the ritual bath. Others began following his example. Some time later, the rebbe paid another visit to the *mikveh.* Some of the men began rearranging and clearing the tables. Others took books and were trying to read or chant some sections from the Song of Songs. Men who a few minutes before had been sunk in stupor, were desperately trying to throw off their drunkenness. Some of them were still staggering and having difficulty concentrating on the text of their books. It was a remarkable exhibition of mind over matter, but the Hasidim had no choice, for Queen Sabbath was due to arrive in just a few moments.

The extra soul offered every Jew on the Sabbath would be descending—if he was ready to receive it. But "the Holy One does not descend upon His throne" unless the Jew prepares himself below, bringing together his scattered thoughts, purifying his mind and heart, and making himself a vessel worthy of the indwelling *shekina.* When the rebbe returned from going to the *mikveh* yet another time, a graybearded elder approached the wooden stand near the curtain-covered ark at the side of the room.

"Bless ye the Lord who is to be blessed," he chanted in a firm but soft voice. "Blessed be He who is to be blessed for ever and ever." Everyone responded, and the murmur of quiet prayer filled the room that a few moments ago had had the appearance of a flophouse.

Everyone read the prayers to himself, the sound merging into a soft harmony. The individual prayers began to approach the point where all would become quiet for the silent benedictions. Then the reader began to chant the doxology, which marked the division between the earlier blessings and the silent benedictions.

"May His great Name be magnified and sanctified," he called out, "in the world which He has created according to His will, and in which His kingdom shall reign, in your life and in your days and in the life of all Israel may it come speedily and swiftly, and say you . . ."

"Amen," shrieked the man next to me. He was doubled over, his face red, yelling at the top of his lungs, "Amen—may His great name be blessed forever, and ever, and ever."

For a moment I thought he was ill, but then I saw that all the worshippers were carrying on in the same way. The room resounded with a cacophony of shouts. My guide noticed my bewilderment.

One of Reb Arele's teachings is that the response, "Amen, may His great name . . ." be recited, as the Talmud suggests, in an utter abandonment of soul, as if one were willing at that moment to die in sanctification of the name.

The yelling stopped as suddenly as it had begun, as the congregation entered into the inner-directed devotion of the silent benedictions. The prayers continued for another fifteen minutes. When they were over, I started to leave.

"No," my guide stopped me. "Not yet. The most interesting part is about to come."

Again the *shamash* began pushing Hasidim aside to make a path for the rebbe, who now walked quickly toward his chair at the head of the table. Someone brought in a wine cup and loaves of Sabbath bread. Everyone in the room began to crowd about the rebbe. A dozen young bearded men hung over his chair, peering into his face. Those who couldn't get to the long table stood up on benches; a few of the boys climbed up to the windows in back of the chair and perched on the ledges. But as yet very little was happening in the rebbe's corner. He had evidently made the blessing over the wine and bread. Now he called out a few names, and handed out pieces of bread to individuals who excitedly fought their way through the

crowd to receive their marks of favor. Some plates of food were passed
overhead from hand to hand until they were placed in front of
him. Utter silence reigned as the rebbe took a spoonful of rice, put
it in his mouth and chewed.

"The *tzaddik*, the righteous man, is the foundation of the
world," says the psalmist. The Hasidim were feeding their *tzaddik*
as if the sustenance of the world, at least their world, depended on
his intake. For more than half an hour they watched in rapt silence
as the rebbe sampled plate after plate. When a plate was half finished
and relinquished by the rebbe, it was grabbed by the Hasidim and
licked clean within a fraction of a second. Finally, the eating part
of the ritual seemed to be over, or at least to have reached a point of
recess.

"The rebbe is about to give Torah," my guide whispered.
Everyone tried to squeeze another inch or two closer to the white-
dressed figure at the head of the table, who was talking in a barely
audible voice. I was far away but caught some reference to Purim
and the biblical verse, "I will hide my face." In Hebrew the word "I
will hide" (*astir*) is related in sound to Esther, the heroine of the
Purim story. Faith, the rebbe seemed to be saying, required a hiding
of God. If God's presence and mercy are obvious, what merit is
there in believing. The rebbe did not speak long; after about five
minutes he fell silent, closing his eyes as if striving for further inlet
of inspiration. The Hasidim waited eagerly. Then the rebbe snored
lightly.

Of course, in Hasidic tradition, rebbes do not usually sleep. In
fact, the man who had taken me to the synagogue that Sabbath vowed
that he had spent several days and nights with the rebbe and never
seen him sleeping. Catnaps, such as the rebbe was now taking, do
not count. Besides, for the Hasidim, the rebbe's sleep is really the
occasion for the ascent of his soul to spheres where it can be refreshed
in the waters of Eden and return with new inspiration; it is,
therefore, reason for rejoicing. So now the *shamash* jumped on the
table. Lifting one hand high and cupping the other behind his ear,
he began a song. Everyone joined in. The wine of Purim joined with
the "extra soul" of Sabbath and produced an outburst of dancing, singing, and clapping which literally caused the benches and tables of the

little synagogue to shake. The noise ascended in a crescendo of gaiety. A few older men jumped on the table with the *shamash* and began hopping about. Others linked arms and swayed back and forth around the table while chanting snatches of biblical verse. The window panes shook and soon became utterly befogged with human steam. Now the muscular *shamash* standing on the table lifted a three-year-old child onto his shoulders and began to dance. The singing reached a still higher level of noise. And the rebbe? He was sleeping—or in heaven.

At that moment I went to the door to catch a breath of fresh air and saw a group of sedately dressed tourists who had entered the courtyard. They stood looking at the dancing shadows and listening to the noise; their guide seemed to be urging them to leave, but they were too fascinated. They were speaking Swedish to each other, though the guide addressed them in English.

"Wild fanatics," I heard him saying.

Moved by some obscure impulse, I went over to a blonde, middle-aged lady. "They are Hasidim, a pious sect, rejoicing with their rebbe," I declared, as if answering a question. "Probably Jesus and his followers looked like that," I added.

She gazed up at the synagogue and at me, her eyes wide. "Ya," she said politely, "ya," and moved back toward her group. After a few moments, the guide succeeded in leading his charges away.

I'm not sure what compelled me to confuse the already bewildered visitor from Sweden. Perhaps my friend's earlier reference to the Jesus-like appearance of the rebbe, or a desire to counteract the embarrassment of the guide. Perhaps I wanted to suggest that there was something going on in that little synagogue which utterly escapes the quick judgment of the outsider.

But, how can even a sympathetic and informed outsider share the sense of holy joy which Buber and others, insist is to be found in groups such as Reb Arele's followers? The mystic Eden within the gate of Hasidism is, in a sense, more closed than the gates of the Kabbala. The latter discourages with intricate symbolic systems, and one can explain the difficulties by complaining about the absence of competent guides or kabbalistic communities. Hasidim, however, although not so hard to find, discourage the visitor with a seemingly impenetrable shell of strange clothes, customs, and ideas. For example, what would an outsider make of a Hasidic text? Would its basic assumptions and seemingly endless interplay of quotations exhaust his patience? The experiment should be tried.

Reading a Hasidic Text

Take the opening of the book entitled *Shomer Emunim,* keeper of faith, a collection of Arele Roth's talks, comments, and notes; the theme of its first pages might be called, "The Importance of Saying 'Amen.'" Before beginning the reading, a warning may prove helpful. The bible, the Talmud, and most classic religious texts of Judaism are not systematic works, but prefer to discuss a subject in a style that resembles the form of a tree, the ideas shooting out like branches and subbranches in different directions, though rooted in a common trunk. Reb Arele's book follows this kind of order.

Shomer Emunim starts with its root quotation, some words from Isaiah, "Open the gates and let enter a righteous people, keeper of the faith. . . ." What follows is based on the mystic's conviction not only that the words of scripture have revelatory power, but that the shape of their letters, even their numerical equivalent—all are essentially connected to the divine mystery. They are, to repeat Scholem's striking metaphor, like the lines which a voice impresses on a gramophone record. With a proper needle and resonance box, these lines can be made to express something of the original power that brought them into being. Obviously, if these lines are altered, the original impulse cannot be as precisely recovered. Hence, all translation of the Torah is a distortion. The real secrets of the divine cannot be conveyed without the Hebrew word. It is an assumption which makes Jewish mysticism almost incommunicable without a knowledge of Hebrew, but helps us see the purpose of what otherwise would seem only complicated verbal gymnastics.

The argument begins with a quotation from the Talmud.

Resh Lakish [a third-century rabbi] says, "everyone who answers 'Amen' with all his strength has opened to him the gates of the Garden of Eden, for it is written in scriptures: 'Open the gates and let enter a righteous people, the keeper of faith (emunim). *Do not read* (emunim) *as keeping faith but as saying 'Amen.'"* [*The Hebrew word for faith,* emunim, *and* amen *are similar.*] *What is the meaning of Amen? Rabbi Hanina says, "God the faithful king."* [*In the Hebrew,* El Melech Neemen, *the first letters of which compose the word Amen.*])

Having shown that the Hebrew word for faith can be linked to Amen, the main theme is established. The next few pages are an intricate filigree of quotations from the Talmud, the Zohar, and various Hasidic rabbis, emphasizing the importance of saying Amen and the disastrous consequences resulting if one neglects to say it. The mystic picture that gives structure to all Hasidic thought is immediately presented—the conception of an upper group of worlds or *sefirot,* from which our world draws its sustenance. The flow of this sustenance depends on the harmonious interrelationship of these upper worlds. The Holy One, the name given to the central and male component of this divine structure (the middle or body part of the *sefirot*), must unite with the *shekina,* the female, the receiver, the presence. Only then can the flow proceed. Man, by saying Amen with the proper *kavannot,* intentions, can stimulate the unification of these upper *sefirot.* Proof for all this is derived from the fact that the numerical equivalent of the Hebrew letters in Amen is equal to a combination name constructed out of the two Hebrew names for God—which are respectively used to designate the Holy One and the *shekina.* Therefore, "he who answers 'Amen' with all of his strength" gives strength to the uniting of these names, with the result that the upper lights unite, as do the *sefirot* of beauty and *malchut* (otherwise called the Holy One and the *shekina*), and through this act the harsh judgment of the seventy years is annulled (the seventy years symbolizes the seven lower *sefirot*). The Hebrew word *neeman,* faithful (from the previously quoted phrase, God, the faithful king), is linked to two biblical references picturing God as sitting and standing, evoking the erotic imagery of the kabbalistic unification of the Holy One with the *shekina.*

In Reb Arele's book this thought is complicated by numerous quotations and side issues. After more word play, the opening quotation is given its fuller interpretation—namely, that he who says Amen will have opened to him all "Gates of the Garden of Eden" (another reference to the upper *sefirot*). This phrase evokes a recollection in Reb Arele's text of a story about the Holy Ari who, whenever he slept, would have his soul conducted by the Angel Metatron through heavenly gates into palaces above. There the Ari learned mysteries of Torah never before revealed and brought them back to earth.

There follow other examples of the salutory effect of the Amen on the upper *sefirot*. A Talmudic tale describes its importance for those who sit in hell, both Jews and gentiles. When they say, "Amen, may His great name be blessed forever and ever" (in response to the doxology), God hears them. He asks the angels, "Who are they that praise God from the depths of hell?" When told that these are sinners, God says, "Open the gates for them, and let them enter into the Garden of Eden." In this way the reader is told again and again that the worshipper must say, "Amen, may His great name be blessed," literally with all his strength, not caring if his loud voice or physical effort provoke laughter or mockery. "For know my brothers and my loved ones that if you stand before the Holy One, blessed be He, and answer, Amen, blessed be His great name with a loud voice and with proper intent of heart, then this voice rises and breaks down strong gates and shatters locks and splits walls above according to the power of your soul. . . ."

The early pages of the book also contain a copy of a letter written by Reb Arele to one who asks what secret intentions he should have when he pronounces his prayers. Reb Arele discourages him from depending upon mystic incantations or thoughts designed to effect unities in the worlds above. Before the time of the Holy Ari, he points out, there were very few who tried to effect unities by secret intentions and yet there were many, "among them women," who attained to the Holy Spirit because of their holiness. And if a person is not unified within himself he can "unify" day and night and they will "laugh at him from heaven."

My dear child, the main things [writes Arele, lapsing into Yiddish] *is that one should be God's soldier and serve Him day and night . . . and struggle with animal desires . . . and make one's speech gleam with integrity and faith. . . .*

It is written, "In Thy light we see light." But what teaching is there for us in the seemingly extra phrase, "In Thy light"? Do we not observe that there are those who see only darkness in our light? For example, there are those who see only darkness in our house of study and in our fellowship, as you know. Therefor did King David, may peace be upon him, pray, "May we see light in your light"—and not its opposite . . . and this is the grace drawn down only to those "who are Thy knowers," who know Thee. They see the light within the darkness. That is why the scripture follows the phrase, "In Thy light may we see light," with the words, "draw Thy mercy down upon Thy knowers." The first letters of the latter three words make up the Hebrew word for bread. This means that even when they sit near bread they will see a great light before them, and holy sparks within it. But if they are not worthy, they will see in this bread only desires and darkness. . . .

Reb Arele's Hasidim are quite aware that visitors to their Meah She'arim courtyard see only wild primitives, but they feel their days and Sabbaths are suffused with light and high meaning. "Better a day in Thy courtyard than a thousand elsewhere" is for them a statement of simple experienced truth. Like the kabbalists of old, they live in a world of "vertical causation." The phenomena of life are linked not only in the horizontal chain of cause and effect postulated by science, but are even more deeply involved with forces of causation from above. Since these causes can be radically affected by what man says and does below, every word, every set of circumstances is filled with portent. "There are no accidents," insisted the Baal Shem Tov.

Time to Shoot

One summer, it occurred to me that I ought to apply the Baal Shem's dictum to the fact that I had found an apartment for my family near Meah She'arim. One Sabbath morning, at the Bratzlaver synagogue, when I saw Gedaliah Fleer, a young American convert to Bratzlaver Hasidism with serious dark eyes and a strong chin, it seemed that providence was showing its hand quite plainly. Since it was Gedaliah who, at Rabbi Rosenfeld's house, had accused me

of a dilettantish attitude toward religion, he would be glad to act as
my guide for a more strenuous excursion into the orchard of Hasidic
mysticism. I invited him to my home for that Sabbath evening. He
agreed to come and bring with him three American-Jewish girls
whom he had recently converted to the Bratzlaver way. I immediately
decided to invite a few non-Orthodox Israeli friends as a counter-
balance in the debate I was sure would ensue.

My Israeli friends were, of course, fascinated by these pretty
young Hasidim who were ready to offer quiet testimony to their
beliefs. One of them, a petite, blondish secretary, had recently accompanied Gedaliah to Rabbi Nachman's grave in Uman, Russia. She
gave a simple explanation of her conversion, timidly looking to Gedaliah for encouragement. Though born to a nonreligious family, she
had always liked to argue with people about religion. One day she
had met Gedaliah and "lost the argument." She had been attracted
by Rabbi Nachman's advice to engage every day in *hisbod'dus,* that
period of aloneness which Bratzlaver Hasidim use for a private pour-
ing out of their prayers or problems. Then, too, she smiled bashfully,
the girls liked the little dance which was customary after prayers.

"You don't dance with the men?" one of the Israelis asked.

"Oh, no, but we can watch the men dance from the women's
gallery. And sometimes," all the girls giggled, "we dance a bit ourselves."

I asked Gedaliah if Jerusalem Hasidim approved of such behavior. It was, he admitted, an "American innovation."

But, I turned to the girls, didn't they feel uncomfortable about
Bratzlaver teaching? I didn't want to get too specific for fear of
embarrassing my guests, but warnings against carnal desires, adultery,
and lewd imaginings occupy so much space in Rabbi Nachman's
Torah as sometimes to appear almost an inverse kind of sexual stimulation.

The young ladies seemed totally unaware of this problem and
again looked to Gedaliah for an answer. But he was interested in
discussing only one question: Did, or did not Moses receive the Torah
in its present condition directly from God? As far as he was concerned, it was on this that the whole authenticity of Jewish religion
stood or fell. The Israelis in the room quickly responded to his

challenge and the argument flared, but without resolution. Only one point did the Israelis concede, and Gedaliah pressed it home. How could one "know the truth" of something he has never experienced? How could a person either accept or reject the divine character of the commandments, before at least "tasting" these commandments in life experience?

Seeing my opportunity, I told Gedaliah that I had long wanted to try the *mikveh,* the ritual bath. Would he take me to one?

Certainly, he said. But he usually went to the *mikveh* after *hisbod'dus,* which occurred late at night or in the early morning, and this might be a bit difficult. It involved rising about one thirty in the morning and walking to Tel Arza, an empty field which at that time joined no-man's-land on the Jordanian border. I had no choice but to accept the challenge.

Preparations

The days passed, and though I saw Gedaliah frequently at services, I put off making arrangements for our night excursion. In mysticism, all depends on the *hachana,* the preparation, and I was a bit worried. The Talmud puts the Hasid, or pious one, on a very high level. It is a stage that one should arrive at only after traversing a number of lower spiritual rungs, such as wisdom, diligence, and purity. To skip levels was a dangerous matter which might bring on psychic and even physical damage. *Hisbod'dus* in Tel Arza, the *mikveh,* and the prayer of the *vatikin,* the ancient ones who arise before dawn to prepare themselves for morning prayer with an hour of private meditation—these were pretty high levels for someone like myself.

On the other hand, I had been attending the Bratzlaver services for several weeks now. The Hasidim there no longer stared at me curiously: they had even stopped asking me for contributions to the building fund of their unfinished synagogue, a sure sign of my having graduated from tourist status. By now I was also familiar with many of the men who made up the inner circle of this group. There was the short, bearded man with the muscular stockinged legs, known as Nachman the *Shosek,* the silent one, a former acrobat, who for forty years had not spoken except for prayer. Another man,

Eliyahu Chaim, a respected elder, stood alongside the ark during prayer, and whenever he said, "May His great name be blessed," he lifted his hands as if physically and personally setting God upon His throne. Then there was a gray-bearded man with a pointed nose and sharp black eyes, who always sat near Reb Eliyahu Chaim when the latter was teaching. He had to be led through the streets because he would not lift his eyes lest they fall upon a strange woman. I was no longer disturbed by the shouted phrases, heavy sighs, and occasional outbursts of clapping which punctuated Bratzlaver prayer. It now appeared obvious to me that such bodily expressions of feeling were more natural than the inhibited schoolboylike recitation with which most of us are familiar. Long before William James, Hasidim had discovered that outer physical expressions stimulate inner feeling, hence, the fervent weaving and bending of the body during prayer and study.

A Hasidic service also allows every person his own rhythm and style of spiritual work. A person who is healthy cannot be expected to linger as longingly over a petition for physical healing as a person who is ill. The individual who is being attacked by the "obstructor," Satan, with feelings of guilt or despair, may find a few deep sighs and a bit of hand-clapping useful in repelling the attack. Why inhibit these needs by a straitjacketing notion of decorum? Since the service also contains many formulae which the congregation must pronounce together, the total effect resembles the style of a gifted jazz band where individual variations and improvisations alternate with moments of orchestrated unity. I had also come to enjoy the perhaps therapeutic release offered by the simple dance which concluded every service, and the study sessions that were conducted between the late afternoon and early evening prayer.

These services were often led by Eliyahu Chaim, a stocky gray-bearded man, whose eyes lit up like shiny brown mirrors behind his spectacles as he talked. The "collected teachings" of Rabbi Nachman served as pretext for reminding Reb Eliyahu of many stories, some of which seemed directed at me. Thus, one passage reminded the rabbi about the time a Jew in Russia made a wager with his comrades that their rebbe could not, despite his claim, always distinguish a Jew from a non-Jew. To prove his point, a Hasid dressed up a bearded non-Jew in the broad-brimmed hat and long cloak worn by Jews, then sat him at the table during the third meal of the Sabbath. After the meal, everyone said the postmeal blessing. The non-Jew followed his instructions to look at his prayerbook and pretend to join them. Later, the rebbe asked who had invited the *goy.*

"How did you know?" asked the Hasidim. "By the fact that he didn't move when he said his prayers," the rebbe answered. "A Jew can always be distinguished by the fact that he is physically moved by a Jewish word. A Jew is not a stone." It seemed to me that Reb Eliyahu looked toward me as he concluded the story, as if replying to the criticism often made of the gyrations that accompany Hasidic prayer.

A few moments later he told a story about a conductor who once asked some Hasidim in a train for their tickets.

"Why don't you ask the engineers in the locomotive for their tickets?" asked the Hasidim.

"But they're driving the train," the surprised conductor replied.

"So are we," replied the Hasidim.

Again, I suspected that the rebbe might be offering this tale as an answer to the charge that Hasidim spend all their time in the synagogue or at study, sustaining themselves and their families on the charitable donations of others. But Reb Eliyahu may simply have been refreshing his Hasidic colleagues about a central tenet of their faith, the belief that the dynamics of the cosmos are set in motion by the prayers of pious Jews.

"If the *goyim,* the gentiles, knew how important Jews were to God's arrangements, they would follow Jews around begging them to keep meticulously all of his commandments," claimed Reb Eliyahu.

Adin Steinsaltz once likened this perspective to a map in which the importance of countries and cities was marked not by the size of the population but by the number of *mitzvot,* commandments, which were performed in each locale. Sitting those afternoons around the rickety wooden table in the Bratzlaver synagogue, I thought of Adin's map, for on such a map New York and London would be hick towns. Some sections of Brooklyn and Jerusalem would be great capitals. And the "White House" would have been the Bratzlaver synagogue in Meah She'arim!

Most of Reb Eliyahu's stories repeated two or three basic themes. One was the inevitability of death: "A man is rushing to another town for business. 'But isn't there a cemetery in your town?' asks the rebbe. 'Of course there is a cemetery,' replies the man. 'Oh,' said the rebbe. 'I thought you were rushing to another town because your town didn't have a cemetery. But if it is only to enter your own cemetery a few rubles wealthier, why rush?' "

Many of the stories indicated familiarity with the criticism of Hasidism as a kind of madness. The rich tourists came to Meah She'arim to watch penniless, threadbare Hasidim. But who is really crazy—the rich visitors, whose faces are dark with worry and dissatisfaction, or the "strange" Hasidim, who are always singing and dancing? A similar point is made in a parable related by Rabbi Nachman about the time a prophet announced that all who would eat wheat that year would become insane. Only one family believed him, but even they realized that the scarcity of food would force them to eat some wheat. Besides, if they were the only ones to remain sane, the others would consider them crazy. What could they do? They decided to eat the wheat, but to mark their foreheads with a sign so that they would at least know that they were acting insanely. Hasidim made the same choice. Living in an insane world, they wore clothing, observed laws, and kept other signs by which they could at least remind themselves of their insanity. Indeed, said Reb Eliyahu, one must look upon the human predicament as being like the situation of a woman who is being raped in the field: "Though nobody can hear her, she must cry out. If she cries out, according to law, she is not punished, no matter what happens to her." Our whole world is being violated by forces it cannot resist; let it, at least, cry out. "And this crying out," said Reb Eliyahu, "was prayer. Prayer and faith are the same."

This is also the implication of the story told in the Zohar about a pupil of Rabbi Simeon Bar Yochai who, bowed down with sadness and ill-health, met a doctor and asked him for advice. The doctor gave him a prescription, "Wash your forehead with the tears of your eyes." The man followed the prescription—that is, he sobbed out his prayers unto God, and he was healed. "For a doctor is not interested in the fact that a man has a fever but in the *source* of that fever." Prayer can change a man's fate by touching the source of that fate, his inner self. For "if there is a judgment below, there is no judgment above."

The consciousness of death, the commandment to be always joyous, and the power of prayer—this was the message communicated again and again during the half hour of study between the afternoon and evening prayers. Although it did not completely convince me of Hasidic sanity, it did whet my curiosity enough to try the kind of "crying out" which Bratzlaver Hasidim carry on alone "in the desert." I finally agreed to meet Gedaliah at two the next morning for an exercise in *hisbod'dus,* ritual immersion, and prayer at dawn.

Hisbod'dus

At one-thirty I arose, and taking a towel and the phylacteries which orthodox Jews don for morning prayers, hurried toward my appointment. Summer nights in Jerusalem can be cool and moist with heavy dew, and I regretted not wearing heavier clothes. A half moon silvered the stone surfaces and dark windows of the buildings. The only sounds came from the scraping of my shoes on the un- paved rock and gravel streets that connected my home to Meah She'arim.

Gedaliah was waiting for me on the steps of the synagogue, and we started toward Zephaniah Street, where we were to pick up a young man who was going with us. His name, Gedaliah told me, was Yaakov, and he had been born in Jerusalem to Bratzlaver forebears; he worked as a *sofer,* a scribe who copied scrolls of the Holy Torah on parchment. Yaakov's home was on the ground floor of a small apartment house surrounded by a stone wall. Gedaliah knocked sev- eral times softly on the door at the side of the house. "Yaakov," he whispered. Yaakov was recently married, and Gedaliah didn't want to disturb his wife's sleep. In a few moments the door opened, and a fragile looking young man with a blonde beard and warmly gleam- ing eyes, framed by metal spectacles, invited us in. He was dressed in the yellow and black striped robe which is still worn by Jerusalemites descended from the "old community." Yaakov asked if there was any- thing I might like in the way of refreshments and insisted that I take at least a glass of soda water. I looked over the rows of books on the upper shelves of a buffet-like piece of furniture that occupied one side of the small room; it was the standard library of an Orthodox Jew: a set of the Talmud; *midrashim* and other classical commentaries on the bible; commentaries, legalistic works of later rabbinic authorities; and a special Pentateuch used by scribes for their copying work.

"It takes a *sofer* about a year to write a Torah, and the going price these days is about three or four thousand dollars," Gedaliah said as he saw me looking at the scribe's Pentateuch. "Would you like to see the parchment on which I'm working?" He opened a drawer at the bottom of the buffet and took out some sheets of white parchment with gleaming, freshly inscribed black letters, decorated with the fine lines called *tagin*. It is the clarity of the letters, plus the accuracy and elaboration of these *tagin* that mark the work of a good *sofer*.

I expressed surprise at the length of time it took to write a Torah. "My grandfather would take much longer," Yaakov replied. "Each time he came to the Name of God, he would first go to the *mikveh* and purify himself. Well, shall we start?"

We left the house and walked rapidly for about ten minutes until the paved streets merged into an empty field. This was Tel Arza, the Hill of the Cedar. Whatever association with trees it might have had in the past, the Tel Arza I saw was now a stony plot of land with hillocks and valleys that merged into a vaguely defined no-man's-land.

"Incidentally," I asked, "how far away is Jordan?"

Gedaliah pointed to some lights on a hill directly on the other side of the valley.

"It seems very close," I said. "In fact, isn't that the muezzin we hear?" An undulating wail calling Moslems to early morning prayer sounded as if only yards away, but my companions didn't appear to share my concern about our proximity to enemy territory.

"Well, here we are," Gedaliah said, after we had made our way single file along a rocky path that twisted and turned between large boulders and small caves. "Now it's time for work, and we can each go our separate ways."

"Yes, here we can cry out and nobody minds," Yaakov said, turning to me with an encouraging smile. Then, sensing my need for more orientation, he offered me a brief introduction to the philosophy of early morning *hisbod'dus.*

"The rebbe says that pure *emunah,* faith, is natural to every Jew, a part of his blood. Through his sins, however, a person can cloud its original purity. Then come doubts and problems. But a man's most natural condition is one of complete faith; the young child believes what he is told until he learns about lies. To recover this original condition of faith, the rebbe recommended *hisbod'dus* at night in an open field. There, away from the noise of the day and people, in the pure air, he can dig into himself, pierce through the surface layers of doubt to his natural faith. That is the purpose of *hisbod'dus:* to ask for a lighting up of the darkness, so that we can see with the clarity of a child, and rediscover the goodness of God, the holiness of his commandments, and the wisdom of his saints. And we do this simply by crying out our questions and doubts. But now, it's a little late and we have to begin."

With that Yaakov turned and walked off into the darkness.

"Come, let's find a good place for you," Gedaliah took over. I followed him to a small cave whose entrance was blocked by some refuse and a rusted bedspring.

"This might do." He pointed to some steps which had been carved out of the rock alongside the cave. "You can sit here if you want, or walk about. Incidentally, you may see some little animals with bushy tails, jackals. If they come close, just throw a few rocks or stamp on the ground. I'll come back in about three quarters of an hour," he assured me and suddenly was gone.

It took me only a few moments to realize that I was going to have a difficult time just talking aloud, let alone crying out. For one thing, there were a number of practical considerations which immediately occupied my attention. For example, the jackals. True, jackals aren't supposed to attack human beings, but still, I decided to pick up a few stones. This act somehow led me to think of scorpions and the likelihood of their being encountered under stones. My fear of scorpions was an old phobia; I had once heard a man screaming for hours after being bitten by one. I then began wondering about snakes, since they are known to inhabit the kind of cave near which I was stationed. Shoes would have been more sensible than open sandals for this excursion, and perhaps it would be just as well to get away from the cave and into the open field. But there was still the muezzin, or rather the record which is used nowadays instead of a muezzin, continuing its melancholy wail. Why offer too clear a target for any adventurous Arab soldiers? Recently, there had been a number of attacks by terrorist bands in border areas, and there were also Israeli border guards who, seeing some figures strolling near no-man's-land at three in the morning. . . .

Suddenly there was a series of groans emerging from some place over the hill. I couldn't make out the words, but it was a man's voice crying like a child, imploring, sobbing. It was, I realized, one of my comrades in the midst of his *hisbod'dus,* while I was worrying about all kinds of nonsense. Of course, I knew who was responsible for raising all these obstacles to my *hisbod'dus*—who but the *Baal Davar,* the Master of the Thing, as Hasidim call Satan, the Obstructor? It is well known to Bratzlaver Hasidim that as soon as one begins to approach truth, this Master of the Thing begins throwing up obstacles. Well, I wasn't going to let "him" spoil this experience; with an effort I wrenched my attention away from the "terrors that fly by night" to the beauties of the dark sky. The stars were out, slightly clouded by the early morning mist, and the moon was clearly visible in the lower quarter of the sky.

"Lift up your eyes and see who has created these." I decided to launch my *hisbod'dus* with this phrase of the psalmist but immediately encountered a serious obstacle, a heresy that I had frequently heard from my old teacher, Dr. Henry Slonimsky. The power and mystery of the cosmic design as expressed in the starry heavens was a good thing, he used to say, "but what has it to do with the Jewish assertion that the Power which made the heavens was also interested in love and justice?" I thought of Slonimsky, who liked to call himself the "last of the Manicheans," because a huge black cloud was beginning to send probing black wisps over the face of the moon. Then the moon completely disappeared. And since every struggle above mirrors one below, was not this conflict between moon and clouds a symbolic representation of the old Manichean claim that the world was divided between good and evil, God and Satan?

A new series of groans from Yaakov's direction reminded me that such doubts were supposed to be cleared up by crying them out in the predawn air. But could one cry out about a semiphilosophical problem? A groan like Yaakov's could only come from a more personal, more specific kind of question. There was a renewed wail of anguish from one of my invisible companions, and then across the valley the muezzin brought his elongated chant to a wavering end. Wasn't his call also something of a crying out, a call for light where there was darkness? The next moment I was singing to myself, repeating the words "to light up." It was only a home-composed melody, and not much of a groan. In fact, it turned out to be a rather cheery little tune calling for a "lighting up" in whatever area came to mind—Vietnam, my home, the soul. Then the moon emerged out of the clouds for a moment, and I entertained the possibility that my singing had some influence on this fact. It probably wasn't very impressive by Bratzlaver standards, but it was the best I could do; I was even rather disappointed to find Gedaliah's silhouette ahead of me. But it was time to leave: the sky above the hills was now that faint green and red which the ancients took as a signal for beginning their prayers. We would have to hurry if we were going to make the *mikveh* and emerge in time to coordinate the silent prayer with the sunrise.

We saw Yaakov waiting for us on the path ahead.

"Now a *rikkud,* a dance," he suggested pleasantly, holding out his hands. "Lift up your eyes and see who has created these," he and Gedaliah chanted as we circled about. I would have been more startled by the coincidence of his selecting the phrase I had used for my *hisbod'dus* if I were not concentrating on not stumbling on the rocky field.

After a few more moments of circling, leaving me slightly dizzy, we began to walk rapidly back to Meah She'arim. The streets were already beginning to lighten, and there was no time to lose. As we walked, I confessed my difficulty in working up a good, loud *hisbod'dus.* Yaakov was consoling.

"Of course. There are many kinds of *hisbod'dus.* The *hisbod'dus* which prays, 'God, open Thou my lips' is also good."

Gedaliah agreed. As far as he was concerned, the important thing was simply to cry out one's problems every night; then, having deposited the burdens with God, go about happily for the rest of the day.

But why should this sort of nightly meditation lead only to joy and faith, I asked. Couldn't it also suggest illness and tragedy, or remind us of the holocaust, clouding rather than clarifying our faith?

My companions hastened to disagree. God's ways were often obscure, but they were surely good in their ultimate intent.

"The important thing," Yaakov suggested, "is to remember that the world is only a passing illusion. There is a teaching—that when a person awakes in the morning, he must quickly think of the first and second letters of the alphabet. The first *aleph* is like the Aramaic *aluf,* which means learn. The second *bet* stands for the number two. We are to learn and remember that there are two worlds, and this world— what is it but suffering and certain death? The best we can hope for is an easy exit."

I had already encountered the Bratzlaver attitude to death. But how, I asked, could such reflections be reconciled with the constant state of joy that Hasidism commanded?

"That's easy," Yaakov assured me. "It's like somebody who is riding on a crowded bus and has no seat. As long as he knows that he will soon get off, why should he feel badly? It's only if he knows that he can't get off, but will have to stand and stand, that he would have cause for worry. Since all our problems in the world are so temporary, why be sad about them?"

His answer didn't satisfy me, but we had arrived at the synagogue containing the *mikveh,* and I was worried about the next activity on our busy agenda.

The Mikveh

All my knowledge about the nature and importance of the ritual bath in Jewish life was secondhand. I knew that *mikveh* meant a gathering of waters, and these waters had to come from a primary source, like rain, a river, a spring, but not from a stored reservoir. When indoors, the volume of the ritual bath was precisely legislated by Jewish Law—approximately two hundred gallons. Married women who live according to Orthodox tradition are obligated to visit the *mikveh* after their menstrual period; this bath makes them "pure" and fit for cohabitation with their husbands. Failure to do so is a serious breach of the family purity, a sin whose effect may be visited on the lives of children born of such an impure union.

The *mikveh* is also used in traditional Judaism for the ceremony of conversion. A person dips into the primal element of water and emerges new born—a conception very much like that which lies behind Christian baptism, a practice that derives from the *mikveh*.

Men may also visit the *mikveh,* but in their case the act is voluntary, and its breach not classed as a sin. Hasidim feel that a man is commanded to visit the *mikveh* after any seminal emission and try to do so after coitus. Not all Orthodox Jews, however, accept this custom as law. In a mystical movement like Hasidism, however, immersion in the *mikveh* became an act of the highest spiritual significance. In Eastern Europe, it was not at all unusual for pious men to cut a hole in the ice of a nearby river or lake and dip in it not only on the eve of a Sabbath but every morning before prayer.

Like most modern Jews, I didn't really know what inner intent a man was supposed to carry into the *mikveh*.

"There is no ordained blessing," Gedaliah reassured me; "all you have to do is to want to be purified." We were about to use the communal *mikveh* of the Satmer Hasidim, located in the basement of their synagogue. Actually, there would be two *mikvehs*: one would be very hot, but the water in it was probably fresh; the other was cold and its water had probably not been recently changed.

We entered through a small anteroom, placed a few coins in an iron box, then proceeded to the larger chamber which had wooden boards stretched across the moist floor. A few elderly men were in the process of hastily undressing; their nakedness, although briefly exposed, was a chastening sight. The long jackets, the fringes of the ritual undergarment that usually peeked through the shirt and fell over the belt, and finally, the skullcaps which Meah She'arim Jews wear under their broad-brimmed hats, all were removed, leaving skinny limbs, ungainly lumps of flesh and hair, and flabby muscles. The clothes worn by Orthodox Jews may not strike an outsider as attractive, but in the eye of the wearer, they are robes of honor, announcing his membership in a sacred fraternity. When the clothes disappear, the body seems to diminish in dignity. No wonder that the rebbe of a Hasidic sect always went to the *mikveh* in guarded privacy. I remembered the Talmudic anecdote which describes the panic of King David when, after taking off his clothes, he suddenly realized that he was without any tangible sign of his covenant with God, a fright that was ameliorated only when he looked down and saw that one token of this covenant was still with him—the seal in the flesh, his circumcision.

A Czechoslovakian Jew, Jiri Langer, who left his assimilated family in the early part of this century to become a Belzer Hasid in Poland, claims that, in addition to its mystical significance, the *mikveh* helped to guard Jewish life from sexual attitudes which have undermined other civilizations. By forcing Jews at an early age to see each other naked in an atmosphere that neither glorified the physical body nor made it forbidden fruit, it discouraged in the context of holiness, voyeurism and perversions. Langer was fascinated by the erotic aspects of Jewish mysticism, particularly its recognition of the basic conflict in the human psyche between hetero- and homosexuality. This natural conflict was kept in viable tension by letting the Hasid spend most of his time in male company, and the rebbe acted as a legitimate love object, while urging him to fulfill the duty to "be fruitful and multiply" with his wife.

My friends were already in the *mikveh* room, and there was no more time for this kind of speculation. Before me were two large square baths with stone steps descending into the water. Gedaliah was already in the *mikveh* with the steaming hot water. I started down the steps but stopped. The water was scalding.

"Hot enough to boil an egg," Gedaliah agreed. "But you'll get used to it." I tried again, but to no avail. An old bearded man brushed by and walked into the water without a murmur. Again I inserted a foot; it was no use. I was fated for the other *mikveh,* the cold one where the water looked murky indeed. I walked into the water and immersed myself two or three times. Whatever inner intent I tried to have in mind was forgotten at the taste of the water, which I was sure was absolutely filthy. Then it was over, and a few moments later we walked out into the pale morning light, hoping to be on time for the *vatikin* service. The synagogue was frequented by opponents of Hasidism, and worshippers offered their prayers in a simple, businesslike fashion.

The Vatikin

There were about a dozen men in the small synagogue when we arrived, and they were well along in their service. The prayer leader stood in front of a small stand near the ark of the Torah and was rapidly reading the introduction to the psalms. Usually about eighteen minutes were allotted between the beginning of the psalms and this silent "standing" prayer, which begins at the precise moment of sunrise.

My companions and I hastily donned phylacteries. The leader and congregation placed their hands to their foreheads, closed their eyes and chanted, "Hear, O Israel, the Lord our God, the Lord is One." A few moments later, the leader, watching the clock on his table, slowed the pace of his words. Then, as he recited the phrase, "Redeemer of Israel," the buzz of prayer faded into complete silence; this was followed by the quiet murmur of the "standing" prayer, which is supposed to be offered on a level of sound no louder than necessary to carry from "mouth to ears." It had been accomplished: the moon, which for kabbalists symbolizes the *shekina* or feminine presence of divinity, had been united with the sun, its divine husband. The inner structure of the cosmos had come together in that mating, drawing the juices of life into the world. Life could proceed.

Our work done, we left the synagogue. The morning was bright. A small milk wagon, pulled by a donkey, clattered its way along the street. A man with a briefcase was running toward a bus stop. The air was cool and fresh. It seemed to me as we walked toward our starting point of a few hours ago that everything was unusually clear, sharply defined—the curve of an old stone archway, some garbage strewn on the street, the sound of our feet on the empty pavement. I expressed my surprise at not feeling tired.

"When there is *chayut,* vitality, time passes quickly and one doesn't feel tired," Yaakov smiled. "But you should rest a while when you get home."

It was five-thirty when I quietly opened the door of my apartment. Everyone was sleeping. Somehow the thought that I had not slept gave me pleasure, as if I had received a bonus. The gift included not only the hours, but the sights and sounds they contained—the silver moonlight on the boulders, the first glow of light on the horizon, the silence of the morning streets.

Judaism refers to sleep as a sixtieth part of death, and Rabbi Nachman's stories are replete with examples of the tragic losses that occur to a person because he falls asleep at the precise moment when his soul could have been redeemed. I recalled the story of the second to the king, who after seeking his lost princess for years, finally sees her and makes an appointment when he will meet her and bring her back to her father. At the last moment, he cannot resist the temptation to drink some forbidden wine and falls asleep. The princess comes at the appointed time, but he is unconscious. Only when he wakes and sees her message "written in tears" in a handkerchief does he realize what has happened. A person may be lulled into sleep, say the Hasidim, by food, by the noise and bustle of crowds, by business, by all that diminishes consciousness. For the Bratzlaver, most of what we call life is really a kind of sleep from which we can occasionally be awakened by listening to tales about *tzaddikim,* saintly men.

A Sabbath in Safed

Whatever the results of this experience with my Bratzlaver friends, it seemed foolish not to try another exercise. Gedaliah promptly suggested a visit to another *mikveh,* one to which Hasidim attributed special efficacy. In the Galilean town of Safed was the *mikveh* used by the Holy Ari, a pool dug out of rock and fed by a natural spring. Visitors had vouched for its authenticity, since it was the only natural spring in the vicinity. It was also supposed to be very cold, but this was compensated for in my mind by the assurance that it was clean.

I arrived in Safed on a Friday afternoon, along with a busload of Israeli tourists who had come here to find relief in the mountains from their land's hot summer temperatures. The rabbis warn that one's Sabbath depends on the labor that precedes it, and I had a number of arrangements to make before sundown—for food in a local restaurant, for automatically switching off lights, for toilet paper which may not be torn on the Sabbath, for a hiding place for my money, and other prosaic details.

Everything was finally in order, and I grabbed a towel to set out for the *mikveh* of the Ari. After half an hour of wandering in and about narrow streets, I passed through some open fields and found myself in the old cemetery, with its above-ground, rectangular body-length markers. All about me were the names of famous disciples of the Holy Ari. In the tradition of mystical Judaism, the Ari and his followers would often walk in the cemetery and come back to report that they had been "impregnated" by the psyche of one or another great rabbi. The idea that one can be united with the soul of great men, or the discovery that one's own soul was really an incarnation of an early Israeli king or rabbinic scholar, was quite common in seventeenth-century Safed, and the Ari would often inform his followers that the lines of their face revealed them to be a reincarnation of King David, Joshua, or some other important personality.

My reflections on this subject came abruptly to an end when I suddenly noticed dozens of black vultures hovering overhead—the city slaughterhouse was nearby. A group of what looked like large rats scampered through some bushes, and I lost all appetite for further wandering among the graves. I finally hit upon a path descending down the hill and saw ahead of me two young men with broad-brimmed black hats and beards. They were carrying towels, and I guessed that they were heading toward the *mikveh* of the Ari. They themselves were not Israelis, they told me, in Yiddish, but *Amerikaner* from Brooklyn who had also come to Safed for a Sabbath. Near the bottom of the hill, we came to a small stone building. Within were some benches and a small pool with marble steps.

I had taken off my clothes and was ready to enter the pool when one of my companions stopped me. "Look," he exclaimed, "that's for *taharah,* purification of corpses." He pointed, and alongside the pool I saw a shiny aluminum table where dead bodies were placed. I tried to shake off the tingle in my spine.

"Do they bring corpses in here while people are using the *mikveh?*" I asked.

"Why not?" the *Amerikaner* replied. "But don't worry," he added, seeing my worried face. "Not on the eve of the Sabbath."

The *mikveh* of the Ari was in an adjoining room. It was a large hole cut into the bottom of a cave and filled with water trickling

out of a crevice in the rock wall. My two companions removed the
last articles of clothing on their bodies, including the black silk
yarmelkes covering their heads. Their foreheads were clean shaven,
forming a crescent which was surrounded by black hair merging into
sidelocks and beards. They entered the *mikveh,* immersed themselves
several times, and returned promptly to their clothes. It was my turn
to enter the pool. There was a taste of vegetation in the water, but the
coolness was so welcome after my hour-long stumbling in the hot sun
that I remained beyond the time required for the actual immersion.

When I emerged, I realized that in my hurry I had forgotten to
bring a change of clothes. In Safed, where all acts are but hints of
deeper truths, the symbolism of putting on the old clothes after a
ritual of renewal was too obvious to be ignored. I climbed up the
hill, depressed by this victory of the Obstructor. When I got back to
the house, however, I managed some sort of shower in a broken bath-
tub, dressed in clean clothes and set out for the synagogue of the
Ari.

Here the obstacles were of a different form. The small building,
with its intricately carved and colored ark, was filled with people,
as was the stone courtyard outside the door. But most of these were
tourists, more interested in watching others pray than in praying
themselves. When the prayers had ended, I asked an old man dressed
in a brown robe, who seemed to be the sexton, if there were any
kabbalists in Safed. He shook his head. "There was one until last
year, but he died." As if in compensation, he offered me a myrtle
branch. I smelled it, remembering this to be a Sabbath custom of the
Hasidim, some of whom have lovely silver vessels formed in the shape
of branches and filled with sweet-smelling spices.

Walking home that evening after services, I reflected on the fact
that smell seems to be one of the senses which has been eliminated
from modern worship. Only the Catholic and Orthodox censers offer a
reminder of the central role which incense and odor once played in
religion. Their importance in ancient Jewish worship can be imagined
by recalling that in the Temple in Jerusalem, with its masses of animals
waiting for slaughter, the "sweet smell unto the Lord" offered by the
burnt sacrifices may not have been sweet in the noses of flesh and
blood worshippers. Hence, the importance of the special incense used

in the Temple precincts, which the bible ordained should be prepared by a particular family, who were forbidden on pain of death from revealing its precise composition. Some remnant of religious attachment to smell may be detected in the snuff which Hasidim will still offer each other on the Sabbath, though the origin of the custom along with the wigs and fur-brimmed hats, is probably rooted in the *haute couture* of the seventeenth and eighteenth century of European aristocracy. This elimination from worship of a sense which mystical literature has always recognized as the most spiritual of men's sensory faculties is probably part of the general disembodiment of religion. To recognize the mood-evocative power of perfume in the relations of man and woman, while ignoring its possibilities in the romance of man and God, is surely a mistake.

The next day, I set out for early morning services, this time hoping to find a synagogue not packed by tourists. First, I tried the one of Rabbi Joseph Caro, the author of the *Shulchan Aruch,* the "prepared table" of laws and customs, which is still authoritative for Orthodox Jews in our day. I had seen the synagogue before, a light and airy room with high, curved arches and lovely carpets. To my surprise, there were only two men present, the sexton and a tourist. The sexton was telling the visitor that his synagogue, like most of those in Safed, was only open during the Sabbath because it could not gather a prayer quorum during the week. I waited for almost a half hour, when, hearing the sound of prayer chanting nearby, I decided to find its source. I found a building with a stone inscription on the lintel announcing it to be the synagogue of Rabbi Moshe Alseich, another of the famous Safed rabbis. But here, too, there were only two men, one of them obviously a tourist and the other a Sephardic Jew who was rapidly, and by memory, chanting the opening blessings and psalms of the Sabbath service. I was about to try my luck elsewhere when the prayer leader called out sharply, "Don't leave." I meekly took a seat along the carpet-covered stone parapet which, in the style of Sephardic synagogues, circles the building and leaves the center free except for an elevated platform facing the ark of the Torah. Gradually, a few other men and some young boys arrived, and the main part of the service could begin. When the Torah was about to be read, the small congregation left their seats and gathered in front of the ark. As the Torah was taken out, they clapped their hands like children at a party and began chanting a lively tune and we followed the Torah in procession around the room. One old man, dressed in a loose brown burnoose, took out a vial of perfumed oil and poured some of its contents into the hands of the men and boys, who anointed their foreheads and heads while following the Torah to the reading platform. Evidently, these North African Jews, recent immigrants to Israel, still had a place for smell in their religion. The Torah was placed upright in a case, and a young man was called to ascend the platform and offer the blessings which precede and follow its reading. His children ascended with him, and after he finished, bowed their heads for his blessing. Later a young boy was called up for a reading; it was evidently his bar mitzvah. Upon descending, he walked about the synagogue and received the blessing of everyone in the congregation by taking their hands, placing them on his forehead, and then kissing them. When the Torah reading was over, the younger children ran up to the old man who had distributed the oil and laughingly sought an extra blessing from his hands.

The involvement of the worshippers was impressive. They were poor people, ordinary laborers, with few opportunities to express their desires, but their lives did not seem empty. I could not help but think of successful suburban fathers who had made comfortable provisions for their children, yet would never receive the honor and respect that had fallen to the lot of the old North African who could offer only blessings.

Before the Ascent, a Descent

"Let us perform an act of loving-kindness," said a second-century rabbi one hot summer day to the students of his Talmudic Academy. The students, ready to obey their teacher's suggestion, were surprised to see him setting out for a swim. "Certainly," the rabbi explained, "let us be kind to this poor thing, the body."

I comforted myself with this Talmudic anecdote when, the next day, I boarded a plane rather than the bus for a speedy and comfortable return journey. But even as the plane lifted itself over the blue sea of Galilee, I knew that I had compromised with the "experiment." In Judaism, at least, there is no ascent of the soul which does not involve the body—all the body, with its sweat and semen and smell, swelling with life juices or putrefying with death.

These attempted encounters with living Jewish mysticism at least reminded me that the most delicate spiritual phenomena can appear when life is confronted in all of its bodily aspects, but evaporates with the attempt to rise above them. Gedaliah had told me a horrible story about a saintly man, who came home every afternoon from his business and shut himself up in his garden for several hours. The curiosity of his neighbors resulted in their peeking over the fence one day. They saw him go to a hole in the ground and lie down in it as if it were a grave. Then he took a vial filled with worms, uncocked it, and let the worms crawl over him. In this way, he kept in mind the inevitable end of his body, his ambitions, and his dreams. Like most stories about the ugliness of death, this was related by Hasidim with high cheer. Most people today find it hard to see the benefit of such practices, but in Jewish mysticism the table for the purification of corpses and the *mikveh* for the rebirth of life belong in the same room. Delicate and exquisitely spiritual fruits have drawn their strength from roots that were deeply immersed in the dark regions of unconscious bodily drives. Some modern writers, such as Celine, have seen the same connection between the sewer and the spirit. The problem is to turn the descent into the ascent. Perhaps the most important thing that Jewish mysticism, or, indeed, classical Judaism, has to offer the world is a better understanding of how to deal with this dangerous dialectic so that life is strengthened and not destroyed.

But this is a secret whose conscious revelation seems to have been reserved only for the few, although many have lived by its formulae without probing the whys and wherefors. Surely, it is a secret that is closed to the odorless, bodiless, sanitized religious expressions of our day. From the refined atmosphere of Martin Buber's study to the groans and sighs, the dances and midnight meditations, the smells and *mikvehs* of flesh and blood Hasidim is a far journey for all but the most strenuous seekers.

Even those born within the world of Hasidism, once they have become accustomed to modernity, will find it difficult to make a wholehearted return. More often than not they become what the Kabbala calls "naked souls," continually shuttling back and forth between different worlds without ever finding their proper "clothing." Occasionally, however, there is a person who appears to build a visible bridge between these different worlds. It is usually a delicate structure and easily destroyed, but while it stands, it offers a way particularly congenial to other "naked souls." This is the contribution of Rabbi Abraham Chen.

9

THE FRAGRANCE OF EDEN

"No two faces, no two voices, no two grains of sand are ever the same. . . ."

And just as there is no repetition and doubling in reality, in nature or in imagination, so also, according to the mystic view, is there no doubling in time. Every moment is new, not just a straight and boring repetition of itself. More, every moment is different. . . .

This simple realization can bring him into depths, or lift him to heights which have yet to be explored. The absence of repetition and doubling in nature is the seal of singularity which lies in creation. Every matter and every event from the ram in the mountains to the lightest rustle of the wind is stamped with the seal of singularity.

Here is the secret of the unity of all being on the one hand, and the individuality and singleness of that being on the other.

Here, too, is the basis for the complete repudiation and invalidation of that polluting point of view—the progenitor of all the horror and filth which appears in our world today—the idea that every individual is as nothing in his own right, only a tool to be used for the larger community. That not only the individual man, but even the individual generation, is nothing but a small and meaningless cog in the large machine.

The absence of identity or repetition in nature proclaims that in reality there is no "detail" in the sense of a part having meaning only in relation to the "whole." For every detail is not just a part, not one part, but—singular. The singular cannot be a cog, cannot even be a detail of the whole—the singular is everything.

And our ancients, even in their day, realized and proclaimed this . . . and deeply illustrative of their view and perception 2,000 years ago was the great pronouncement, that is to say, the great doctrine deriving from this view that every man is not just one but a singular; the pronouncement that he who destroys one life destroys that which is singular and solitary. . . .

—ABRAHAM CHEN, *"In The Kingdom of Judaism"*

That Rabbi Chen was different, I realized the very first time I saw him. That was in 1947, when the stony fields between Jerusalem and Bet ha-Kerem still gave the appearance of an ocean bed, especially at night as they reflected the white of the moon. Today most of these empty spaces have been filled with blocks of apartment houses and new roads, but then one walked on the Sabbath through quiet, tree-lined streets to the local high school, where prayers were conducted in a chapel-like synagogue on the second floor. On my first Sabbath morning there, I noticed a man standing between the pulpit and the window overlooking the school courtyard, a bit apart from the rest of the congregation. The large prayer shawl covering his head was carefully draped over the upper part of his neatly pressed black frockcoat, and dark sunglasses contrasted incongruously with his prayer shawl and the gray beard. Later in the service, he was called to the Torah. The congregation watched respectfully as he walked up to the pulpit stairs, and closed his eyes; then he began to chant the blessings in a low voice, his Hebrew a mixture of old European and modern Israeli with a twanglike pronunciation of the guttural *ayin*. Throughout the remainder of the service, I was conscious of his voice; his prayers lagged a bit behind the others, and the cantor would wait for him to finish before going on to the next section. When the morning service ended, the cantor announced that Rabbi Chen would offer a lesson on the code of Maimonides. I guessed that Rabbi Chen was the bearded man with the sunglasses and joined the seven or eight men who waited while Rabbi Chen carefully folded his prayer shawl. Finally, he walked over to the table on which the cantor had place a large, brown leather folio. He sat down and leafed through the pages, humming under his breath. Finally, he began reading from the text with a rhythmic lifting and falling of voice.

"A man should be especially careful of his behavior toward widows and orphans, for their souls are exceedingly depressed and their spirits low. Even if they are wealthy, even if they are the widow and orphan of a king, we are specifically enjoined concerning them, as it is said, 'Ye shall not afflict any widow or fatherless child. . . .'" At this point, the rabbi broke off his reading and removed his dark glasses. He had almond-shaped eyes, very gray in color and a bit watery.

238

Looking over our heads, he began his commentary with the same rise and fall of tone which he used in reading the text.

"So does Maimonides speak here about the treatment which must be afforded to a widow and orphan, for they are the weakest elements of society and therefore the test of that society's civilization. And this is the secret of Jacob's ladder, the order of the rungs, but there is much to say here." He paused as if wondering whether to say it, then continued. "Yes, it is the perversion or confusion of the rungs which is the cause of all our troubles. For evil is simply good out of place. Peace, for example, so high an ideal on our rung of values, may, if it is placed too high, become evil, as when Aaron wanted peace above all and gave the people their idols. And it is the confusion of the rungs which will often cause difficulty. As when one tries to satisfy a spiritual hunger through the physical, or," he looked at us, "when a person tries to satisfy a physical need through the spiritual."

From the courtyard below came the sound of wood smacking against wood and the bark of the drillmaster's voice. On Sabbath afternoons, local youth gathered for gymnastic exercises in the courtyard of the school. The British military authorities allowed them to use wooden staffs in this type of training, and the Haganah, the unofficial Jewish defense corps, took advantage of this opportunity to give the young people some semimilitary exercises.

The rabbi was obviously disturbed by the noise and tried to lift his voice above it. "However, the worst of all the plagues which result from the defect in the ladder occurs in the realm of community: placing the honor of the flag or the prestige of the "group" ahead of the life of an individual man; placing economic production, paved roads and parks, theaters and perfume shops, national monuments ahead of the misery of multitudes of individuals. And a *moshel,* a parable, will illustrate.

"Rabbi Yochanan went to Rome and there saw a pillar of marble which during a storm was covered with cloth to protect it from the weather. Near the pillar lived a poor man with a grass mat for his feet and grass matting for his clothes. And this is all the difference between Rome and Jerusalem. Not that Rome did not value human life, nor that Jerusalem did not value marble pillars, but the order of priority, what is first and what is second, this makes all the difference. This is the secret of Jacob's ladder."

The shouting below had now become too loud, and the rabbi closed his book with a sigh. One of the men thanked him for the "lesson," and the rabbi lowered his eyes and raised his hands as if warding off praise. "The ears open the mouth, an old secret every teacher knows, and the ears can close the mouth. Actually, a teacher is only a drill; the water must already be there."

On the way home from the synagogue, a member of the congregation told me that Rabbi Chen was descended from a distinguished rabbinic family that traced its lineage back to the Riv, a famous North African scholar of the fourteenth century. His grandfather, Rabbi Peretz Chen, had belonged to the inner court of Schneur Zalman, the founder of the Lubavitcher sect of Hasidism. His father, a saintly scholar, had followed his son to Israel and died in the old city of Jerusalem some years ago.

"If you can find a little book which the son, the present Rabbi Chen, wrote about his father, you will have found a treasure," my informant added.

I asked about Rabbi Chen's present occupation.

"He writes a bit. He knows Russian and German. He works for the religious department of the Jewish Agency, but he doesn't belong to them," my companion concluded enigmatically.

As the weeks went by, I learned that Rabbi Chen didn't offer a lesson every Sabbath. There were some Sabbaths when he didn't come to synagogue at all, for he was in poor health and his eyes bothered him. Occasionally, I would see him on the bus which traveled between Bet ha-Kerem and Jerusalem. He usually sat on the wooden seat in front near the driver. He carried a small briefcase on his lap and wore a Homburg-like hat which, with his dark sunglasses and proud, straight back, made some of the people on the bus wonder whether he was a foreign diplomat. I never addressed him personally but was eager to hear him speak again. One Sabbath, therefore, when the sexton announced that Rabbi Chen was inviting the congregation to his house to mark the anniversary of his father's death, I went. Mrs. Chen, a petite gray-haired woman with smiling eyes that were the same color as those of her husband, opened the door of their white-washed cottage. There were only three other guests in the house and Rabbi Chen asked me where I was from. When I told him, his eyebrows lifted. "My misfortune was that I never learned English and had to read my Carlyle and Beaconsfield in Russian translation. If some of my pieces could be translated into English . . ."

I offered my services and the rabbi looked interested. He walked into a small bedroom that stood off the dining room and returned a moment later with a typewritten Hebrew manuscript. It turned out to be an imaginative description of the terror that could befall a person from whom a government wanted to extract a confession: his fear of torture, his worry about the fate of his loved ones, and all the other motives that might affect him. Rabbi Chen's main point was that Jewish Law, anticipating an era of faked confessions and other temptations to use the third degree, had simply ruled that any man's confession against himself was legally invalid on the ground that "a man is too close to himself." When I returned Rabbi Chen's essay, and presented him with my translation, I asked where I could find more of his writings, and he referred me to a publication called "Sinai." That week I exhausted my limited student resources by purchasing every issue that contained his articles.

Judaism that Breaks the Ear

At first what intrigued me most about Rabbi Chen's writings was his way, as the rabbis would put it, of "breaking the ear" with a startling phrase or insight. His essays, some of which are now published in two Hebrew volumes, deal with classic rabbinic themes: what is man; what are his obligations, personal and social; what is Judaism; what are its basic principles, commandments, rituals? The themes were old and their illustrations all drawn from the main stream of Jewish literature, but the perspective was nearly always fresh and unexpected. A minor example would be the question Rabbi Chen asks about the well-known episode in the bible describing the sacrifice of Isaac by Abraham. The story relates the reactions of Abraham and Isaac. But what about Sarah, the mother? The bible says nothing, explicitly, but one can draw some interesting speculations on the basis of what is not said, for the narrative seems to hint that after the attempted sacrifice of their son, Abraham and Sarah lived in different towns. Had, then,

something happened to estrange husband and wife? Could this have
been Sarah's reaction to Abraham's readiness to slaughter their son?
The bible makes no direct statement, but Rabbi Chen's suggestion is
intriguing.

He even takes a subject as well-worn as the Jewish holidays, and,
without adding new information, is able to help the Jew, who may
have observed these holidays and their customs all his life, suddenly to
see them in new light. The rabbi begins by asking if anyone can convey
the taste of gefulte fish by words; if not, how much more difficult is
it to communicate the flavor of "days of heaven upon earth," of which
it is said, "he who tastes them, tastes life." It may be possible, however,
to touch them with "the tip of the fork," and this is what Rabbi Chen
proceeds to do. Thus, a common goal of all holidays and festivals is
"the attempt to raise oneself, if only by a hand's breadth, above the
ground; if only for a moment, above the day. And this attempt has
two aspects: first to rise above—to lift oneself up above the differences;
second, to raise up what is lower, to sanctify the ordinary. Not to flee
from it, and not to dismiss it, but sanctify it. The sanctification of the
wine—the *kiddush*—is deliberately performed at the festive table. It is
the place of food, of the ordinary physical act, that is made holy. An
altar is to be made of the table."

Holidays also share a feeling of newness. This theme is emphasized on the Sabbath by the white tablecloth and by the *kiddush,* which
is a birthday song celebrating the creation of the world. Rosh Hashanah, the New Year, is entirely a chapter of newness dedicated to the
renewal of life, and Passover calls for new dishes and asks that people
eat green herbs.

Another thread which runs through every holiday is poverty.
Here, most interpretations of Judaism stress its antagonism to asceticism,
but Rabbi Chen points out that Judaism has always associated the at-
tainment of deepest truths with a measure of separation from wealth
and possessions. Recalling that money is not to be touched on the Sabbath and holidays, he asks, "Is there another people who in their days
of rest and joy refrain from handling money?" Emphasis is given to
the Talmudic view that "the son of David will come only when there
are no coins left in one's pocket":

"And behold, the Messiah himself, the fulfillment of prophecy and the peak of perfection, is described as 'a poor man, riding on a donkey.' Not a lofty lord flying on eagles of fire, from whose nostrils pour forth flame, whose clothes are laden with all the treasures of Korach and armed with the bows of Nimrod—no, only a poor wretch, riding a donkey."

Another theme common to all Jewish festivals is *sod,* "mystery." It is the Sabbath, however, that most strongly emphasizes this element: "A person must not leave his place on the Sabbath," states the Law. "No loud sound is permitted on the Sabbath." The Kabbala in particular stresses this aspect of the Sabbath, and Rabbi Chen delighted in quoting the poem of the Holy Ari: "the mystery of the Sabbath . . . the table wreathed with precious mystery. Deep and hidden, beyond the reach of the word; the Bride crowned with the upper mystery . . . the hidden Menorah . . . shall we speak secret and guarded words— words spoken in whispers, sealed words which reveal thoughts?'"

Another characteristic of Jewish holidays is that the cycle of festivals does not mean repetition. The knowledgeable Jew understands that every Passover is different from every other, depending on its place in the seven year and forty-nine year biblical cycle. Every week has its peculiar type of Sabbath—the Sabbath of Song, the Sabbath of Repentance, and the like; each represents a unique "gate to Heaven." With this kind of awareness firmly established, Rabbi Chen is able to develop his favorite theme: the singularity which is the "seal of all creation."

The Importance of Singularity

Rabbi Chen argues for the superiority of the child's vision over that of the adult. He compares Plato's conjecture that all poetry, music, and holy yearnings come from the "song of our soul, from that place which is the treasure house of everything," with the statement of the Kabbala that Elijah the prophet remembered what was "there—when I stood before the Lord." Similarly, Oscar Wilde's garden where "every blade of grass, every plant, every flower . . . sings its song," is linked to the biblical and Talmudic imagery of angels as children. "For the child knows how to be amazed, everything to him is new—the sky, the sun, the stars, mother, father, the doll. He participates in the biblical statement, 'And God saw all that He had made and it was very good.'"

Adults, unfortunately, have ceased to be astounded. They see no mystery; freshness is hidden under names and categories. As for Judaism, its purpose is constantly to tear away the outer layer with which the years, society, and books have swathed the inner wonder—what the mystics call the "upper whiteness," that primal openness which contracts as soon as script or sound is imposed upon it. But can this attitude of childhood last, or, if lost, can it ever be recovered? Yes, says Rabbi Chen, through a kind of second birth. There can be a sudden tearing apart of the veils of oldness, and the secret of this rebirth consists of a return to "man's essential point." Carlyle is quoted for support: "There is an inner point which makes all creation one within and makes every individual different and unlike any other without." This is what the Kabbala calls, "The oneness of the soul."

There are two things which can so shake a human being that he touches this ultimate level of being. The first and most successful is a great love; "He who loves knows the art of prophecy," says Carlyle. The second is great tragedy, which in Chen's words also has the power to rip away the "pasted-on externals" and open the soul to mystery. An individual who has been struck by tragedy or confronted with death can undergo an inner revolution. Of course, this does not hold for the man who is just an onion made up of layer upon layer with nothing underneath; he is simply destroyed by tragedy. But for someone who has an "inner point" to which to return, the childhood of second birth can be more fruitful than the first. Hence the importance of Judaism's call to *tshuvah,* often mistakenly translated as repentance, but which really means return—the return of one's essential self that has been covered over by neglect, sin, or habit. This is what Rabbi Nachman of Bratzlav meant when he said, "It is forbidden to be old."

To be in touch with one's hidden uniqueness, to find one's personal God, and to refrain from serving the gods of others, this is Rav Chen's constant admonition. In a religion that forbids man to separate himself from the community and prefers the *we* to the *I* in most of its prayers, his position might strike some as a heresy: "To the degree that a man associates with others, he annuls something of himself." Everyone must seek his "unique portion" in God; to appropriate somebody else's idea or way to God is to worship "the god of others."

This sense of singularity must continually saturate man's consciousness. Every moment of time is irreplaceable, every leaf and grain of sand is utterly different—the realization of this idea can bring man to the depths of the pit or the heights of heaven. What is most important and difficult is to understand that every human being is a complete cosmos. In recognizing this truth, we come to see that, even if the goal is something as important as the state, "the teaching which places goals or principles above the sacrifice of human beings is the fountainhead of all the world's sins."

In 1947, when the Jewish community in Palestine was struggling with the British mandatory authorities, this thought had agonizing implications. The Haganah and other paramilitary organizations were urging Jews to die or even to kill, if need be, in order to establish a Jewish state. Arguments about the justice or injustice of such calls were heard in every household, even penetrating the Sabbath third meal at Rabbi Chen's home.

The Third Meal with the Rabbi

I had been looking forward to this third meal, not only because of having read the rabbi's eloquent description of the Sabbath, when Israel is united with "the bride crowned by mystery from above," but also because he had himself tasted of this kingdom of the "secret"— his family came from the inner court of a great Hasidic dynasty. No doubt my expectation was further sharpened by the fact that I was preparing to leave Israel; and I waited impatiently until five o'clock that Sabbath afternoon. The door to Rabbi Chen's home was half-opened, and Mrs. Chen responded smilingly to my knock, "Please, please enter." I walked through a narrow, dark foyer, past a small, white icebox, and into a dining room lined on one side by shelves of books. The room was almost filled by a large table covered with a white cloth. I looked for the traditional herring and "burning wine" which I assumed were a part of a Hasidic third meal, but there were only some empty metal holders for glasses and two small jars of hard candy.

I was also surprised to see that again only three other guests were at the table, none of them from the congregation. One of the men was sitting with his hat pushed down to his ears. It was hard to determine his age, for he kept his eyes lowered to the tablecloth on which his fingers were nervously arranging breadcrumbs in patterns. Opposite him sat a tall, thin-faced man of about fifty, whom we often saw at the university hurrying from class to class as if he were trying to retrieve something he had lost. The students called him the *kibbutznik,* since he told people that he had been given a year's leave of absence after twenty years in his *kibbutz,* but the rumor was that he had left it permanently for personal reasons. Sitting quietly nearby, with a half-amused smile on his face, was a younger man with a long bushy haircut and rimless glasses. A chemistry student at the university, he kept the sleeves of his white shirt rolled up, revealing a blue concentration camp number tattooed on his arm.

The rabbi was not in the room, but we could hear his voice through the door of the adjoining bedroom while we sipped the glasses of tea which the rabbi's wife put in the metal holders. Then the door of the bedroom opened and the rabbi walked out, accompanied by a man wearing a sporty brown hat that matched the color of his suit. If Rabbi Chen was disappointed at the attendance, he didn't show it. With obvious pride, he introduced his guest as a distinguished scholar and colleague at the Jewish Agency and offered him the chair on his right. The honored guest bowed smilingly and thanked him. We all continued drinking our tea, and the rabbi's friend, leaning back in his chair, began humming a little tune. The rest of us sat still, as if waiting for some program to begin. After a few moments, the silence became uncomfortable and the *kibbutznik* tried to make conversation by referring to the latest episode of the strife between the British authorities and the Jewish community. Posters had been plastered on building walls that week announcing the trial and execution of a Jewish informer by the "jury" of a Jewish underground group. Rabbi Chen put down his tea with a snort and his gray eyes narrowed. "Idiots," he said angrily, "they're all idiots, these patriots of ours." His outburst surprised us. Many in Israel were troubled by the terrorist tactics of those days, but they usually qualified their disagreement by some kind words about the ideals of the terrorists.

The smile on the face of the refugee student hardened a bit. "What, then, shall we do with the informers, rabbi?" he asked, his soft tone not disguising its irony.

The vehemence in the rabbi's voice did not subside. "What to do? Shoot them, of course. And if we make a mistake—why, what's lost? Just another screw in the machine, not something irreplaceable, immeasurable—a life."

We all remained quiet, and Rabbi Chen lifted his tea to his mouth, as if trying to calm himself. When he spoke again, it was as if to explain his outburst.

"It is through these 'legal' little wars that *gehenna* has been brought on earth. All the 'holy blood crusades,' from the war with Amalek to the Ukrainian terror and the German horror, they all arose from this view, and it may be that the little murders, the 'legal' ones, planted the seed for the larger." He looked away from us to the books on the shelves. "From the prohibition against killing to the permitted killing, there is a difference so great that it is beyond measure. But between a kosher murder and an illegal murder, I doubt if there is a difference of even two hairs."

The rabbi's friend made an effort to change the conversation. "*Sabuni, sabuni—sovvunni*—they have surrounded me all about," he sighed, as he quoted from the Psalms. "But politics we can hear any place, and it isn't often that we sit at Rabbi Chen's table for *shalos seudah*. Perhaps our rabbi can honor us with a little study. Perhaps with the Tanya."

The rabbi's frown faded as his friend spoke. He sipped his tea, raised his hands in a self-deprecating gesture, then rose and went to the bookshelf. He brought down several copies of the Tanya, the book written by Schneur Zalman, his grandfather's rabbi and the founder of the Lubavitcher sect of Hasidism.

"It is hard," he began, "but perhaps we can touch it, even if only for a moment with the tip of the fork." He began reading. "*Tanya*, there is a teaching, before his birth a man is told be righteous and not evil; and even if all the world should say you are righteous, in your eyes, consider yourself to be evil. And this must be understood, for have we not learned in the *Ethics of the Fathers*, 'Do not think of yourself as evil,' and that a person who is evil in his own eyes is liable to fall into sadness and then be unable to serve the Lord in joy and goodness of heart. . . ."

The man with the hat pushed down to his ears began swaying
back and forth as the rabbi read. The rest of us bent closer to hear
the words.

"Be not evil before yourself," the rabbi repeated, lifting his
head. "Perhaps the meaning here is not what the world thinks—
namely, that we should think well of ourselves. Perhaps it means that
a person must be good, particularly when he is before himself—that is,
when nobody else is watching. Here, a little *moshel* will help.

"Some men came to a cave, sealed with a rock. As they approached, they saw rays of light coming from the crack between the
rock and the cave. As they came closer, they saw that the rays were too
strong to endure, and they knew that they had found the cave where
Moses was buried. We may ask why these people were unable to stand
before the cave where Moses was buried, when the bible tells us that
the people saw the face of Moses and the rays of light streaming from
his face. Perhaps the reason is that when Moses was with other people,
his essence was somewhat diluted."

The rabbi paused and looked around. "To the degree that one
is associated with others, he annihilates something of himself."

The *kibbutznik* leaned forward and licked his lips as if he were
going to say something. He had spent twenty years of his life in a
community built on the principle that man attains his deepest self-fulfillment through association with others. But before he could speak,
more tea was brought in, and the rabbi had turned to the text. "Be
not evil in your own eyes. And even if all the world should say to you,
'You are righteous,' be evil in your own eyes."

Again Rabbi Chen looked away from the book. " 'There is no
man who does not sin.' This is the proclamation of Solomon, builder
of the Temple. No man, without exception, even the most righteous.
And he that congratulates himself in his heart that he has reached the
top of the ladder, reveals that he doesn't even grasp the nature of the
ladder—its infinite height and depth—and again a small *moshel* will
explain."

Rabbi Chen swayed a bit as he chanted the parable. "A poor
man worked at digging sand and sulphur. Once, while digging, he
found a great treasure. He piled up a large amount of the treasure in
his wagon and brought it home. His wife went out, looked at the

wagon, and her soul departed from her. There was a trial. The prosecutor blamed the husband, saying that he had killed his wife, that when he got rich he developed contempt for her. For if, the accuser argued, it was the shock of the sudden treasure that caused her soul to depart, then the husband's soul, too, should have left him, for he had been as poor as his wife. 'Let us go to the quarry,' replied the defending lawyer. They went, and they saw the difference between the reaction of the husband and the wife. The joy of the husband at finding the treasure had been diffused and dissipated by his sorrow at leaving behind so much more than what he could put in the wagon. The wife, however, saw only the loaded wagon. There was nothing which could take away from the great shock of her success. The meaning of the Tanya's teaching is that it is important to recognize one's sins and defects because only in such recognition is there the possibility of healing and renewal. But it is also necessary to refrain from being paralyzed by the knowledge of our defects, because despair can paralyze. The secret then is to know what is in our 'wagon,' but at the same time to remember that the treasure we have obtained is but an infinitely small part of the great quarry from which we have taken so little."

The room had darkened while the rabbi spoke, and from a nearby house we heard a voice on the radio singing, "Come to us, Elijah, the prophet." The sun had set and the Sabbath was over, but for the Hasid this was the time when the third meal really begins, and he "adds holiness to the ordinary" by songs and words of Torah. Again the Rabbi's friend leaned back in his seat, closed his eyes, and began to hum. We knew that this was the signal for the singing to begin, but none of us sang. The solitary humming of the rabbi's friend continued for a while and faded away. The silence was heavy and guilty. We knew that we ought to help create the proper atmosphere for the rabbi's Torah, but we didn't seem to know how to do it. Rabbi Chen lowered his eyes to the tablecloth. After a moment, he raised his head, smiled a bit, and suggested that his friend "lead us in a little song." The friend hastened to oblige while protesting that he was a poor singer. He would try to teach us a *"litvsche niggun,* that is, a tuneless melody." We laughed with him, and he began humming a song which did, indeed, seem to lack a melody. This time the rabbi nodded his head in accompaniment, and all of us tried to join in. The *kibbutznik* sang loudly and out of tune, and the man with the hat over his ears nodded his head in time. Twice we tried to learn the melody, but our efforts were a failure. The rabbi's friend made another attempt. "It's almost time for *havdalah,* and Rabbi Chen has already spoken to us, but perhaps if he is not too tired, he will honor us with yet a few more words before the Sabbath is completely gone." We hastened to murmur our approval of his suggestion. Rabbi Chen, who had been looking at the table, feebly lifted his hand. "It's already late."

"Please," pressed the scholar, "a few words about Hasidism." The rabbi bent his head in surrender, then turned his eyes toward the leather-bound folios sitting on the bookshelves.

"The most basic idea in Judaism is the expression in the Talmud, 'there is no place empty of Him.' It is this thought that Hasidism expanded and deepened. Why did the Holy One, blessed be He, the Midrash asks, teach Moses by speaking to him through a bush? In order to teach that there is no place empty of the presence of God, not even a bush. And it is this thought and its implications that caused the enmity of the Gaon of Vilna, who saw in it the danger of pantheism. But it remains the commitment of Israel to seek God in every place and to know that His law and sovereignty must therefore exist everywhere."

It was quite dark in the room now, except for a small light that filtered in from the corridor. Rabbi Chen's voice rose and fell, his sentences often trailing off so that we couldn't hear their end.

"In the bible it is written that at Sinai 'all the people saw the voice.' This phrase 'saw the voice' is not an accident nor does it speak of a miracle. It points to a deep and great Torah. The need to 'see' what is 'heard' and 'hear' what is 'seen.' It is precisely the 'seen,' the visible, that they did not see. It appeared to them like a distant impression. But what humans usually only 'hear' about—out of books and through faith—it was this that they 'saw' clearly. At Sinai the veil was broken, and even as a man recognizes that it is the sight which is the essential quality of the eye rather than the black and white matter, so, too, at Sinai did they see the soul of the creation through the created, for they 'saw' what was heard and 'heard' what was seen."

I looked at the people sitting around the table. In the darkness one couldn't tell whether the refugee student was still smiling, but the *kibbutznik* was leaning forward trying to catch the rabbi's words.

Rabbi Chen shook his head. " 'Nu, the ears have opened the mouth too much.' May we again climb the ladder of Jacob and Sinai and redemption come to Israel and the whole world, Amen."

"Amen, Amen," the rabbi's friend said, and Rabbi Chen leaned back in his chair, visibly tired.

The rabbi's wife entered, carrying a lighted *havdalah* candle in one hand and a tray with spices and a cup of wine in the other. As she approached, the rabbi rose, and we stood with him. He took the cup from the tray and began chanting softly, "Behold the God of my salvation, I shall not fear. . . ." The light from the candle reflected itself on our faces. The man with the hat over his ears moved his lips automatically as the rabbi chanted the blessings dividing light from darkness, the Sabbath from the profane. He held his fingernails toward the candle so that they might reflect the light, as prescribed by tradition. The *kibbutznik* stared at the candle, his mouth open. Near him stood the refugee; the half-ironic smile which had been on his lips all evening had now drooped into sadness. The rabbi's colleague stood behind his chair, his face lifted upwards and his eyes closed, as if remembering something he had heard before. Everybody seemed to be remembering or trying to 'see what was heard' once. Rabbi Chen's wife, meanwhile, simply stood at his side, her face glowing with pleasure as she looked at the people who had come to show respect for her husband.

The rabbi chanted the final blessing, went to the wall, switched on the light, and we wished each other "a good week."

I walked across the garden with the chemistry student and on to the main road which ran from Jerusalem toward what was the Arab village of Ain Kerem. We talked for a while about the weather, and then my companion suddenly shifted ground, asking, "Did you notice that there were no Sabras, native-born Israelis, in the rabbi's house?" He shrugged his shoulders. "But I don't know why people should complain about our Sabras. They say that they are not spiritual enough or that they are too conscious of physical strength. I don't know." He seemed to be arguing with himself rather than speaking to me. "Every age brings out of a people what it needs for its survival. We're lucky we don't have the type of Jew now who goes to *shalos seudah* with the rebbe, and holds out his fingernails to the *havdalah* candle."

I didn't say anything. The student limped as he walked and seemed much slighter in build than I had thought. His shoulders were drawn together as if they were chilled, but he continued talking. "And you know, maybe it isn't only a new type of Jew, like the Sabra, that we need in Israel. Maybe we need a new kind of God. The God of *dvekut,* to whom we must lovingly 'cling' was all right for the ghetto and for the twilight hour 'between the suns.' But it's not the God of the concentration camp, and maybe not the God for a land with rocks like this." He motioned to the empty fields filled with pockmarked stones. "You know, I used to go to a *yeshiva* in Europe, and it seems to me that the God I knew there is not the kind of God we can meet in Israel. It's the fierce, demanding God of Isaiah or Job that we need now."

The quietness of the night enveloped us, softening the hot, bitter words of my companion. We walked along in silence, and I heard him humming lightly. It was the song which the rabbi's friend had tried in vain to teach us.

"I used to know that melody," he said.

Before leaving Israel, I saw Rabbi Chen and his wife once more after that Sabbath. Quite by accident, I met them in a corridor of the Hebrew University. The rabbi, neatly clothed in a black coat and homburg, was walking somewhat ahead of his wife who was dressed in a thin coat and an old-fashioned flowered hat. She was looking timidly at the students in their khaki shorts and barefoot sandals, who were bustling through the corridor. When she saw me, she paused, as if eager to say something.

"Are you going to hear the rav?" she smiled proudly. "The university has invited him, you know, to give a lecture."

I changed my schedule and accompanied the little lady into the classroom, where we sat down in some desk chairs at the back of the room. Her husband sat in the front row. After the bell rang, Professor Scholem, for it was to his class that Rabbi Chen had been invited, introduced his guest as a descendant of famous Hasidic rabbis. The rabbi stepped in front of the blackboard, slowly removed his black hat, and replaced it with a large velvet yarmelke. He presented a handsome and dignified figure, standing straight in front of the class, his eyes turned toward the window as he spoke in a slow, half-chanting fashion which made the students bend forward to catch his words.

His wife's eyes were fixed on his with shining pride throughout the lecture. At one point, when the class became unusually quiet, she nudged me to make sure I noticed the effect her husband was having on the students. Actually, Rabbi Chen had antagonized the class, who were postgraduate students in Jewish mysticism.

"A scholar of mysticism," he had told them, "is like an account-ant—he may know where all the treasure is, but he is not free to use it." Having thus put all the would-be scholars of mysticism in their place, he outlined some of his ideas about Hasidism which, he said, "took Kabbala and turned it upside down. Whereas the kabbalists wanted to study the nature of God and from it deduce truth about man, the Hasidic rebbes did the reverse."

The professor thanked his guest somewhat perfunctorily at the end of the hour. In back of me, one of the graduate students whispered, "*Kvatch,* old-fashioned nonsense." Fortunately, his wife had not heard. She had gone to join her husband in the corridor.

An Appointment Missed

During later visits to the Holy Land, I caught an occasional glimpse of Rabbi Chen at public functions, and one summer I decided to call upon him again. Mrs. Chen's eyes brightened with pleasure when I told her that I had been a student at the Hebrew University and had never forgotten her husband's words and writings. She brought me into the combination study and bedroom where her husband was sitting behind a small writing desk, bare except for a brass inkwell and a quill pen. He took off his glasses and squinted his gray, catlike eyes, trying to remember me. I told him I wanted to translate some of his writings into English, and a flicker of light came into his eyes. He had received a CARE package the previous year from an American rabbi, he told me, with a note making the same suggestion.

"The package was appreciated; things are not easy here. But if something could be done for this—" he motioned toward some piles of manuscripts and magazines lying on shelves which were built over a narrow bed with a high, European mattress. "Maybe," he rubbed the

eyes which were always giving him trouble, "maybe the time has come
for these writings to be redeemed."

We fixed an appointment for the end of the week, but the next
day I learned that I would have to leave Jerusalem the following night.
When I came at noon to say goodbye, no one answered my knock, and
I assumed the elderly couple were resting. I placed a small package of
cigarettes and candy on the doorstep and left.

Somehow, I always felt guilty. When, in 1958, someone mentioned Rabbi Chen's death, I rushed to a New York library and looked
up the obituary in the Israeli papers. I found it in a small black-
bordered box:

> *On Yom Kippur Day, 5718,*
> *Rabbi Abraham Chen*
> *was requested to appear*
> *at the* yeshiva *on high.*

There were several articles in the paper about the rabbi, most of
them using the clichés which he so carefully avoided in his writings.
Rabbi Zevin, however, one of Jerusalem's rabbinical patriarchs, had
based his remarks at the funeral on a quotation taken from *To My
Comforters,* which Rabbi Chen had written after his father's death. In
this book, Rabbi Chen compared his father to "fragrant flowers—
which are not for eating, of no use for the stomach, even of no taste to
the palate; their fragrance is Eden—delight. Their essence is beauty, a
beauty which does not disturb, the beauty of quiet yearning and the
returning of the soul, joy, and beauty of holiness."

Rabbi Zevin had said that this was true not only of the father,
but of Rabbi Chen himself. The eulogy went on to quote the Song of
Songs: " 'My beloved has gone to his garden, to pick the flowers.' My
beloved—that is the Holy One. His garden—that is this world; to pick
flowers—to take up his saintly ones . . ." But where is the atmosphere,
the eulogy concluded, which can now give gardens and flowers like
these?

More than his ideas, I wondered, was it this fragrance, with its
hint of a garden that was no longer cultivated in this world, that had
always intrigued me about Rabbi Chen? The phrase used by the student in Jerusalem after our third meal came back to me—the rabbi

was a man born "between the suns." That was also how the Hebrew poet Bialik described the Jewish generation of Eastern Europe born toward the end of the nineteenth century. They were destined to live out their lives in the twilight zone between the setting sun of one world and the not-yet-risen sun of the new, yearning for both and at home in neither. Abraham Chen was of that in-between generation, entranced by the Russian and Jewish dreamers of a brave new society, but reluctant to surrender the beauty, pathos, and holiness of the Jewish religious home. Impossibly, his life tried to combine the delicate fragrance of Judaism's mystic garden grown in the "between the suns" atmosphere of the East European diaspora, with the harsh conditions of modern Israel.

At the time I had not read *To My Comforters*, but I wondered if the comfort which friends tried to offer Rabbi Chen when his father died might not be equally related to the predicament of the son. Although the book was out of print, some friends suggested that I visit Mrs. Zahavi, a niece of Rabbi Chen who lived in Jerusalem. When I was in Israel the following summer, an afternoon was arranged when I could meet not only her but her brother, some friends who had known Rabbi Chen, and his widow.

"You've heard, have you not?" the little gray-haired lady greeted me with a sweet smile. "On the day of Yom Kippur, as they were reading the Torah." She opened her gray eyes very wide and looked at me to see if I understood the significance of such a death. To return to God on Yom Kippur, the great day of Return was a sign of singular grace. And Yom Kippur, Rabbi Chen had written, was a day which was all "singularity," the day when "the high priest enters into the one holiest place, the Holy of Holies, to be one alone with the One."

"And he always said that death was the world's greatest injustice," Mrs. Zahavi's brother remembered.

"He had a lot of experience with unjust death," Mrs. Zahavi explained. A soft-spoken young widow with sad, dark eyes, her feelings for Rabbi Chen clearly extended beyond the accident of the family bond. She told me that her father, Rabbi Chen's brother, had been killed, literally "for the sanctification of the Name." There had been a pogrom in a Russian town. Her father, a gifted young rabbi, could have

saved himself by seeking shelter in a church. But he would not do this
and was slain. Rabbi Chen had by then left Russia. Later, his father
had gone to live in Jerusalem, where he died before his son could come
to visit him. There had been another brother who had died suddenly
a few days after his marriage, and a sister who had died because she
had been treated incorrectly by a physician. The mother had suffered
illness for years.

I spoke of my eagerness to redeem, if possible, some of his
writings by translating them, and asked Mrs. Zahari for a copy of
To My Comforters.

"It is my only copy," she hesitated, "and it has a personal inscription. But, you may have it for a few days."

I took the book with me and read it quickly. Some parts left me
impatient, but I was entranced with others and toward the end,
puzzled.

To My Comforters

It was a brief pamphlet rather than a book, containing only
seventy pages. The title, which in Hebrew is only one word, was un-
derlined by a thick black line, and the author's name was also under-
lined in black in the middle of the page. The inside cover contained
an inscription in a delicate and neat script, "To the daughter of my
brother and soul. . . ." Another page had the dedication, "To my
sister, Rachel—an inner quiet altar."

At the outset Rabbi Chen explains that his book is both an
answer to the personal expressions of condolence that had been sent
to him on the occasion of his father's death and an attempt to draw a
picture of "one of the last of the Mohicans of ancient Judaism." The
early pages contain rather repetitious expressions of anguish, not only
at the loss of his father but at the inability of words to express the
awfulness of death. The author seems angry that, even when somebody loses a close and precious friend, he is only mourning a partner
not his whole existence. "Even he who bewails the loss, eats, sleeps,
laughs, and sins as before."

Rabbi Chen makes a sharp distinction between friends, even
one's relatives and loved ones, and the single and singular man. There

is one person who, from the first to the last day, is for you—singular. Everything else was for you peripheral to that central wonder.

He eats, he sleeps, he speaks, he is troubled, he is traveling, he returns, he is sad, he begins, he feels better, he agrees, he refuses, he seems to agree, he doubts. . . .

"He, he, only he."

This is such a strange paragraph that one might almost think that Rabbi Chen resents the central position of his father, but that is not what the son is trying to say.

"In his life he was to me—all, and in his death—all died for me. . . . To people in the market place, such a relationship between father and son seems strange, and even more strange that it should exist between son and father. . . . In my inner, inner depths, I wanted nothing for myself but the privilege of being the dust under his feet. At the same time, he was to me as a comrade and friend of the kind which has no parallel among young people. And also a lover and beloved of the kind which has no example among the young of the same age."

The book continues with a number of movingly written pictures of "star moments." They are little prose poems which capture the mystic atmosphere of Jewish religious family life at its finest and most intense.

A Sabbath early in my life. It is a moment "between the suns"— twilight—the third meal.

The room is filled to overbrimming. Throughout the great hall a great ocean of heads stand and sway at moments like the waves of a quiet sea or like the tops of trees at the moment of a light breeze.

Complete silence.

And a voice, sweet and true, pleasant and sad like a violin, breaks through the darkness and stillness.

Rabbi Chen recalls the words of his father: "And there is the joy of the rose, that is, the joy of the end result. Then, there is the leaf of the rose, the bearer of the beauty and the odor of the beauty. And there is the stamen upon which the leaf rests, and the stalk upon which the stamen rests.

"And there is the root and the ground, and there is the seed, and the inner part of the seed, and there is the ground of the first seedling.

"And there is that which is 'before' all these, the water which waters the ground. In the writings of the Holy Ari, this level is called 'the waters which make all the joy to grow.' And there is also the source of the water, and there is the primal well, and there are the walls of the well and there is the ground of the well, and there is the source of the source, the beginning of all beginnings, and that is called 'the Well of the Well.'"

I and my brother, may his soul rest in peace, little children, are leaning against the suitcase of a visitor in the house. I have hardly understood a word. I have only "seen" the voice, "seen" that which is "heard," and these things are impressed into my mind without my understanding them.

This impression of the "moment between the suns" I cannot express. A sweetness close to fainting. I was so riveted by the sweetness that I could not leave the room.

Another memory picture from that period:

A young man, really just a boy, goodly of eyes and of appearance, with curly locks of hair, came to request permission to be married.
"Who are you, and who is your father?"
And, behold, my father is as pale as white lime, upset, or, more correct, shaken to the foundations. A terrible war rages in his soul.
It turns out that the would-be bridegroom is a bastard. Broken and shaken, my father comes close to the lad who, by the way, was far from empty-headed. With a tremendous effort to overcome the tears in his voice, he decrees the Law.
"My son . . . it is forbidden for you to marry."
"How?" cries out the unfortunate one, paralyzed with bewilderment. "This Miriam is forbidden to me? Why?"
"Not this bride, but in general, forever. . . ."
I look at the face of my father and understand then the words "in the hour when a man is troubled, what does the presence of God say—woe is me, my head hurts me." And from his good eyes flow tears, hidden, but hot. Suppressed rebellion is mingled with deep bowing before He Who created man and his sorrow together. "The tear of the oppressed."
There is no doubt that if there were consultation above, they

*would have been abashed before the vision of my father filled with
pity and moved to change the evil of the decree.*

*But what is there to do when the Torah, so holy and good and
precious, is so explicit?*

*"What do we, dwellers in houses of gross matter, know?" Un-
doubtedly even in this there must be some hidden good thought.*

*The bridegroom is shocked. My father continues to try to recon-
cile the tender child with the hard Torah. . . .*

*At that time, there was a typical devout, Orthodox Rabbi Zalyah.
He was the head of the burial society. He knew the exact dates of the
holidays, and the exact times of the sinking of the sun and the blessing
of the candles, and the exact time when one must stop eating leaven
before Passover. This Rabbi Zalyah, whose piety was his "trade" did
not find it pleasing that so much attention should be paid to a* mamzer,
a bastard.

*It was then that the patience of my father, which literally had no
limit, came to an end.*

*To my teacher and father, it was always painful that so many of
the pious did not grasp the simple meaning of goodness and graciousness and mercy in the Torah. His heart was always saddened by the
faithful who "did evil for the sake of heaven" and who thought they
were carrying out the mission of God. The righteous who tasted a taste
of holiness in pursuing and breaking and smashing. . . .*

*"It is still not clear to me who is really holier in this case," said
my father to the pious one.*

And my father did not rest until he took his book, the Yalkut
Shimoni, *and almost sat the young man who wanted to marry upon
his knees and read to him.*

*" 'And I have seen the tear of the oppressed and he who has no
comfort. . . . Daniel from the village of Chayta cried out against the*
mamzerim, *the children of illegitimate birth. One of these children
stood up before him and cried out, 'Master of the Universe, in what
way have I sinned?' . . . and the Holy One, blessed be He, says to
him, 'Upon Me let thy bitterness rest, my son. Let thy tears be upon
me, and in the future thou shalt sit next to Me.' "*

*In the end this boy became almost a great man. Quietly he sep-
arated himself from the world and withdrew into his inner chambers.*

Rabbi Chen offers other memories and then tries to describe the focal point of his father's personality: "Absolutely no artificiality, no pretense, not the slightest bit of forgery in speech and voice, in his eyes and his lips, in the lines of his forehead, in his face." He tells of an incident when a non-Jewish artist came to his town in Russia in order to seek a face which would remind him of the biblical patriarchs. By accident he saw his father walking by and said afterwards that there was only one man whom he wanted to draw, and he would not give him permission. The frustrated artist later explained to a Government official what it was about Rabbi Chen's father that struck him: "In this man's face there is not the slightest sign of role playing."

Toward the end of the book come pages that are puzzling. They begin with a recital of the sufferings and tragedies which fell to the lot of the Chen family in Europe, beginning with his mother:

Our mother, the pure and vital spirit of the house, was paralyzed. Taken from her was her speech, her walking, and her ability to move her hands.

And this tragedy came upon her only as a result of previous wounds.

For thirteen years she bore her sufferings in silence, without complaint—there were only two words which she could express all these years, and they were "Amen" and "One."

Rabbi Chen lists the other tragedies: a talented young sister is killed through the mistake of a doctor and dies with terrible pain in her twentieth year. There was also a younger brother in the family, who was gifted with genius for painting and drawing. "He had two black, pure eyes, and every soul which looked at them dipped into the depths of purity, the beauty of purity. He was greatly gifted, and to draw was the greatest longing of his life, but the son knew that his father did not approve. So the son offered up as a great sacrifice the great fire in his heart—offered it up without complaint. This son later died, a few days after his wedding."

There was another brother, who was the father of Mrs. Zahavi, and Rabbi Chen speaks about him with love and respect as a genius of his generation. On his way to seek help for his people during a pogrom, he was set upon and killed.

This son was slaughtered, and the father reads the Sh'ma, *the Hear, O Israel, the Lord our God, the Lord is One . . . and the heavens are quiet, and the earth is silent, and the children of men continue along their ordinary paths. For two and a half years after this event [writes Rabbi Chen], my father did not write to me about it, and then he hinted in one letter by quoting from a psalm, "From the Lord was this, it was wondrous in our eyes. . . ."*

[Then Rabbi Chen tells about his mother.] Oh, my mother, my mother, would that I were in your place. Our mother, our mother . . . who knows what this silent dove was like. Who knows her spiritual level, for she was the mother of us and of very many . . . and the children of men did this . . . this fragile old woman could not and perhaps did not want to resist, she who always trembled before a goy (a gentile), sank like a stone underneath their blows. She hoped that they would wound her flesh so that she would feel that which her son felt. It was forbidden for her to do it to herself, but at the hands of others. . . . And after thirteen years of terrible suffering and torture of body and soul was this silent song broken off. . . . Without even having her only son left in life, the atonement of all her suffering, present to close her pure eyes.

Finally, Rabbi Chen describes the trip of his father to Israel, uprooting himself from the family and land with which he was familiar. His father, too, died suddenly in Jerusalem, "and the son was not present."

There is something strange about these closing lines. For reasons which he does not offer in the book, Rabbi Chen was absent from his family during all these incidents. For years he did not see this father who was to him "all," despite the prayer which his father offered before the ark every Yom Kippur, "that they might soon see each other in peace and life."

And I had closed my heart with seven locks. I had hoped that there would come a day when I would tear open the lock of my heart for him, for him alone. . . .

For seven full years I lived with this long dream. . . .

And he also, without doubt, his great heart was closed up in the

latter years, after the sacrifice of his son, his crown and his glory. . . .
And for the opening key of a single beloved he waited. . . .

To what does Rabbi Chen here refer? What were the locks which separated father from son? The last lines of the book are even more puzzling. "For a small thing was their blood spilt," Rabbi Chen quotes from the liturgy describing the death of the ten martyrs during the Hadrianic period and applies the lines to the tragedies in his own family. "For a small thing, a thing which could have been prevented, were each of these great tragedies brought about." It was a small thing, he writes, which brought about the death of his brother and his sister and his mother, and perhaps even the death of his father. In each of these cases, it was a small mistake or a coincidence of time and place, and even with the death of his father, it was a small thing, small, indeed, that I had not come to Israel to see him one last time before this eternal parting. "And this is the main thing about our family," closes Rabbi Chen, "and you are trying to comfort me with words."

What is the small thing which cut Rabbi Chen off from his father?

I returned *To My Comforters* to Mrs. Zahavi and tried to suggest this question. She seemed to understand but did not elucidate. We spoke again about her uncle.

"He had some favorite phrases," she told me when I expressed my desire to write about Rabbi Chen.

"For example, he liked to apply to Judaism the words of Maimonides, 'He who knew her, would be hers!' I think he slightly changed Maimonides' words."

Abraham Chen had made a change. Maimonides had written, "He who knew Him [God] would be His." Was the small change Rabbi Chen had made important?

For Maimonides, the wondrous central point was God, as it was for the father of Rabbi Chen. But in Rav Chen's teaching, it is the infinitely precious, irreplaceable human soul, "before which all principles and ideals must bow, but which must not give way to any other needs or goals." His father, however, did have a central goal before which even the infinitely precious human soul gave way. Is it possible that the great difference which separated Rabbi Chen and his father was not some unmentioned family circumstances, nor the fact the son had read some non-Jewish books or even belonged to a different age, but that he was unwilling to surrender the "wondrous central point" in man to an even more wondrous center—the mystery his father called God?

"Perhaps," Rabbi Chen says in one of his essays, "it is all gates within gates." Perhaps everything below consists of a gate through which we may enter into gates above; and the upper gates are also "gates to gates." This is the perspective of the Kabbala. The kabbalist was sure that beyond and within all the gates there was a reality which cared for and responded to the human cry. Was Rabbi Chen?

But who can ask such intimate questions even of himself, let alone of another? Even if what was central to the father was no longer central to the son, whose fault is it that this happened, and can we even speak of fault? The bible speaks of man hiding from God, but also hints at times when God hides from man.

There are twilight moments in the history of a faith, moments when the sun of an old faith has sunk and the sun of a new faith has not yet appeared. In such a period, Rabbi Chen wrote in the final essay of *The Kingdom of Judaism,* idols are broken or must be broken, and a great and pure truth, different from all which has been received until now, must appear to light up the darkness.

In such a time, he continues, there is an almost physical thirst for a human being formed in the "upper image—like unto the mystic figure of Jacob which is engraved under the heavenly seat of glory." By such a human being even little people can be brought to reveal what is highest and most ideal in themselves.

Such a man, he insists, came to Palestine before the first World War and died in 1935, "a giant of reconciliation," capable of bringing about the great *yichudim,* joining left and right, flesh and soul, law and spirit. Perhaps, Rabbi Chen suggests, time will prove that this man was able to bring together the different and apparently clashing values of fading and rising worlds. The name of this man was Abraham Isaac Kook.

10
THE VIEW FROM THE ROOT ABOVE

He who feels, after many trials, that the soul within him can find repose only when it is occupied with the mysteries of the Torah, should know that for this has he been destined.

May no obstacle in the world, fleshly or even spiritual, confuse or turn him from the pursuit of the fountain of his life, his true fulfillment.

And it is well for him to know that not only his own self-fulfillment and salvation wait upon the satisfaction of this tendency within him. . . . The saving of society and the perfecting of the world also depend upon it. For a soul fulfilled helps to fulfill the world. True thoughts, when they flow without hindrance into any one of the corners of life, bless all of life.

But should he abandon his search, and wander about seeking water from wells which are not really his, then, though he draw water as much as the ocean, and take from streams in every part of the earth, yet will he not find peace. For like a bird who has wandered from his nest, so is the man who wanders from his place.

—ABRAHAM ISAAC KOOK, *Lights of Holiness*

Rabbi Zvi Yehudah Kook, the son of Palestine's first Chief Rabbi, endorsed my hope to use a chapter about his father's ideas as a way of synthesizing much of what has gone before in this book.

"For, he included all—all," the gentle, white-bearded rabbi said to me the day we first met. "He was original, altogether original. But also, all of Judaism—law, philosophy, poetry, mysticism, Hasidism—poured into him like springs feed a well. Thought, feeling, logic, practical details, all came together in him in an harmonious whole."

Rabbi Zvi Yehudah had waved his hands in circles to graphically illustrate his father's inclusiveness, then patted my shoulder as if to congratulate me on recognizing this quality. I did not tell him that he was somewhat mistaken; it was not Abraham Isaac Kook's powers of harmonious synthesis that had attracted me, but the apparent contradictions and splits in his personality and in his ideas that had really quickened my interest. How was it, for example, that a rabbi, immersed all his life in the minutiae of legal phraseology and ritual detail, could burst out with words like:

"Son of man, let not names, words, phrases, and letters swallow your soul. They are in your power. You are not in theirs. . . . Lift upwards, rise. You have the wings of spirit, the wings of mighty eagles." How could a pious, saintly, Orthodox mystic tell his people that they had become "over-spiritualized" in the diaspora; that they ought now to expand their "gross, animal" qualities? And how could the first Chief Rabbi of Palestine assert that atheism might be a fine thing; that the "winds of God-denial" ought, on occasion, to make "heaps of rubble" out of traditional religious institutions?

Nor were these merely theoretical observations on the part of Rabbi Kook. He had often visited nonreligious *kibbutzim* and joined the young "atheistic" settlers in their dances. On the other hand, at the Universal Yeshiva which he had founded in Jerusalem, with the purpose of wedding rabbinic disciplines to the scientific and humanistic insights of the twentieth century, he asked his students to study carefully the details of the animal sacrifices that would commence with the imminent restoration of the ancient temple.

What brought me to the Universal Yeshiva that summer day was the conviction that Kook's orthodox faith had not been facilely achieved. His ultimate religious position was that "God's in his heaven; all's right with the world"—especially right, he might add, with those Jews who lived in the land of Israel, fulfilling the commandments of the holy Torah. But he seemed to have known the argument of what the kabbalists called "the other side," even in his own life, always talking and writing about blissful joy but struggling often with a "sadness that burdens the soul."

Zvi Yehudah Kook: First Impressions

Rabbi Zvi Yehudah was talking with a young student from the Yeshiva, when I was brought into his office. On his hand and arm were the prayer phylacteries that he must have put on hours ago, then forgotten in his conversation. An untouched and by now cold glass of tea stood on the rickety little desk. In appearance, at least, the son was

quite different from his father. The photographs of Abraham Isaac
Kook show him to have been dark, with an oval face, full beard, and
large, sad eyes. Zvi Yehudah Kook was light-complexioned, short, with
round face and twinkling, almost mischievous brown eyes.

He was holding the student's arm, and his words seemed to be
tumbling over each other in eagerness. Apparently I had a long wait in
store, and I looked around at pictures in the room, trying to match
them up with the biographical material I had picked up in my reading
about the famous chief rabbi. One photograph had obviously been
taken in Russia. It showed a young man with a short, dark beard,
dressed in a Russian-style visor hat and long brown coat. Kook had
been born in Latvia in 1865. He had attended the famous Volozyn
Yeshiva, where he had been known as the "squint-eyed genius," a
reference to the peculiar set of his eyes, as well as to his talents as a
student. But the picture on the wall was probably taken after he had
left the Yeshiva and become a rabbi in the town of Boisk, Latvia. That
was the time when he had gone about trying to sell his first publication, anonymously written—a pamphlet urging Jews to be extremely
careful about putting the prayer phylactery in the exact position of the
forehead required by law. Strange that the person who would occupy
himself with such a theme, would also write, "Expanses, expanses—
enclose me not in cages of mind, spirit or word. . . ." It was said, too,
that in the Yeshiva he would occasionally scratch his own face to help
drive out "strange thoughts" about the other sex, another peculiar trait
for one who was later to urge the development of fleshly qualities.

Nearby was a second picture taken, I surmised, after he had
become the Rabbi of Jaffa in 1917. This time the rabbi's headdress was
the fur-covered *shtreiml* which Orthodox Jews had imported from
Eastern Europe and insisted on wearing, even in the semitropical cli-
mate of Palestine. Those early years in Jaffa were Rabbi Kook's most
fertile literary period. Here he wrote several important legal works,
poems, and most of his private meditations. These meditations were
filled with ecstatic exclamations about "heavenly joy, and divine bliss,"
for Kook had achieved his youthful dream—residence on the holy soil.
While he was still a student at the Yeshiva, his comrades had noticed
that Kook's feelings for the land of Israel far exceeded the normal
religious yearnings of his day. On Tisha b'Av, the fast day marking

the destruction of the Temple, he would stay up all night, crying bitterly. When one of the students had asked him about his extraordinary feelings for the Holy Land, he exclaimed, "You wouldn't understand; you are not a *cohen,* a priest."

In 1917, Kook was appointed Chief Rabbi of Jaffa. Though now a "servant of the holy people on the holy soil," there was still a great sadness in the eyes and face of the rabbi. His dream was encountering reality, including the onerous petty details and labors which went with religious officialdom. A letter has been preserved from this period asking a friend in Jerusalem to find him a small store where he could earn a simple living and devote himself to the pure study of Torah. But Kook did not believe in dodging everyday reality. Even when composing his legal works, he refused to let others do the routine checking of quotations and references that important lawyers usually leave to their clerks. He wanted that to be part of his "black work," his bond with those who carry on jobs as humdrum as street-sweeping or weeding.

The real challenge to Rabbi Kook in dealing with religious realities in the Holy Land was more serious. He could not avoid recognizing the fact that many rebuilders of the land, many of its most idealistic *halutzim,* were anything but pious. They respected muscles and physical courage more than skill in Talmudic dialectics. Was this the time when Rabbi Kook began to try to reconcile the concrete phenomena about him with the assertions of traditional faith? He explained, to others and to himself, that this increase in the "fleshly" qualities of his people had to take place before the coming of the Messianic era. "Only a strong and vigorous spirit, and a healthy and firm body can contain, without being crushed, the most powerful spiritual illuminations." Were not the prophets, including Moses, possessed of husky outer bodies? Was not King David, the sweet singer of the psalms, a man of lusty appetites? Vessels had to be "thickened," so that they could contain without cracking, the high-powered spiritual charges destined for the Israel that had returned to its own soil.

There was a third picture of the rabbi on the wall, sitting in a chair, chin in hand, his large eyes meditative, sad. I seem to recall this photograph as having been taken in England during the First World War. He had been visiting in Switzerland when the war broke out and, after some months there, had been asked to assume an important rabbinic position in London. This period of his life had produced some of his most interesting essays and meditations, including one called "Rosh Milin," the "Beginning of Words." It was a kabbalistic discourse on the alphabet, vowel signs, and musical notations used in the reading of the Torah, quite incomprehensible to most readers. Rabbi Kook had not meant it to be a popular work, calling it simply a bit of writing inspired by "memories of the Holy Land in the diaspora."

There was one other photograph, Kook wearing a large, fur-encircled *shtreiml,* now Chief Rabbi of Palestine, a post to which he had been called in 1921 and occupied until his death in 1935.

Stories about Rabbi Kook's behavior and responses to the challenges which he met in this position have become a part of Israeli folklore. People remembered his words to the British high commissioner at a public event following a massacre of Yeshiva students by Arabs in Hebron. The commissioner, despite appeals, had refused to provide the Jewish community with weapons for self-defense. Seeing Rabbi Kook on a public platform, the commissioner had come forward to shake his hand. The rabbi, usually on excellent terms with the mandatory authority, had turned away, later explaining his actions with words from Isaiah, ". . . and they stretched out to me hands, covered with blood."

Probably the most famous of the stories associated with this period of Rabbi Kook's life was the illustration he used to answer those who criticized his friendship with the nonreligious elements of the land.

"There is a place for distinction between the pure and impure," the rabbi would say to them. "In the temple, there was a Holy of Holies into which only the high priest could enter and then only on the day of Yom Kippur. But what was the situation when the Holy of Holies was being built? Did not even the most ordinary of masons and carpenters enter freely and contribute their offering to the total structure? We are building today in Palestine and have not yet completed our 'Holy of Holies.' All have a portion to offer in this building and none has more right than another in bringing his offering."

Now at last the conversation between Rabbi Zvi Yehudah Kook and the student appeared to be terminating; the rabbi accompanied him to the door and turned to me. I introduced myself and told the rabbi that I had been reading his father's writings for years and wanted to learn more. Zvi Yehudah nodded his head in eager assent and took my hand while telling me how his father had, indeed, combined the various streams of Judaism "all together." Then, still holding my hand, he inquired as to my first name and my work. He would be glad to talk with me at his home that Sabbath afternoon.

"Receiving" from Abraham Isaac Kook

Visitors who meet the son of the famous Rav Kook are liable to be disappointed on first impression. He does not possess that aura which Hasidim call *malchut,* the air of royal authority, and even accomplished Hebraists have difficulty in understanding the rapid flow of his words and sentences. "An overabundance of *shefa,* of the desire to give," is the way one perspicacious observer has analyzed this characteristic of Zvi Yehudah's speech. But all that he wants to give to others, he insists, is his father's teachings.

The places and occasions where I did my "receiving" from Rav Kook's son were many and varied: a twilight hour conversation in his home, a class with some students in the Merkaz ha-Rav, a walk through Jerusalem streets—in fact, every meeting became an occasion for Torah.

At the beginning I would come to Zvi Yehudah's house alone, usually on a Sabbath afternoon. His apartment contained a little kitchen where he often prepared his own meals, a small foyer, dining room, and bedroom. We sat in the dining room, whose walls were lined with books. The furniture consisted of an old broken sofa, a roughhewn wooden table with benches, and a broken-down cabinet on which were strewn some knickknacks, books, and small pictures.

One evening, Zvi Yehudah saw me examining the pictures. "That's the Hofetz Chaim"—he told me, as I picked up a small photograph of a white-bearded rabbi. The Hofetz Chaim, whose real name was Rabbi Israel Meir ha-Cohen, was a late-nineteenth-century Polish scholar who "specialized" in the battle against the sin of *lashon harah,* the evil tongue. His name came from the opening words of the psalmist's phrase, "He who desires life (*hofetz chaim* in Hebrew), let him keep his tongue from speaking evil. . . ."

Rabbi Kook's eyes crinkled with delight as he told me about a rich American Jew who once visited the famous rabbi in his home that consisted only of a book-filled room, a table, and a bench.

"Rabbi," said the American, "where is your Eminence's furniture?"

"Where is yours?" asked the Hofetz Chaim.

"Mine?" replied the American in surprise. "But I'm only a visitor here. I'm only in transit."

"Me too," said the Hofetz Chaim.

Rabbi Kook chuckled as he told me this story, then asked me to sit on the bench at his side. "Nu?" he began, placing his hand on mine and squeezing it. "Nu?" We would then go on to almost any subject: an interpretation of one of his father's texts; a discussion about the status of women in Jewish tradition; the latest battle between the religious and nonreligious camps. The latter topic frequently served as a springboard for the exposition of what Zvi Yehudah called his father's way of analyzing problems from "the roots above."

The View from "the Roots Above"

The state of Israel is broadly split into so-called religious and nonreligious camps, the former being identified in Israel with Orthodoxy. The religious camp is, in turn, divided into a spectrum which varies from liberal groups, such as the Mizrachi Party, to the extremely conservative Neturei Karta, the Keepers of the City, some of whose members will not let the money of the "atheistic" Zionist government touch their hands. The war between the so-called religious and secular segments is continuous, only the battlefront changes. The struggle may be joined on the problem of public transportation on the Sabbath, the prohibition against civil divorce, exemption from military service of *yeshiva* students and religious girls, or the insistence that visitors to the Wailing Wall in Jerusalem be separated according to sex. The elements of this conflict already existed in the East European environment which bred the first pioneers and leaders of the Jewish state. In the Czarist Russia of Rabbi Kook's day, many idealistic Jewish youth were attracted to revolutionary ideals which envisioned a world that would burst the limiting fetters of bourgeois values. Others, who remained emotionally committed to their people's destiny, were alienated from religious leaders who felt that the movement to establish a Jewish state was "pushing the end" that should properly wait the coming of the Messiah. This attitude had even produced some Jewish nationalists who felt it necessary to desecrate Jewish religious laws "on principle."

In Palestine, Abraham Isaac Kook quickly found himself in the midst of this struggle. Though pained by their disrespect for traditional religious values, he could not help but recognize the personal idealism of the young pioneers or the fact that they were the element which was actually constructing the new Jewish state. His openly expressed sympathy for these *halutzim* quickened the antagonism of some Orthodox to the point where one extremist group actually put him, the chief rabbi, under a ban of excommunication. Even more crucial for the rabbi, however, was his own effort to reconcile the paradoxes of holiness in the Holy Land. What helped him, Rabbi Zvi Yehudah explained, was the way he could clarify details in the light of *hachlala,* an all-inclusive perspective.

Hachlala comes from the Hebrew *k'lal,* meaning generalization or principle. Kook's inclusive thinking can be illustrated by various images; the onion whose inner layers are "included" by successively encompassing layers; the tree whose branches are "included" within the trunk; or the human cell that is "included" within a limb, that is in turn "included" within a body, that is in turn part of humanity, and so forth. With Rav Kook the concept of inclusion is broadened to encompass not only human phenomena but the totality of creation. "The life which slumbers in minerals, which is slightly awakened in plants, and which already strongly pulsates in animals, is one and the same; a tree of life reaches from these lowly creatures, over mankind, divided into ever so many peoples and parties, to the angels on high, one living, pulsating, organic unity."

This view of reality as an organic unity, as one "bundle of life" is called by Prof. S. H. Bergmann panentheism, which he defines as an assertion that "everything is in God, though God is more than everything." A corollary of this view is the assertion that everything, since it is ultimately rooted in the divine, is ultimately good, and evil is not real but a veiled or a lesser good.

There is nothing original in this thesis. It is a classic Jewish belief which, as we have seen, Hasidism carries to its extreme in asserting that "there is no place empty of Him." What is original is Rabbi Kook's application of this thought to such problems as the conflict between the religious and nonreligious camps in the Holy Land. An example was offered me by Rabbi Zvi Yehudah one summer afternoon not long after the founding of the State. On the way to the rabbi's house, I had passed a demonstration by several dozen Orthodox women, dressed in the Meah She'arim uniform of long-sleeved dresses and bandanna-like head coverings. They had gathered in front of the Israeli parliament building to protest the drafting of their daughters into what they called the brothel atmosphere of the army. The civilian bystanders, whose sons and daughters were serving in the army, had shouted angry insults at the women who, in turn, had called them and the police Nazis. The near violence ended only when the fire department arrived and sprayed the scene with water.

I arrived at Rabbi Zvi Yehudah's house visibly depressed, and the rabbi must have noticed both my exhaustion and my mood, for he hurried to get a glass of water before asking for the cause of my dejection. When I told him what I had seen, his face saddened and his words came more slowly than usual.

"Yes," Rabbi Zvi Yehudah had sighed, "believers should have more belief. That is, those who proclaim their faith in God should have more confidence in His power. They should have enough confidence to believe that God has a place in his providential plan for all kinds of people, including the nonbelievers or 'free thinkers,' as they call themselves here in Israel. And the free thinkers, too, should break through the little ideological formulae by which they define the world. They should press beyond the limitations of their political and economic catchwords and glimpse vistas which are not encompassed by small definitions. More belief for unbelievers, and more freedom of thought for the free thinkers—and, above all, more love. The sages said that Jerusalem was destroyed because of 'causeless hatred.' Therefore, my father always said, it would have to be rebuilt with the help of 'causeless love.'"

"Yes," I agreed halfheartedly, "but meanwhile it is all so discouraging."

"Discouraging?" His face brightened. "Listen, did you ever visit a chemical factory, a place where they synthesize different elements? Do you know how it smells?"

I confessed that I came from an area of New Jersey where it is well known how chemical factories can smell.

"Then you realize that in such a place one cannot avoid bad odors or explosions. Well, we are here engaging in resynthesizing a people that has, over thousands of years, been broken into more than seventy different elements: Kurds, Germans, Yemenites, Iraquis. Do you think this can possibly take place without bad smell, without explosions? This is what my father meant by trying to see the branches which extend into the world below from the roots above, to see the individual phenomena, from the perspective of the overall whole."

Abraham Isaac Kook's view of all problems in what the Kabbala calls "the world of division" from the perspective of the upper "world of unity" also helped him explain the revolt of the new Jew against traditional values. He was keenly aware of the contempt in which so many Israelis held the *yeshiva* student, who poured all of his energy into the study of Torah, and how the younger generation admired the man who was able to swing a pick and shoot a gun. This was inevitable, Kook explained; in the diaspora, Jews had almost died from overspiritualization. Now the pendulum had to swing toward the opposite extreme. The increase of *hutzpah,* brazenness, was a necessary part of this process. The end, however, would be the "swallowing up of the bodily and secular by the holy, resulting in a holiness of strength and power."

This same view from above made it possible for the chief rabbi to insist that even atheism had a certain right to existence. For religious institutions could become so cluttered up with inadequate definitions of the divine that they hid rather than disclosed real divinity. Only when the winds of denial have purified religious institutions will the "higher knowledge of God build its Temple upon the rubble heap."

The need of the holy to achieve power in the world by including within itself the strength of the outer world helps to explain Rabbi Kook's interest in externalities such as the office of a chief rabbi or popular journalistic techniques. He insisted that the war with secularism could not be won simply by denouncing the values of the non-religious world. The representatives of the "inner kingdom" must learn how to use the techniques of modern communication, technology, and organization. They must include within themselves the good points of the enemy; "if they are lacking in us we will not be able to stand against him, let alone conquer him."

The acceptance of an overall inclusiveness also applied to the vulgar and wicked of the world. "Just as it is impossible for wine to be without lees, it is impossible for the world to be without the wicked. For even as the lees ferment the wine and keeps it at its proper strength, so do the vulgar desires of the wicked bring sustenance and strength to the vital current of all men. . . ."

The Veiling of the Light

The problem of reconciling apparent evil with the existence of an all-powerful and all-good God is, of course, the supreme challenge of the monotheistic faith. Dostoevsky's claim that it is impossible to justify "the tears of even one innocent suffering child" has often been given a "religious" answer, but no one, neither questioner nor answerer, is really satisfied. And Dostoevsky's problem is raised to the nth degree in the case of the genocide of Jews in Europe. Even "knights of faith" in Judaism have preferred to sidestep the problem by saying, "it is not for us to understand either the reward of the evildoers or the suffering of the innocent."

Almost inevitably, the claim that there is an all-powerful and all-good God leads to the conclusion that what men call evil is not really evil in the perspective of a higher reality. I understood that this would have to be the ultimate position of Rav Kook, but was nevertheless eager to hear it stated in his own terms." That opportunity occurred one afternoon when I happend to meet Rabbi Zvi Yehudah as he was leaving the Yeshiva for his daily walk home through the center of town. Our discussion began with his observation that attempts to define Judaism in terms of a way of life and a set of *mitzvot,* or commandments, could produce only a flawed religion. There was also the obligation to have a "full faith." To be sure, this full faith had to be substantiated by evidence and the most powerful evidence which a Jew could adduce for his faith was the singular fate of Israel. God's providence was manifest everywhere but was concentrated in Jewish history and, within this history, in the relationship between Jews and the land of Israel. When the bond between the Jewish people and their land is warped, exile is the result. The relationship must be cleansed and purified, and this is a process which encounters many obstacles from both within and without. Nevertheless, this cleansing process is the meaning of Jewish history, its process of evolution toward the final establishment of the bond in its most purified form.

I asked the rabbi how events like the Nazi holocaust could be adduced as proof for faith in God. Zvi Yehudah nodded. "The process of God taking us out of *galut,* exile, sometimes requires a strong hand —with the fingernails, so to speak; and the pain of the removal is great."

Such a view, I protested, denied the reality of evil and weakened attempts to resist it. Zvi Yehudah dismissed my argument with a shake of his head. In the world of division, we had to react to evil as evil, for that was the level of reality on which we lived. But the effort to impose our partial vision on God was childish.

"There are so many worlds being discovered now, and all of them touch each other, have an effect on each other—who can judge only by this world alone?" The only way to resolve all problems, Zvi Yehudah assured me as we arrived at his home, was *berur* and *hachlalah,* the clarification of details by setting them in the perspective of the whole.

Once inside his apartment, the rabbi drew open the shutters and asked me to sit at the table. He left the room to return a few moments later with a small book entitled *The Lights of Repentance.*

Did I know of this book? he asked. "My father wrote it, but looked upon it as a gift of God. He would study it himself before the High Holy Days." He opened the book to a specific passage, one which evidently bore on the subject we had been discussing during our walk:

At a moment when a man sins, he is in the "world of division,"
and then every detail stands by itself. Evil is then completely evil and
it possesses the quality of doing harm. But when man does repentance
out of love, then there shines upon him the cosmic light of the "world

of unity" where everything is combined into a oneness: and in this general binding together, there is no evil as such, for evil combines with and gives tone to the good and raises it to an ever higher value.

After letting me read these lines, Rabbi Zvi Yehudah turned to another page toward the end of the book:

It is the function of the righteous, the saintly ones in the world, to recognize that the pure light is too strong for the world to endure. Yet it must somehow illuminate the world. Therefore it is necessary that there be many veils to soften the light, and these veils are what we know as evil and its causes. [Consequently, the explanation continued, these veils have a place in the total arrangement and order of the world. Our difficulty is that] we who possess a limited perception of the intensity of the light, do not have the ability to see that all evil is but a veil needed in order to adjust the flow of light.

Now the rabbi closed the book. "Look, a few moments ago we came into this room and it was dark. Then I pulled open the shutters. It does not mean that we no longer clearly see the furniture of the room. On the contrary, what seemed hazy is made clear by letting in the brighter light from without." In the same way, the rabbi explained, an "ascent to the roots" did not mean that a person could no longer function in the world of division. It simply helped him to make clearer judgments about affairs in this world.

Problems of Partial Thinking

The converse of the view from the roots on high is partiality, the isolating of a detail from its overall context. Such thinking, Rav Kook had insisted, led to a tragic misunderstanding of the apparently great antinomies of existence—life and death, good and evil, flesh and spirit. It could even cause considerable misunderstanding in a matter like the status of women in the Orthodox Jewish religion.

The setting for a discussion on this latter subject was quite unusual. One summer I asked Zvi Yehudah to meet with a group of Christian ministers and tourists. He had hesitated and wanted to know if there would be any Jewish converts to Christianity in the group. When I assured him that these were born and bred American Christians, he consented to a meeting at the Universal Yeshiva on a Sabbath afternoon; I didn't realize how strong his reluctance was until I brought my group there for our scheduled discussion.

Two or three young men were studying some Talmudic tomes when we arrived and I asked one of them where the rabbi might be. After a few moments he returned to say that the door to the study was closed, but that the rabbi might be inside. I urged him to announce our presence, but he hesitated. Instead, he knocked very gently on the door, peeked through the keyhole and came back to tell us that the rabbi seemed to be either studying or praying. I finally prevailed upon the student to knock more strongly on the door of the rabbi's study. A few moments later the little white-bearded man emerged and greeted the tourists with a respectful *"shalom."*

"Every people," he began with a timorous smile, "has its favorite expression of greeting; as the visitors knew, *shalom,* peace, was the Hebrew greeting. But the meaning of this salutation must be understood in its fullness. Now, Martin Luther, in his commentary to a translation of the Psalms, had commented on the unique characteristics of the Hebrew language in that it had so many names for God, while most languages had only one or two names. One of the Hebrew names for God was *shalom.* This meant that wherever there was peace between people or within society, there God revealed something of His essence. It was in this sense that he wanted to say to them, *"shalom."* And now they could ask any questions they liked.

The group applauded the rabbi's statement, and a Lutheran professor of bible raised his hand.

"Has the rabbi read Martin Luther?"

I translated the question and Zvi Yehudah Kook's face crinkled happily.

"Well, I didn't hear about Luther's commentary from the Holy Spirit."

Everyone laughed and the ice was broken. From then on the questions came rapidly.

"What is Judaism's main disagreement with Christianity?"

"The identification of God with man."

Would the rabbi tell about one or two of his most moving religious experiences?

"Every prayer can and should be a moving religious experience."

As we went along, the rabbi's answers grew longer. Finally, one woman rose to ask a question that occurs to many Western visitors when they encounter the synagogues and religious gatherings of Orthodox Jewry.

"Why are women given such a secondary position in the Jewish religion?"

I translated the question, and Rabbi Zvi Yehudah cleared his throat.

"Everything must be seen in the category of 'wholeness,'" the rabbi began, "and one example of the relationship between the organic whole and the details would be the heart and limbs of a human being. They both have different functions, but they constitute a whole. In the same way, man and woman make up one whole, what we call *Adam* in Hebrew." But though they make up one whole, they are also different. Women were more sensitive, more inclined to feelings, more passive. Men were more practical and logical.

"Of course, there are exceptions," Zvi Yehudah interrupted his line of thought. "Madame Curie, for example. But, in general, men are more logical, and logic is something that can be communicated and shared. On the other hand, feelings cannot be commanded; in this realm it is individuality which is exercised. That is part of the reason why women are not obligated to perform some commandments that must be performed at a certain time.

"To be acted upon," Zvi Yehudah continued, "does not mean to be subjected. It is but another way of becoming a part of the total building. Now, a *chacham,* a rabbinic sage, is in the category of those who create and do work. But there is another category of religious life which is higher—the prophet. The prophet is one who has risen to a level where he is 'worked upon.' Hence, to become a passive recipient rather than an active creator, is a higher spiritual category. This is the category of the blessing that women offer up in the morning, thanking God for 'having made me according to His will.' That is to say, they thank God for being made as to be an instrument of His will. Is that clear?"

Most of the group, despite my efforts at translation, had long ago lost the thread of the rabbi's argument, and a few were looking at their watches. The rabbi was ready to proceed further, but I hastened to draw the meeting to a close by thanking him for his time. Everyone applauded, and he seemed pleased. In the corridor, the rabbi admitted to me that this was the first time in his life that he had spoken with a group of Christians. "But it is good to do this. Every meeting between people of good will can expand the boundaries of the mind and soul."

When I returned to the group, everyone politely assured me that they had enjoyed their meeting with the rabbi. "I like his sense of humor and the smile lines around his eyes," one minister told me.

"He's really read Luther," another said. "He must be a liberal rabbi."

I didn't want to disillusion the minister about Zvi Yehudah Kook's "liberalism." Furthermore, I did not then know that there were some painful lessons about Rabbi Kook's liberalism in store for me. Besides, the group had received quite enough of that *shefa* which could, on occasion, be overabundant even for his own students.

Rabbi Kook's Definition of Mysticism

The students who attended regular classes at Zvi Yehudah Kook's house were usually reconciled to their teacher's fulsome approach to almost any subject. Officially, their classes were supposed to center about a specific text—like the *Kuzari,* a philosophic defense of Judaism written in the twelfth century by Yehudah Halevi, or books authored by the sixteenth-century Rabbi Yehudah Loew of Prague. These two men, Rabbi Zvi Yehudah liked to say, were part of the "triple-linked chain," of which his father was the third link. More often, the text came from the written legacy of Abraham Isaac Kook. Whatever the subject, however, half the evening would pass before we got to it. The good-natured rabbi was well aware of his propensity for straying from topic to topic, and one evening offered a rationale which linked it with his father's system of thought. The most elevated ideas, Rav Kook had once written, were received as flashes that enter into the bodily limited forms of life only to "turn and flee again to their source before they are fully embodied. Then a new flash comes to take their place. . . ."

Many of Kook's meditations were received as such flashes which he scribbled at odd times into notebooks. "He had a compulsion to write, and rarely attempted to organize these thought flashes, considering such 'ordering' a secondary level of creation." But all "primal Jewish creations," Zvi Yehudah Kook insisted, such as the bible and Talmud, and many high level "creators" like the Vilna Gaon, revealed this seeming indifference to systematic presentation. But this apparent lack of order was actually the "order of the spring at its source." Only when the stream has come far from its source and become somewhat placid and lifeless can it be packaged into neat vessels.

"Once, I was sitting in a doctor's office," said the rabbi by way of illustration, "and a little girl came in and began cutting up a pile of papers. When the doctor asked her what she was doing, she said she was arranging things—making order." His eyes twinkled. "You see, what is order on one level, seems like disorder on another."

One evening this order in disorder led us to a definition of mysticism. A student's remark provoked the rabbi to take out a notebook of dreams. Nobody in the room had ever known that he kept such a book, and the rabbi spoke softly as he read from a few of the entries, so softly that we had to lean forward in order to catch the words. One of the dreams was about the house that his family had occupied in Jaffa before the First World War. Zvi Yehudah was a young boy then, and in the dream he "remembered everything—the courtyard, the stairs, even the fish peddler who knocked at the door." Zvi Yehudah had wiped his eyes as he read these lines. A few days after the dream, he had found himself in Jaffa at night and taken a walk. Suddenly, he was standing near his old home. Nobody seemed to be in the house, and so he had entered the courtyard and walked about. "Interesting, yes?" He smiled at the students. "What would you call it—telepathy?"

The conversation veered to another topic when one of the students asked the rabbi's opinion about a recent newspaper article attacking the Canaanites, a small group of native-born Israelis who denied all bonds with traditional rabbinic Judaism and even with Jewish communities outside of Israel. Zvi Yehudah, as was his custom, immediately tried to show the other side.

"Even here there is an angle that deserves clarification. This antidiaspora rebellion stems partly from the realization that there is something really new being formed here."

Another student then reported that the Lubavitcher rebbe from Brooklyn might soon be visiting Israel. Zvi Yehudah shook his head gently. The Lubavitcher rebbe was known to be something less than a fully committed Zionist.

"Believers should have more faith in the deeds of God, in the history and divine providence that brought us here. There are *tzaddikim,* saintly men, who meticulously fulfill all the commandments but lack faith."

Mention of the Lubavitcher rebbe led to some general observations on Hasidism. "Their mistake," Rabbi Zvi Yehudah suggested, "is not that they are wrong in wanting lively prayers, but in forgetting that there is also value in the act or prayer that is not on this level. Even in the temple there were various levels of sacrifices. The highest were indeed animals, but there were times when one composed of inorganic materials, such as oil and flour, was also in order."

The discussion went on this way from subject to subject until the students tactfully tried to interrupt Zvi Yehudah's endless train of associations.

"Doesn't the rabbi feel cold?" one young man asked.

"If you say so," Zvi Yehudah grinned impishly, closed the windows, and returned to his *shmuess.*

Finally a student tried to bring Zvi Yehudah around to the purpose of the evening by asking what page in the *Lights of Holiness* we were about to study, as if he didn't know. The little rabbi chuckled and opened his book to the page scheduled for that evening. "I can remember this page in my father's notebook. It was on the left side." Zvi Yehudah shook his head nostalgically.

After invoking the "view from above," he began to read a passage subtitled "The Soul of Life":

The soul of the world shines; it is filled with glory and beauty, filled with light. It is the residuary of souls, the treasury of the holy spirit, the wellspring of strength, greatness and beauty. . . .

"The introduction is a poetic flight," Zvi Yehudah interrupted, and reminded his listeners what his father meant when he spoke of soul. "The soul is the inner man, the inner essence, out of which the outer forms evolve, even as man is only superficially to be identified with the shape of his clothes, or even with the form of his body, or even with his expressed thoughts, but is to be identified with some deeper intangible, less visible entity, the essential truth of his being." It is this inner, less visible, but more real source spring of existence which Kook calls the "soul."

To be sure, this soul cannot be perceived by the superficial, external glance which sees only the outside. It requires a relationship. This is the mistake of those who would like to know with objectivity. If by this objectivity they restrict themselves only to surface facts, then their knowing is partial. To know a person more fully requires penetration into his inner being, and such penetration involves closeness, rather than objective distance. In this sense, said Zvi Yehudah, "true objectivity, the objectivity which wants to know more fully, leads one to subjectivity."

I remembered Professor Scholem's insistence on objectivity as the prime condition for understanding historic truth.

"In general," the rabbi continued his discourse, "the more deep, the more hidden; the more inner, the more truth. And conversely, the more superficial; the less penetrating, the less truth. In this sense, the deepest truth, what some might call the mystic insight, is to be identified with the lyrical perception that sees the inner unity of things, rather than with the external and more partial glance that sees only unconnected surface facts."

Nor is there a contradiction in Jewish mysticism, Zvi Yehudah continued, between the feelings and reason, or between reason and the moral imperative. The rabbi illustrated this by turning to another passage in the book. "All ethical darkness is in itself mental darkness . . . where there is evil, there too is foolishness . . . the divine life cannot reveal itself in that life which is morally defective, for, says the Zohar, the 'presence does not rest in a polluted spot.' "

Here is the difference, Abraham Isaac Kook had written, between the Holy Spirit of the Jewish prophets and that of non-Jewish religious leaders. In the case of the latter, the incursion of the Holy Spirit was often sensed as something which annulled logic and even transcended moral strictures, tending to blur the claim of the petty detail. In Jewish prophecy, the divine flash illuminates and strengthens the power of the mind on all its levels, logical and imaginative. It expresses itself in ethical demands and insists on seeing these demands translated into minute detail. The prime example is Moses, who is permitted the greatest of mystical visions, yet expresses his illumination through laws which embrace the smallest as well as the largest of life demands, the details of clothes and ritual sacrifices along with the Ten Commandments, the trivial along with the tremendous, the high with the low. That is why, claims the Talmud, the rabbinic scholar who is concerned with details is more important than the prophet.

"Nor must we underestimate," Zvi Yehudah Kook concluded, "even the smallest detail in the totality of conditions which produce or take away the possibility of connection with life, growth, and freedom. We know, for example, that with a seed planted in the ground, or an egg in a human body, if the temperature is just the slightest bit off, or if a minute quantity of a certain chemical is missing, then all possibilities of life can also be missing." In other words, the smallest details of Torah, the seemingly pettiest laws and most insignificant traditions, are absolutely essential for the living soul of the Jew.

It was this point of view, I reflected after the class, which could make the same rabbi who wrote, "Expanses, expanses—enclose me not in cages of mind, spirit or word," also the author of a tract urging Jews to be careful about placing the head phylactery on the precise spot on the forehead prescribed by law. The high and the low, the universal and the particular—all are connected in the Jewish way. Any attempt to embrace one level without the other led to the sin of partial perspective.

The Withdrawal of the Light

We have met the question at the beginning of this journal and we must meet it again at the end. For it is *the* question which must be confronted in any attempt to establish a meaningful connection between the *yesh,* the inner life substance claimed by those who dwell within the inner chambers of Judaism and those who stand outside. Can this *yesh* be acquired or even discovered without a commitment to the full structure, the hundreds of negative and positive commandments of the Law? More, can the Law be obeyed without a full commitment to the premises that have traditionally undergirded the Jew's acceptance of the commandments, that is, without the faith that at Sinai "God spoke and Moses wrote."

The Orthodox Jew offers an affirmative reply to such questions. But there remains a question, as real for the Orthodox insider as for the outside observer. Does Orthodoxy show sufficient evidence, even to those who approach it closely, of the vitality and inner substance that it claims to possess? This is a mystery that presents itself not only to those who visit out-of-the-way Hasidic houses but also to one who may visit the family of Rabbi Kook.

I recall a Sabbath meal with Rabbi Zvi Yehudah and his family. Rabbi Zvi Yehudah's sister, a kindly woman with watery blue eyes and face that bore a strong resemblance to her father, had invited me to dine with them after morning prayers. Zvi Yehudah, a widower without children, was frequently at his sister's home. I met the rest of the family at the table. The late chief rabbi's son-in-law, who called himself Rabbi Raanan Kook, a white-bearded, good-natured man, listened with a timid smile to our conversations. Rabbi Kook's daughter, a woman in her seventies and in poor health, served the meal and was a gracious hostess. Her daughter, sitting at the table, had her mother's red-rimmed, slightly puffy eyes. She, too, was listening to our conversation and occasionally interjected some questions about America. She was married, but her husband, who had entered the room for a few minutes, was evidently eating somewhere else. Her brother, now the only grandchild of Rabbi Abraham Isaac Kook, was eating with us. He was a good-natured, simple young man, then unmarried, who kept his eyes on a picture magazine during most of the meal.

I watched Rabbi Zvi Yehudah put his hands on the bread and mumble the blessings. Then, as we began to eat, he asked me where I had prayed that Sabbath. I told him I had been with the Dead Hasidim in the Bratzlaver Synagogue and added that I saw strong similarities between his father's ideas and the teachings of Rabbi Nachman. The Hasidic rebbe and his followers liked to go out into the fields where, by their prayers, they would try to "bind the life that was in each blade of grass and flower into a garland for the Lord." Rabbi Kook, too, had rhapsodized how man, when he prays, "unites within himself the pent-up desire of all that lives, every blade of grass and every clod of earth to return to its source. . . ." Rabbi Nachman called himself a moon man subject to periods of waxing and waning and advised his followers to use the troughs of life as opportunities to strengthen oneself for a new leap upward. Rabbi Kook also fought with melancholy and asked why a person should not take advantage of this mood of his soul and "lift pearls out of the murky depths . . . for, after all, in whatever manner and wherever a man's soul makes itself evident, there is evidence of the beginning of deliverance. . . ."

Then, there was Rabbi Nachman's insistence that true piety could be found more in the cowlike faith of simple people rather than among the sophisticated intellectuals. Kook, too, had said that "the healthiest instincts for righteousness would be found among the untutored, "gross" elements of society.

The little rabbi's eyes crinkled with pleasure as I quoted from his father's writings, but denied that Rabbi Kook had borrowed Rabbi Nachman's ideas. All Jewish ideas were included within his father's Judaism. Rabbi Kook was like the Hasid who, when asked how he should preach, was advised to turn himself into a "huge ear into which all the voices of tradition could pour and find transmittal." In the same way, all the streams of Judaism had been poured into Rabbi Kook as underground water pours into a well. But in the case of his father, the well was also a spring continually bubbling with new and original ideas.

The meal was pleasant, but I could not help sensing an absence of joy around the table. This was probably due in great part to a recent tragedy that had taken the life of the younger son in the family, Abraham Isaac Kook. He had been a gifted student, and all had sensed in him "sparks" of his grandfather's soul, but less than a year before, he had drowned in the Mediterranean while swimming with some soldiers of his army unit.

But I could not help feeling that there was another less personal reason for this lack of vitality, which was not peculiar to Rabbi Kook's family. True, I had witnessed examples of profound prayer and intellectual acumen in many traditional synagogues and homes, and even what Hasidim call *lebedigkeit,* liveliness. But this *lebedigkeit* was often accompanied by an atmosphere of degeneration. Again and again, it seemed like a world that had once been flooded with creative power, but then, as in the cosmic kabbalistic imagery of the Ari, this power had been withdrawn leaving only an "impression" in empty space. There was still enough force emanating from the impression to supply the inhabitants of this world with a *yesh* more substantial than could be found in the more glamorous dwellings of the non-Orthodox, but the light was fading, the "space" was widening.

All this, I realized, could be the superficial judgment of an outsider, but I recalled young Rabbi Adin Steinsaltz telling me that the old Hasidic houses were undergoing a biological crisis. They were not producing the physical heirs to their dynasties. It was as if the stream of creative vitality which had produced and sustained the Hasidic movement for more than two hundred years was entering a *cul-de-sac*. The same thing, he pointed out, seemed to have happened in the house of Rav Kook. Not that there was less vital force here than in other Orthodox quarters. On the contrary, students at the Universal Yeshiva were far more alive to the problems of the world about them than other Orthodox students of Torah, and the teachings of Rav Kook remained a constant call to let in the creative force of a new and changing world. But for this very reason, because the students and the teachings were so eager for rebirth, the reality was all the more painful. Despite criticism of the religious Establishment and the call for rejuvenation, in the last analysis, when life pushed against the structure of the old Law, it was the Law which had to conquer, even if the result was the very opposite of Rav Kook's dream. And so we were back to the basic question: can this Law, even if it offers the only way to Judaism's inner substance, even if a rediscovered faith declares it to be divinely inspired, can it really construct a viable house of life in our modern world?

Not One Dot or Tittle

Not long after this Sabbath came a moment which I knew was inevitable, when my own inability to share the full Orthodox faith of Rabbi Kook would involve a fundamental change in my relationships with my teacher.

Zvi Yehudah knew all along that I was a Reform rabbi in the United States and even assured me that, "There is undoubtedly room for such work there." On several occasions he had suggested that I remove my yarmelke—"After all, we don't believe in national imperialism. Why should we believe in personal imperialism, in the effort of one person or group to impose its way of life upon another. As long as you keep the hat on, I feel there is a *mechitza,* a boundary, between us."

Actually, I had the impression that Rabbi Kook was rather intrigued by the interest of a liberal rabbi in Abraham Isaac Kook. *Tshuvah,* return, the return of vegetation to its roots, of a people to its ancestral soil, of an individual to his people, of a sinner to the laws of the Torah—this was the central doctrine of Judaism. On the other hand, an individual who not only fails to make the full return himself but engages in activities which may mislead others is no longer welcome. In the winter of 1962 I came to Israel as the administrator of the newly built Hebrew Union College in Jerusalem, an institution which the Orthodox press quickly denounced as a "beachhead for Reform Judaism." Not long after my arrival, a student from the Universal Yeshiva left word that Rabbi Zvi Yehudah Kook wanted to see me.

I came to his home the next evening with considerable apprehension, and I was right. Zvi Yehudah did not invite me to sit near him as we talked. Instead, he paced about the room. Finally, the question burst out: was I trying to bring Reform Judaism to Israel? I explained that the primary purpose of the Hebrew Union College in Jerusalem was biblical and archaeological studies, though there would also eventually be religious services. He wanted to know what kind of prayerbook would be used, and I described it. Still troubled, he took down a volume of his father's letters and showed me some paragraphs from two letters. One was to a Jew in Australia who had asked for advice. There were two synagogues in his town, the Australian Jew had explained; one was Orthodox, where the sexes were separated, and the other was traditional, but was mixed seating. The rabbi of the Orthodox congregation was, however, a public desecrator of the Sabbath and a man known to be unobservant and even unethical. What the Australian Jew had wanted to know was whether he should continue to attend the Orthodox synagogue, despite the blatant hypocrisy of the rabbi, or join the other congregation. Rav Kook's answer had been unequivocal: any attempt to seat women and men together was absolutely forbidden!

The second letter was even stronger in tone, denouncing the spreading plague of organs in synagogue services. There were other expressions of Rav Kook's disapproval of liberal religious innovations.

Even the sound of a woman's voice singing in synagogues was forbidden by Law on the grounds of lewdness.

I never had any illusions about the elder Rabbi Kook's feelings on such matters but was taken aback by the violence of his language. His son must have sensed my shock, for he made an effort to explain. Is it not historic fact that the Reform movement had been responsible for the assimilation of large Jewish communities in Europe? And to bring this Judaism "to the center, to the very apple of the eye"—his voice trembled at the thought.

It was no use, I knew, expressing my disagreement with this teacher whose warm friendship had meant so much to me. I had to face the fact that Rav Kook had expressed contempt for that kind of religious "tolerance which was rooted in spiritual indifference or weakness." I had been able to walk together with his son all these years because I had agreed, at least in his presence, to play the game according to his rules. But the courtesy was a one-way affair. There was no other path, no other rule; I was again an outsider.

The Descent

Every treasure hunt should lead from the projection of a goal to its accomplishment. But what if the hunt does not go according to plan? Then there is a tempting alternative. Offer maps, describe the manner in which others have succeeded, and close the book. After all, why should it matter if the person who writes a journal has personally accomplished the quest on which he set out? The important question for the reader should be: is there a treasure? Are the maps that lead to it accurate? If he is still interested, let him join the hunt for himself.

Perhaps this should be the way this journal closes. For the continued mingling of subject matter with personal reaction involves an uncomfortable confession, the story of a "falling." Whether or not it is the kind of falling which Hasidim claim must precede every ascent is a question I must leave open for myself, as well as for the reader.

Signs of this falling have, I suspect, already made their appearance during the last few pages, but the real descent occurred several years later in the winter and spring of 1967, weeks when I was trying to finish this book in Jerusalem. And I was not alone in this descent; there were others, many others, in Israel and in other lands. How to describe the mood of that period? A well-known passage by Rav Kook may help:

> *There is one who sings the song of his own soul, and in his soul he finds everything, full spiritual satisfaction.*
>
> *And there is one who sings the song of the people. For he does not find the circle of his private soul wide enough, and so goes beyond it, reaching for more powerful heights. And he unites himself with the soul of the community of Israel, sings its songs, suffers with its sorrows and is delighted by its hopes. . . .*
>
> *And there is one whose soul lifts beyond the limitations of Israel, to sing the song of mankind. His spirit expands to include the glory of the human image and its dreams. . . .*
>
> *And there is one who lifts beyond this level, until he becomes one with all creation and all creatures, and all the worlds. And with all of them he sings a song. . . .*
>
> *And there is one who rises together with the bundle of all these songs. All of them sing out, each gives meaning and life to the other. . . . And this completeness is the song of holiness, the song of God, the song of Israel. . . .*

It is difficult to pinpoint the exact time of the year 1967 or the precise causes which brought about the weakening of this multilevel song. The news of the world—war in Vietnam, race riots in the United States, chaos in Africa—was certainly a factor. The weather in Israel had something to do with it, endless weeks of cold rain, which continued long beyond the season when the sun of spring usually appears in that land. There was economic depression and the continuous bickering of that land's dozen-odd political parties and its leaders. They were good leaders, many of them were the founding fathers of the Jewish state, but they were old. And more important than their physical age was the oldness of ideas with which they were trying to solve the problems of their country. Of these problems, none was more depressing than the virtual cessation of immigration and the rise in emigration. A joke circulated through the land during those months—someone had hung up a sign at Lydda Airport: "Will the last Jew to leave the country please turn out the lights." The joke expressed a definite mood. The Jewish state, so boldly conceived and amazingly established only a few years earlier, seemed to be facing its demise. For without immigration, the island of Jewish existence in the Middle East would inevitably be inundated by the vast Arab population that pressed about its borders.

But it was more than the song of Israel which was at stake. It was also the song of God that was overtaken by a sense of ending. Again, although the feeling was not consciously expressed or analyzed, its roots were clear. They went back to an historic event which, though heavily discussed, had never been really digested by the individual Jew, namely, the genocide of six million Jewish men, women, and children in Europe. When I say "not digested," I mean that Jews who want to make some sort of sense out of their history, and out of the claim of this history that there is some sort of moral arithmetic "up there," have not really been able to shake off the "lesson" of the Nazi holocaust. For this lesson, on an individual level, would logically lead to an agreement with Heine's definition of Judaism as a "misfortune"; on a group level, it would seem to teach that there is no sense in Jewish historic existence; and, on a theological level, it seemed to say words that would end the song of God, namely, the forbidden assertion that "there is no Judge and no judgment."

From this abyss of negation, Jews were saved by one fact, the emergence of the state of Israel. Not that Israel was able to straighten out the moral balance sheet; but it would not have come into being without the European catastrophe. Therefore, the existence of the state was an opportunity to give some measure of meaning to the suffering of the innocents who perished in Auschwitz and Treblinka. And the end of the new state was not only an end of another Jewish community but the end of all attempts to make sense out of four thousand years of Jewish effort to survive.

Until the spring of 1967, all of this was a matter of mood. But in the middle of May, this half-intuited possibility became concrete probability. Egypt demanded that the United Nations withdraw its troops from its border with Israel. The government in Israel was obviously surprised and unprepared. It had scarcely finished announcing that the Egyptian move was mere "window dressing" when Egypt moved its main forces into the Sinai Desert close to the borders of Israel. It was still predicting that Nasser would never go so far as to blockade the

Straits of Tiran when the Egyptian government announced that the straits were blockaded. By the third week in May, every Arab nation had agreed to join military action against Israel, while the United Nations was locked in impotent debate. Outflanked both diplomatically and militarily, Israel stood alone with France, England, and the United States all proclaiming neutrality.

There was little fear in the land, but there was a mood which went deeper than fear. If war broke out, Israelis felt they would survive. The cost of survival, however, would be the flower of their youth—the future of Israel. And if there was no war, there would be economic strangulation, a complete cessation of immigration, and an increase of emigration, in brief, the end of Israel, of Jewish history, of the claim that the universe made any kind of moral sense, the end of Israel's multileveled song.

During these weeks, I continued my visits to the chambers which claimed to house the treasure of Judaism's inner world. Naturally, the mood of the outer world had penetrated into these chambers, but the program of study continued as before. In class with the Nazir whom you met at the beginning of this journey, we had reached a passage in Rav Kook's *Lights of Holiness* that discussed the revelation of mystery that would take place in "latter-day generations."

> *In the latter-day generations, occupation of the heart and mind with the highest and finest thoughts, whose source is in the mysteries of the Torah, will become an absolute necessity for Judaism. . . .*
> *In those days it will be necessary to realize that there is nothing in the world which is not holy. At the same time, we will find out that all our conceptions of what is holy and secular will be as nothing in the light of high holiness, the infinite source.*

Reb David had sighed when we read that passage and hinted that we were dealing with the deepest and most dangerous doctrines of the hidden wisdom. The statement that there was no real difference between the holy and the nonholy came close to the pantheism of "the Amsterdam philosopher." The idea that the full revelation of holiness required a merger with the nonholy could lead to the most terrible abominations, even to "plagues" like those which Shabbatai Zevi and Jacob Frank brought into the world.

"Should we, dare we, talk about this?" the Nazir had asked. After a few moments of hesitation, he decided to try it. After all, we were the latter-day generation. And did not the rav say that the generation which preceded the light of the Messiah should try to reveal that which was hidden and try to raise the revealed to the level of the hidden?

At this point one of the students had risked a question. "But how do we know we are the latter-day generation? Did not the kabbalists of the seventeenth century also interpret the 'impudence' and 'darkness' which characterized their times as a sign of the imminent dawning of the Messianic light?"

"Ei, Ei," the Nazir had sighed, and clapped his hands. He directed us to a passage where the rav described the advent of the Messianic age.

When the people is awakening, and all the world is quivering in the throes of wars whose ultimate purpose is known only to God, this is the time for the establishment of God's Kingdom on earth. . . . The chains which bind the feet of the Messiah are broken. They are shattered and become like wicks for fire, like fine threads of flax which are consumed by burning flames. . . . This is a sign that the light of the soul in all of its aspects is in the process of being rebuilt and the light of a heavenly salvation proceeds to reveal itself in a host of golden sparks.

The room was quiet as we listened to Rav Kook's lyrical prophecy. Some golden sparks accompanied us as we walked into the hallway and out into the dark street. Meah She'arim was empty that night. A few days ago every able-bodied young man and woman had been conscripted into the army. All day the Jordanian radio had been broadcasting victory marches announcing the end of Zionism, the end of the Jewish state. Walking home through the silent streets, the golden sparks seemed to evaporate and disappear into the darkness.

The next night, I attended a class at the home of Rabbi Zvi Yehudah. Contrary to his usual custom, the rabbi turned immediately to the text. The boys around the table were obviously disappointed.

"Won't the rabbi speak to us about the 'matter of the day'?"

Zvi Yehudah shrugged and made no immediate reply.

"The students at the Yeshiva are uneasy," someone added. "They don't know whether under the circumstances they should continue the usual order of studies."

"Continue?" The little rabbi looked up and shrugged again. "Why not? Israel is all one organism, but it has inner and outer aspects. There are 'people of the body,' those who must specialize in its physical requirements, and there are those who keep the soul, the inner being. Everybody has his task, and all the tasks are holy. Why should the 'people of the inner being' leave their task? Why change the order?"

"But what if a person can't keep his mind on his studies? What if he is worried, nervous?" a student asked.

"Nervousness is a waste of man's powers. Better to use the opportunity to intensify and lift up the task to which we have been assigned. Why break the order?"

The students received the rabbi's advice in silence. We began to read a passage from Rav Kook which spoke of the constant "lifting of the world." Everywhere and always, Rav Kook had written, there was a constant ascent. But there is a class of people who see this *aliyah* better than others. "Every poet of faith" sees the ascents. Others, looking only at external matters, may not see it.

"Rabbi," a student interrupted, "can we speak some more about what is happening today? Last night I was at a Hasidic synagogue and they were all excited. Their rabbi had said, 'This is the end, the eve of the coming of the Messiah, the final war.'"

Everyone in the room laughed and Zvi Yehudah Kook smiled with them.

"What does the rabbi think?" the student pressed.

"What is there to think? That the redemption will come through wars, we are told by the sages. It is good that we have, at least, some pauses in between the war." For a moment, Rabbi Zvi Yehudah hesitated, then continued. "Whether or not this will be the last war, nobody knows. What we do know is that the previous wars in our generation have all been steps in the return of Israel to its ancient borders. There was the First World War, and after it the Balfour Declaration, which made possible the beginning of the modern Jewish resettlement in the land. Then came the Second World War, and the establishment of the state. Then the Sinai Campaign in 1956, and a little more territory was

returned. What will happen this time we do not know. But the sages
have told us how the light of redemption will come. 'Like the dawn,
kima, kima—at first slowly, step by step, then suddenly, a great shining.'"

The students asked no more questions. I had the feeling that
they were disappointed. Not that the rabbi could have said anything
else. He was, after all, committed to the words of the holy books. The
problem was that they suddenly seemed so irrelevant to the reality. An
hour before the class, Premier Levi Eshkol had addressed the nation.
His three-minute speech had been a repetition of diplomatically
phrased formulae. His voice had broken, and he had stuttered as if not
believing himself in the assurance he was trying to give the nation.

That night, awakened by the rumble of tanks in the empty
streets, I thought of the biblical phrase, "and a people walked in darkness."

Aftermath

The story of the Six Day War, which returned Israel to its biblical borders and brought battle-hardened, nonreligious paratroopers to
press tear-stained cheeks against the wall of the Temple restored to
Jewish sovereignty after two thousand years of "exile," has been told in
numerous places. All the stories offer testimony to one fact. Jews in Israel and abroad, but especially in Israel, experienced the psalmist's
phrase in its fullness: "A people that walked in darkness saw a great
light." Clearly, it was not the final outburst of a Messianic dawn. Nevertheless, it was an experience of great light bursting through utter
darkness. There had been a descent, as deep as any which Jewish History
has encountered. It began with the Nazi holocaust and reached its nadir
in May, 1967. It was followed by an ascent, as high and higher than the
measure of the descent. That experience is now in the past, and Israel
has returned to a future that will surely offer more trials of darkness
and more descents. The question I ask myself is why it has seemed
necessary to conclude this chapter on Rav Kook and my account of
attempts to know the "hidden" world of Judaism with a reference to
the fall and ascent associated with the Six Day War.

Is it simply a way of telling the reader that I, along with many
others, learned that the seemingly old formulae of the Nazir and Rabbi

Zvi Yehudah, derived from their inner evidence, turned out to be more correct than those who drew their conclusions from external evidence? That those who said that light can suddenly spring out of darkness were right?

This is not much of a conclusion for an inquiry into the nature of Jewish mysticism. However, the lesson I want to communicate goes beyond a confession of personal experience and concerns an aspect of Jewish mysticism that has been neglected in these pages, for I have discussed Jewish mysticism in terms of its basic insights and interpretations as a personal, subjective experience. All these patterns are present, but it has been forgotten that at its core is an experience centering about actual historic events, such as the event at Mount Sinai or at the Red Sea in the time of Moses, or in Israel during the six days of June, 1967. Obviously, there are different accounts and interpretations of such events. The fact remains that in Judaism it has been the concrete historic event, the existential experience of a people, which has given it a sense of contact with the deepest level of truth.

The reader will recall the Holy Ari's picture of creation as the result of a primal outburst of light, a going out followed by a *zimzum*, a withdrawal. In this imagery, the divine affluence is withdrawn, leaving a seemingly godless space in which there remains only a *rishima*, a feeble impression of this primal light. In one of his commentaries to the prayerbook, Rav Kook compares the light available in our world to shining, fluctuating waves, something like the aurora borealis. Accepting this image, Judaism might be called an enterprise devoted to the detecting and revealing of this wavering "impression" of light. Jewish mystics, "who turn sour into sweet, darkness into light," are the specialists of this enterprise, that is, they "see" with a sensitivity which can, at least in their vision, make all the darkness as nothing.

Rav Kook was such a seer. What makes him of particular value to the rest of us is that his vision, though strong, was aware of the darkness confronting less talented seers. This understanding enabled him to work out a way that did not automatically exclude doubters or even negators of the hidden light. Because he shared their darkness, he was able to encourage their attempts to glimpse what the specialists seemed to see with discouraging ease.

The point that I have been trying to make in these latter pages,

however, is that Judaism's "seeing" ultimately depends on at least an occasional bursting of light through darkness in a concrete historic context. Afterwards come the teachers and systems which can husband the
memory of that historic flash, and make sure that it can illuminate the
darker periods of history, affecting that slow "tenderizing of the heart,"
which, one Lubavitcher rebbe suggested, is preferred by Jewish mysticism to the "searing flame." In other words, although Judaism insists
that man constantly try for a "quickening below," at least occasionally,
there must be a "quickening from above."

EPILOGUE: "... AND SO?"

"U'v'chen, and so?" is an expression which Lubavitcher Hasidim like to append to the end of every theoretical discussion. It is a phrase spoken with raised eyebrows. It asks the individual what he plans to do, in concrete terms, about all his theories and observations.

"U'v'chen, and so?" is the question with which this kind of a book should end, not with conclusions. Conclusions imply that a search has ended, but the kind of search recorded in these pages, for *shefa,* light, joy, truth, can have no end. It can only lead from gate to gate until one reaches a gate that opens with one's last breath. Still, even a journey without end must, after a while, affirm direction lest it wander aimlessly toward weariness. And so? What has been learned that will help in moving toward those "unifications" of thought and act that, the kabbalists said must occur at least from time to time if life is to receive its flow of *shefa.*

On my cluttered desk as I begin this last chapter are two books utterly unlike each other in form and content. One is a large and expensively bound volume with an elaborate cover design juxtaposing the green-lettered title, *Psychedelic Experience,* against a reddish photograph of the "Hevajira Buddha in ecstatic union with his Shakti." It announces itself as a manual describing how the Tibetan *Book of the Dead* may be used in conjunction with drugs such as LSD, Psylocybin, mescaline, DMT, and the like, to offer a "journey to new realms of consciousness." One of the book's coauthors is Dr. Timothy Leary, former teacher of psychology at Harvard University and self-proclaimed founder of a new religion involving the use of hallucinogenic drugs.

The other book is a small pamphlet printed in London. Its Hebrew title is *Rosh Milim, The Beginning of Words.* It is a meditation on the esoteric meanings of the Hebrew alphabet, vowel signs, and musical trope. Its author is Rabbi Abraham Isaac Kook, and it begins with a laconic quotation from Maimonides, "Should you fail to find herein anything that helps you in any way, consider it never to have been written."

297

Of course the fact that these two books happen to be on my desk as I write may be sheer accident, but the Baal Shem has taught us that "there is no accident." What appears as a coincidence is only a hint of hidden relationships, whose significance one must try to understand.

Can one then discover a connection between the worlds of Timothy Leary and Rav Kook, a connection that might help to derive out of the encounter with Jewish mysticism some lessons for one's own life?

The very proposal of the idea evokes personal memories that appear to make such a juxtaposition terribly artificial. There comes to mind, for example, a summer afternoon in Jerusalem, in 1966. A small crowd has gathered in the library of the Hebrew University for the opening of an exhibition displaying samples of Abraham Isaac Kook's writings; it is the one hundredth anniversary of his birth. Most of those in the room are bearded men wearing hats or black yarmelkes, many of them officials of Jerusalem's religious establishment. They are well-dressed, dignified, and politely interested in the display of manuscripts and photographs that have been arranged in the glass-covered cases. They wait quietly as the main speaker, a short, white-haired man wearing a brown fedora, mounts the platform to read his scribbled notes into the microphone. Shmuel Joseph Agnon has not yet been awarded the Nobel prize for literature and his words are received politely but without great excitement. Besides, he is a poor speaker, and I manage to catch only a few phrases of his highly stylized Hebrew. He seems to be recalling his first glimpse of Rav Kook in a Jaffa synagogue: "a face shining, translucent with goodness," and then he recalls a visit to the home of the Kook family shortly after the rabbi's death, when the widow whispered a tribute to her late husband—"*a za heilegen guf,* such a holy body."

Rabbi Zvi Yehudah Kook, the son of the former chief rabbi, is not present. He has not come, it is said, lest his appearance be interpreted as an endorsement of the Hebrew University, an endorsement he does not want to give because the university is not committed to an Orthodox presentation of Jewish values and literature.

Yes, this is Rav Kook's world, the self-enclosed, rigidly structured world of Jewish Orthodoxy. What could it possibly have in common with the "turned-on underground" of Timothy Leary and his colleagues? Another memory comes to mind.

It is the same year—1966. This time the setting is a theater near

Greenwich Village in New York. A large audience has come to witness a psychedelic celebration advertised as "the Illumination of Buddha." Most of them are young people carefully dressed in the casual clothes that proclaim their liberation from bourgeois society. They watch the projection on a large screen of undulating shapes and colors, alternating with glimpses of Indian statuary. Sitting cross-legged in a corner of the stage, a young man twangs the strings of an electrically amplified Indian sitar. There are flower petals in the aisles and the faint odor of incense in the air. A mimeographed program explains that psychedelic art uses "smell, light, amplified and mixed sound waves in order to speak directly to the trembling membranes of the sense organs." Now Leary, dressed in tight-fitting white jeans and an open-collar shirt, walks on to the stage, a miniature microphone strung around his neck. He introduces the program of the evening, a drugless, psychedelic "trip" into the world of Indian Buddhism which, he hopes, will help us "contact the ancient strands of energy within," encourage us to abandon those "games" concerned with the accumulation of money, possessions, honors, and other goals that dissipate an individual's contact with genuine reality.

Later in the evening I meet Leary. The graying, long-haired psychologist has sincerity in his voice as he tries to explain how hard it is to found a new religion. One must find small groups of people who are interested in genuine self-sacrificial human relations. We go down to the lobby where Leary is immediately surrounded by his young followers, girls in miniskirts, boys with long hair falling over their eyes. On tables in the lobby are pamphlets and magazines presenting psychedelic lore, their language clogged with slang and pseudoscientific jargon. Cosmic energy, Leary writes in one article, is "programmed" into the nature of the cosmos, of which the body is a microcosmos. This energy may be tapped not only by chemicals but with the aid of "codes" which have been deposited into the wisdoms of ancient cultures.

"Those of you whose bag is meditation," another psychedelic enthusiast proposes, "might try using one of the prayers [composed by Leary] as a focal point for your attention. Read them to your children especially once they are in school. Keep the book on the mantelpiece . . . keep it in the bathroom."

"L'havdil, a thousand separations," a traditional Jew would gasp

if presented with the proposal that there might be a relationship between such ideas and the hidden wisdom of Judaism. But it was seen
that the kabbalist also wants to contact a level of reality deeper than
what is offered by the usual games of society. He too has his "codes"
for evoking a flow of *shefa* from the macrocosm of the universe into
the microcosm of the body. He too is suspicious of "psychic roller-
coaster rides." "With us," Rabbi Nachman once said, "the real problem
is not the *r'tzo,* going out, but the *shuv,* the return."

The analogies, however, must not be strained. There are still a
"thousand separations" which divide the experimental, often puerile,
psychedelic world from the inner space of Jewish mysticism. Not the
least of the differences is implied in Rav Kook's widow's description of
her husband as a "holy body." It is not likely that the chastity, the
discipline, the concern for Law, and the self-offering that is involved
in Jewish holiness will enthuse Leary's young followers, and the suggestion that religious experiences may be achieved by drugs, breathing
exercises, or other external techniques is likely to remind a traditional
Jew of Canaanite paganism, which used all kinds of orgiastic rites,
including drugs, to produce states of so-called expanded consciousness.

Nevertheless, the question perists: Is there not something which
unites as well as separates these different worlds?

Rav Kook and Timothy Leary

A Hasidic master has suggested a technique for making unities
out of what appear to be utterly disparate or even contradictory elements. One must seek, he taught, a third and higher element, a root
into which the first two are subsumed and from which they both
derive their strength.

It seems to me that there is such a root from which a chain of
descent leads, not only to an interest in inner visions and consciousness-
expanding drugs, but to all actions and ideas that promise an exit from
the prosaic patterns of an outer-layer existence. In its mildest form, this
root impulse involves a dissatisfaction with all surface relationships,
surface truths, or the surface facts of history, and seeks something more
real, more vivid, more significant. It is not content with anything that
can be circumscribed, delimited, or completely comprehended. For most

people such a hunger ends with the passing of youth, withered by suffering or surfeit, forgotten in the bustle of the marketplace, and dissipated by the bright lights of entertainment.

But there are those in whom this hunger for "more" gnaws without cessation. "Children from the chamber of yearnings" is the name which the Zohar applies to those so afflicted. Such children appear among every people, in every culture, and in every age, but there are times, Rav Kook has written, when the "burning thirst for an inner substance and vision that transcends the surface of existence" wells up with terrible force. Such a time occurs in an "end-of-days" period, when the structure of one civilization begins to crumble and the foundations of the new world have not yet been revealed. Such a period produces an increased hunger for the innerness which can quicken the "dry outer skeleton of existence." It also witnesses an incursion into this world of "souls from the world of formlessness."

For the chamber of yearnings is connected to what the Kabbala calls the world of *tohu,* that state of chaos which, in the mystic scheme of creation, precedes our world of *tikkun,* or order. Souls which are rooted in this higher world cannot reconcile themselves to the given order and arrangement of things. They yearn for more than guardians of the establishment, those whom Kook calls the "masters of proportions and good manners," can endure; more even than they, "the souls of chaos," can handle. Rav Kook's words, though couched in kabbalistic terminology, can bear direct quotation.

> *The souls of* tohu, *of chaos, are higher than the souls of order (they are very great). They seek much from reality, more than their vessels can endure. They seek very great illumination. Everything which is bounded, delimited, and arranged they cannot bear.*
>
> *They see that they are bound by laws, by limiting conditions which cannot be endlessly expanded . . . so they fall into sadness, despair, anger, and—out of rage—into evil, deliberate sin, degradation, ugliness, abomination, destructions, every kind of evil . . . but the essence of the force which is within them, is the point of holiness . . .*
>
> *Particularly do [these souls] reveal themselves in an "end-of-days" kind of period, a time which precedes the remaking of a world. . . . On the eve of redemption* hutzpah, *impudence, increases. A storm*

broods, becomes stronger, there is breach after breach, and hutzpah
escalates. . . .

　　*These fiery souls show their strength before which no barrier
and no limitation can stand, and the weak of the "built" world, the
masters of "proportion" and "good manners," are appalled. . . . Who
can dwell with consuming fire? Who can dwell with those who would
burn up the world! . . . But the truly powerful will know that this
revelation of strength is one of the phenomena which appear for the
purpose of perfecting the world, in order to strengthen the power of
the people, of the individual, of the world. Only at first this strength
appears in the form of* tohu, *but finally it will be taken from the evil
ones and given to the righteous, who with the heroism of lions, through
a forceful and clear reason, with the strong feeling, in a practical, clear,
and ordered way, will reveal the true order of construction.*

Make Room for the Aberrant

　　The language and imagery comes out of Rav Kook's inner world
but the truth it expresses is universal, applicable to Mao's Red Guards,
American hippies and demonstrators, psychedelic beatniks, and religious revolutionaries, but in the context of our own subject and the
question *u'v'chen,* what can it mean to people in our day?

　　The answer might go something like this:

　　Make room for the aberrant. Make room within the Establishment for those souls whom the "masters of proportion" tend to label as
abnormal, extremist, dangerous. More often than not, these irritating
"souls of chaos," these "children from the chamber of yearnings" bear
within themselves those spores of creation which society needs for its
own regeneration.

　　The prophets, the followers of Mohammed and Jesus, men like
Jakob Boehme, al-Ghazali and the Baal Shem Tov, all found it necessary to expand, if not altogether to burst, the inherited and accepted
structures of faith. They alarmed and outraged the Establishment, but,
when not altogether ejected from its framework, they were able to
infuse its old forms with new vitality. A church or society which can
expand and strengthen its structure so as to include such yearning
spirits will be lifted on the wave of the future.

　　But it is not only aberrant souls for whom room must be made.
There are times when society as a whole must make an exit from the

"world of order." Only the civilization whose life force has been altogether weakened or tranquilized by excess of bodily comfort, artificial
games, entertainment, will feel no need for an occasional "turning on."
Primitive communities instinctively provided rituals, religious ceremonies, celebrations which made it legitimate to "take a trip." They
also provided rites of passage for a safe "reentry." To disregard this need
for a periodic "going out" will result either in a total diminishment of
life force or a bottling up of emotions which will burst out in acts of
chaotic destruction.

"Make room"—this is the first lesson for life which can be
extracted out of our journey. Let the structure and Establishment permit and even encourage that periodic *r'tzo,* going out, which is motivated by the human need for something more than is offered by the
surface patterns and truths of daily existence. At the same time, let it
provide the rites of passage, the wisdom and structural strength that
will make possible not only a safe reentry, but a way of using the *shefa*
tapped during the moment of the high, so that the low is also affected
and lifted. And now, having come again to the need for uniting highs
with lows, we are back to the particular "secrets" of the Jewish inner
way.

The Well-Cooked Heart

That potpourri of psychosomatic phenomena which the world
sometimes associates with the term mysticism is not usually thought of
as a Jewish specialty. This fact derives in part from ignorance, an ignorance which in our day may be shared by learned and pious Jews,
as well as outsiders. But it also has a great deal to do with the fact that
Judaism accorded speculation and interest in hidden matters a very
limited and circumscribed place in its scheme of values.

I have seen in the course of my own limited encounters that this
kind of warning was often ignored, even by the classical masters of
Jewish teaching. Rabbi Akiva, Joseph Karo, the Vilna Gaon, and other
distinguished normative teachers of Jewish tradition did occupy themselves with "hidden matters," and there were times, as in sixteenth-
century Safed, when the mysteries were discussed and felt with as
much urgency as the problems of the revealed law. The fact is that
during most periods of its history, the Jewish community did make
room for those of its children whose souls were deeply rooted in the

chamber of yearnings. The rabbis of the second and third centuries reserved an honored place for the descenders of the chariot. The seventeenth-century Joseph Karo reported that he was regularly visited by a preacher from the higher world, but this did not disqualify him from being appreciated as the author of a legal work which still guides the Orthodox world of our day. As for Hasidim, they were, in a sense, the "turned-on underground" of their day. Rebbe Shmelke of Nickolsburg, it was told, never really heard his teacher, the Maggid of Mezritch, finish a thought because as soon as the latter would say "and the Lord spoke," Shmelke would begin shouting in wonderment, "The Lord spoke, the Lord spoke," and continue shouting until he had to be carried from the room. The Baal Shem Tov and many of his disciples, including a supposedly brain-oriented figure such as Rabbi Schneur Zalman, were ecstatics in the full sense of the word, seized by fits of cataleptic-like trembling during the course of their prayers. But it was not only the Hasidim who made room for the "queer ones." The so-called normative Jewish community also tolerated and gave status to those whose soul roots required a stronger diet than what they could obtain within Judaism's central chambers. There were separatists who wanted to share the fate of the divine *shekina* and wandered about in exile. There were *matmidim* who held candles in their hands to prevent themselves from falling asleep during the all-night study vigils, and ascetics who wore hair-shirts and fasted from one Sabbath to another. All were given a respected place within the house of Judaism.

It was this tolerance and even encouragement of the individual's need for a "trip" out of this world that made it possible for Rabbi Nachman to say, "with us, the problem is not the *r'tzo*, the going out, but the *shuv*, the return." And in saying this, he put his finger on that characteristic which indeed distinguishes Judaism from other mystical systems. Judaism believed in the need for "turning on," but it specialized in the return. How to transmute the lofty illumination into prosaic this-worldly terms was the problem which concerned Judaism. It is this emphasis which can and did give the outside world the impression that Judaism was an outer-directed faith more interested in legal detail than in spirit, and indeed the danger of such a misbalance did exist, but it was preferred to a fruitless wallowing in vague emotions and visions. One Hasidic analyst of the psyche, himself a mystic, phrased the ideal of Jewish mysticism in a simple but effective image: "Not the transient upshoot of a straw flame but the well-cooked heart." Not the sudden and searing flame but the transmutation of that flame into slow warmth which "tenderized" a human being and made him sensitive to the need of other human beings for bread, pity, and justice—this was the ideal.

The vessel which was used to accomplish this result was the Law, the yoke of commandments derived from the bible, and interpretations of the sages. It was this revealed wisdom which helped the mystic make a safe exit but also anchored him to earth. And even as this Law could transmute the flame into effective heat, so could it serve to warm up and frequently evoke a spark out of reality's dry tinder, for the same Law which insisted that the high of an inner experience be involved with problems of the kitchen table, the bathroom, and the workshop, by that very fact forced a person to pause in awe before the heavenly mysteries involved in every so-called low.

U'v'chen—and so? Returning to the main question and asking what Jewish mysticism can offer children from the chamber of yearnings in our day, one might reply: not only a way of going out, but a tested and quite effective system of return. A way of preventing the ecstatic flame from consuming the soul. A way of using every high so that it lifted the lows. The desire to tie heaven to earth is not, to be sure, an exclusively Jewish goal, but the stubbornness, energy, and measure of success which accompanied this attempted unification in Judaism is perhaps singular in the history of religion. Its secrets, in an age which has seen the bankruptcy of so many attempts to balance spirit and flesh, its exits and reentries, would seem worthy of serious consideration.

How Much and What Kind of Salt?

Rabbi Schneur Zalman, founder of the Habad school of Hasidism, uses an interesting analogy to explain the place and value which mystical studies ought to occupy in Judaism by calling it the "salt" which helps to make the "meat" of Jewish Law more palatable; that is to say, there can be no doubt but that the Law is the major substance of Jewish existence. Salt without meat is altogether valueless. On the other hand, meat without salt not only lacks taste but lacks the quality of preservation which salt gives to meat. Men need both.

This is the position of classical Judaism, but Rabbi Schneur Zalman and other mystically inclined thinkers have made a point about the relationship between this salt and meat which is of great importance in regard to the question placed at the beginning of this chapter. It appears, they say, that the latter-day generations require far more salt than did the earlier. It is as if appetites and sensitivities which were once healthy have become jaded. The deep truths and illuminations which once came naturally and easily to men in biblical or even rabbinic society are no longer perceived by our sickened and degenerate spiritual organs. We require more help, more explanation of truths which in earlier time could be conveyed merely by a hint or by direct confrontation with simple reality. How else to explain the fact that the bible and the Talmud make such sparse references to doctrines and theories which were elaborated by the kabbalists of Spain and Safed? It was the spiritual illness of the later generations which made it necessary to receive a stronger dose of mystical teachings. The use of such strong medicine was dangerous, and that is why the sages discouraged its use among the masses, but what alternative is there now that the masses have become so unhealthy, except to risk its use?

It was this theory which underpinned the determination of the Hasidic movement to let the "waters of the wells spread outward" and to clothe the mystic doctrine in forms and life patterns which could reach the masses. It is this same thought which motivated Rabbi Ashlag's call for a Judaism which gave its inner wisdom a prior rather than latter place in modern Jewish studies. Rav Kook, too, felt that the time had come to "reveal the hidden and to lift the revealed up to the level where it reveals its mysteries."

In short, it is time to increase the proportion of salt to meat. For the generation of King David, Rabbi Akiva, or even Rabbi Nachman, the "going out" may have been no problem. This generation does have a problem. It needs stronger medicines in order to be "turned on."

U'v'chen, and so? We come again to the question, what can be done? But now we can narrow it down. What is the nature of the salt which Judaism can offer? And what is the proportion, the relationship between salt and meat which can feed Jewish souls in our day, particularly those children from the chamber of yearnings.

To Find a Chevra

How Jews tried to answer this question in past ages has been described. They looked for a teacher, and this teacher, I have suggested, had at least two qualities. First, he was a great "translator," able to build a bridge of communication between the language and values of different worlds, the world of the past and the world of the budding future; the world of inner space and the world of outer surfaces. Equally important, he was able, in his own being, to embody this stretch, to offer a living example which others could emulate.

"Everything depends on *mazal,* luck," said the sages, "even the Torah in the ark." Without the luck of finding such translators, the secrets of Judaism's inner wisdom are likely to remain locked and sealed in old texts, a source of interesting material for talented accountants, but unavailable for use by ordinary men and women. Without such luck, the hidden wisdom will remain hidden; its insights and games either ignored or abused by dilettantish play. The individual searching for salt will find himself impelled to look in other places, bottles of chemicals, multimedia stimulation, exotica of other lands and cultures.

But what if some gifted translators do appear? The problem is still not resolved, for, as we know, a game needs not only explainers but players. Where do we find them?

It is only the rare soul that can go it alone. Most people require a nutritive environment. It is not only faith, as the Lubavitcher rebbe pointed out, which must constantly be fed. Moods, rhythms, ideas, values, all require constant feeding if they are not to wither and blow away. How an historic structure like Judaism can, through its laws, prayers, and ceremonies, build the palace and chambers of such a nourishing environment has been seen, but it is hard to live alone even in the loveliest of palaces. Nor—except for an occasional Setzer—is the company of books enough. Most people need a living *chevra,* a relationship, or, in the more elegant language of the religious Establishment, man needs a "covenant community."

Judaism came into being and managed to survive through the instrumentality of such covenant communities, groups that assumed a commitment to a common code of values and laws. Abraham, Moses, the prophets, the rabbis, all saw the purpose of Jewish existence in the keeping of such a covenant. The Essenes and other Dead Sea groups were groups who formed special covenants within the larger consensus. Mystical groups of the Talmudic era and later periods also formed such "cells." The usual structure of such a cell included a "righteous teacher" or rebbe, an askesis or particular pattern of discipline, and a nutritive body of literature. Many such communities were formed and then fell apart, but sometimes they became the seedbeds for ideas and values which made their way into the larger society, and there were times when the power of the smaller group was so strong as to eventually transform and take over the total community. To find such a community would be the "practical" step that a searcher for Judaism's *shefa* must take in our day.

How can he find it? It seems to me that a person seeking such a *chevra* will see before him alternative roads. One will be well trodden, for it is the way used by past generations. It is clearly demarcated by the *halacha,* Jewish religious Law. It assumes that the person who uses this way will grant to this *halacha* supreme authority, agreeing that its every detail comes from a source of wisdom which transcends man's finite powers of judgment. That is not to say that the traveler along this road will avoid confusion. Jewish religious law in our day is subject to many differing interpretations, and there are areas of modern life for which it has no clear guidance. So there will be some stumbling, searching, and questioning. Still, the walker along this way assumes that there is a "king's highway" to which he has been given an accurate map, namely, the Torah. He may believe with Rabbi Nachman and other mystics that this map is a copy of a higher map which will some day be revealed, but meanwhile the copy is all he has. He will, therefore, follow its directions and examine its every line for hints as to the hidden paths by which he can trace and personally encounter the flow of that *shefa* which sustains the world.

As has been noted, this way of the king is a multilane highway. It can include those who prefer the lonely walking of a Nazir or the traveling *en masse* of various Hasidic schools. As to nourishment, the traveler can select the diet needed by the roots of his own soul. He can, so to speak, add salt according to the needs of his palate, but his basic food remains the *halacha,* the Law, as this law is defined by the Orthodox rabbinic world and interpreted through the generations by sages who believed in a Sinaitic revelation.

To the individual who finds it possible to search for *shefa* along this clear path may be applied the ancient words: "Blessed is he, and it is well for him." Others will have more trouble. An individual unable to believe that the Law is divinely inspired in both its form and content finds that the writings of the mystics, concerned as they are with the "true" interpretation of the Law, have lost much of their power. Not believing, perhaps, not observing the commandments which tradition has warned must be assumed by anybody who would venture into the "orchard," he will be unsure of his direction, in doubt as to his ability or worthiness with respect to receiving "secrets." He may feel guilty, he should be afraid. If he is neither, then he is unaware of that characteristic which truly distinguishes the Jewish from other mystical ways, for, when all is said and done, it is the Law, with all of its commandments and customs, that is the gate to the Jewish *pardes*. Take away this Law and what remains is little more than a collection of data, interesting to accountants, or a body of ideas, insights, and moods whose like may be found in many other places. Gone is the vehicle which gives Jewish mysticism its peculiar flavor, the instrument which enables it to influence the form and quality of real life. Knowing this, he finds himself in a dilemma. To be sure, he can play a game of "let's pretend" and observe the forms of the Law without believing that they represent divine will. Such a game is not illegitimate from the Jewish religious point of view. That observance of the Law, without conviction or out of improper conviction, will lead to an observance with true conviction is a premise accepted by the rabbis. Some individuals will be able to resolve their dilemma this way, but he who is unable or unwilling to play the game on these terms is left with his problem. What can he do?

What can he do but walk what Buber calls "the narrow ridge." Only he must take care to feel the full tension of his predicament. He must be aware of the tempting abyss on either side of his path. On the one side, there is the pull of the ready-made answer, the old but comfortable structure of tradition; on the other is self-indulgence, mind-diminishing emotional "trips," or anarchy. Both offer the kind of "sleep" which Rabbi Nachman correctly sees as the antithesis of life. Whereas the narrow ridge itself offers only constant self-doubt, constant questioning—especially that kind of questioning illustrated by a story taken from that Hasidic tradition which asks "and so?"

Once, say Lubavitcher Hasidim, the old rabbi, Schneur Zalman, was imprisoned because of false charges brought against him by the opponents of Hasidism. There he was visited by a government official who, impressed by the appearance of the holy rabbi, tried to engage him in conversation. Their discussion turned to the biblical description of the dialogue between God and man in the garden of Eden. How was it, asked the official, that an all-knowing God had to ask man, "Where art thou?"

"You must understand the meaning of this question," answered the rabbi, "for it is a question asked by God of every man in every generation. After all your wanderings, all your efforts, all your years, O man, where are you?"

Tradition relates that the official, confronting the searching eyes of the old rabbi and remembering perhaps how man confessed to God that he had been hiding, began to tremble.

That the story related in these pages, told by an outsider to other outsiders, may have a similar effect on its listeners is quite unlikely, but neither of us, neither the storyteller nor the listener, should hide from the point which the Lubavitcher tale makes. That point is that there is a garden of Eden, an inner and higher world from which man, even in his state of exile, can draw waters of life. That much, I hope, has been revealed by the testimony of the people which this journal records. But he who wishes to find a personal gate to this garden by asking questions will ultimately have to hear a question—a question addressed to himself.

Completed on the thirty-third day of the counting of the Omer, 5729.
On this day the Holy Lamp, Rabbi Simeon bar Yochai, departed
to attend the great wedding feast Above,
and all the worlds came together.
And this is what is told in the Zohar:
Rabbi Abba said, "scarcely had the Holy Lamp finished saying 'life,'
when his words were stilled.
I wanted to write more, but heard nothing.
I did not lift my head, for the light was so great I could not see.
And I was shaken.
I heard a voice saying, "length of days and years of life."
Then I heard another voice:
"He asked of you life, and you gave it to him, even length of days
forever and ever."